28,500 MILES
TO GALWAY RACES

By Dave and Angie Conroy

The adventures of Dave and Angie
as they visit every racecourse
in Great Britain and Ireland
over a six year period

First published in Great Britain in 2012 by
J&B Print Ltd.
info@jandbprint.co.uk
www.jandbprint.co.uk

ISBN 978-0-9574323-0-7

Printed by
J&B Print
32a Albert Street
Newton Stewart
DG8 6EJ
Tel: 01671 404123

INTRODUCTION

I was eighteen years old when I first started going to Newcastle races. Back then it was normally just a boozy day out with my mates which usually ended with either a taxi into town for a big night out or walking home and asking my parents for a sub to last me until payday.

It was two years later and at the grand old age of twenty while on a works outing to the St. Leger meeting at Doncaster that I got hooked on going to the races. Standing among the huge crowd in my shiny shoes, Levi sta-prest trousers, collar and tie with almost two weeks wages in my pocket I felt like the bee's knees, and even now thirty five years later I still get the same buzz when I go racing.

Attendances at race meetings are on an upward curve which I think is thanks to the number of younger people that are coming along to the different theme days that seem to be the in thing at the races these days, and also the sudden realisation by some people that a day at the races is a fun day out.

While on holiday in Ibiza years ago I was chatting to a Dutch couple who asked me what my interests were. When I told them one of my pastimes was going to the races they asked me if I was an aristocrat. The nickname "The Sport of Kings" is a name that has stuck well with racing but in my mind it has done the sport no favours as a lot of people still think that racing is a hobby for the rich and not somewhere to consider taking the family. This was evident in my own family for even though he loved a bet on the horses my father never attended a race meeting, which was strange as he often took my sister Elaine and I to greyhound meetings when we were young. I think he was just old fashioned and his perception of horse racing was a one of scoundrels and blackguards like those who frequented the race meetings of Victorian England. Thankfully today's generation are a lot more open minded and with a lot more emphasis being concentrated on the leisure industry these old fashioned virtues are fading away.

I'd always fancied the idea of visiting all the courses in the UK but had never made any effort to push myself. It was a conversation that Angie and I had while sitting in the bar on Waverley railway station in Edinburgh that finally got the ball rolling.

We both love going to the races, in fact the first ever date we went on was to the Fighting Fifth hurdle meeting at Newcastle, a meeting we try to attend every year.

No matter what walk of life you're from it will be full of ups and downs, so if you can create a few more ups for yourself it will tip the balance in your favour to have a more enjoyable life, racing has done that for us.

We are a working class couple with two grown up kids, Hollie and Grant. I work continental shifts at a pharmaceutical plant in Cramlington, Northumberland. The continental shift work gives me good blocks of days off, including five blocks of seventeen throughout the year. Angie looks after our home in Dudley, a one time mining village a few miles north of Newcastle and looks after (spoils them rotten) our two boxer dogs, Cassie and Zak. Although Northumberland isn't the ideal location to use as a base for touring the length and breadth of the country we are quite close to the A1, plus Newcastle airport and Central railway station are just a few miles from our house.

This is the story of our journey around the racecourses of the UK and Ireland and some of the highs and lows we encountered in our life on the way.

Dedicated to our loyal and faithful dogs Cassie and Zak and to those who cared for them in our absence.

Acknowledgements

Thank you to the staff from all the racecourses we contacted for sparing us their time.

A big thank you to:

Paul Struthers from the British Horseracing Authority for his kind assistance and the encouragement he gave us.

Lynda Fraher from Horse Racing Ireland for the useful information she forwarded to us.

Clémence Rémy from France Galop for her kind help.

Thanks to everyone else who has given us support and advice.

PAGE		PAGE	
025	AINTREE	236	HAYDOCK
240	ASCOT	199	HEREFORD
097	AYR	179	HEXHAM
364	BALLINROBE	141	HUNTINGDON
145	BANGOR	043	KELSO
187	BATH	153	KEMPTON
244	BELLEWSTOWN	359	KILBEGGAN
050	BEVERLEY	404	KILLARNEY
203	BRIGHTON	337	LAYTOWN
017	CARLISLE	212	LEICESTER
055	CARTMEL	296	LEOPARDSTOWN
070	CATTERICK	316	LIMERICK
135	CHELTENHAM	105	LINGFIELD
207	CHEPSTOW	399	LISTOWEL
062	CHESTER	271	LUDLOW
378	CLONMEL	077	MARKET RASEN
276	CORK	007	MUSSELBURGH
221	CURRAGH	280	NAAS
085	DONCASTER	348	NAVAN
266	DOWN ROYAL	183	NEWBURY
288	DOWNPATRICK	021	NEWCASTLE
342	DUNDALK	093	NEWMARKET (July)
232	EPSOM	127	NEWMARKET (Rowley)
157	EXETER	191	NEWTON ABBOT
301	FAIRYHOUSE	073	NOTTINGHAM
163	FAKENHAM	031	PERTH
384	FFOS LAS	261	PLUMPTON
108	FOLKESTONE	059	PONTEFRACT
149	FONTWELL	255	PUNCHESTOWN
410	GALWAY	046	REDCAR
111	GOODWOOD	035	RIPON
354	GOWRAN PARK	321	ROSCOMMON
370	GREAT LEIGHS	195	SALISBURY
089	HAMILTON	305	SANDOWN

5

PAGE

013	SEDGEFIELD
325	SLIGO
123	SOUTHWELL
115	STRATFORD
160	TAUNTON
228	THIRSK
284	THURLES
329	TIPPERARY
175	TOWCESTER
394	TRAMORE
066	UTTOXETER
119	WARWICK
039	WETHERBY
333	WEXFORD
171	WINCANTON
080	WINDSOR
131	WOLVERHAMPTON
217	WORCESTER
167	YARMOUTH
101	YORK
292	AUTEUIL
248	LONGCHAMP
311	VELKA CHUCHLE

Sunday 6 February 2005

Musselburgh Racecourse
Linkfield Road
Musselburgh
East Lothian
Tel: 0131 6652859
www.musselburgh-racecourse.co.uk

I have often been referred to as a gambler, and if you take the word gambler literally I am, but so are the millions who buy their £1 lottery ticket every week. I think of myself more as someone who likes to have a bet, and in my opinion a bet only turns into a gamble when you can't afford to lose your stake money.
One thing I do enjoy is a day at the races and I have done ever since I was a young man when I went to Newcastle Races and got my first taste of "The Sport of Kings."
It had always been a secret ambition of mine to visit every racecourse in the UK, an ambition that I thought I would never fulfil. It's funny how things work out.

My sister Elaine and her husband Tam live in Creetown, South West Scotland. Tam's birthday just happens to fall on the same day as Angie's, Feb 6th, and although we don't usually have a joint celebration we decided to do something together on their birthday weekend. The decision was made to stay overnight in Edinburgh then go to Musselburgh races on the Sunday. Friends of theirs, Howden and Lisa also decided to join the party, their decision being boosted by the fact it was the week of Howden's 40th. They drove to Edinburgh in two cars. Angie and I decided to travel by train and agreed to meet them in the bar at Waverley Station on Saturday afternoon. We boarded the train and managed to find ourselves seats with a table and got ourselves settled for our one and a half hour journey north. Five minutes after the train left Newcastle Central Station Angie poured a

7

couple of vodka and lemonades (our favourite tipple) from a water bottle in which she had prepared the mix earlier.

A couple of months previous to this, Elaine and Tam had been to Carlisle races where Elaine had won a share in a racehorse through a prize draw. The horse, Youwontcatchmenow had been entered that day for a race at Chepstow, and Elaine had been told it was fancied to run well. We would still be on the train when the race was due off, so Tam told me he would put a good bet on for us, and I could square up what I owed him when we got to Edinburgh.

We arrived at Waverley station to be greeted on the platform by Elaine and Tam, who handed me a bundle of banknotes, Youwontcatchmenow had won at 11/2.

We joined Howden and Lisa who were waiting in the station bar and had a few drinks before hiring taxis to take us to our hotel, the Holiday Inn which is adjacent the zoo. Thirty minutes after checking in we had freshened up and regrouped in the hotel bar for a quick drink before hitting the big city for the birthday celebrations.

The next morning Angie and I were prematurely woken by the sound of chimpanzees that had been let out of their overnight pens and were noisily patrolling their territory. Both suffering from hangovers we made our way down to breakfast, of which we ate very little. Instead we decided to grab another hour's sleep before checking out, loading the cars and heading for the races.

We travelled the 9 mile from our hotel to the racecourse on what turned out to be a warm sunny day for the time of year, with luckily no icy winds blowing across the North Sea, even though Angie still thought it was freezing. I don't know if Musselburgh is always busy or if it was because the days sponsor John Smiths were giving away free pints, but a really good crowd had turned out.

At the time I had no particular system for betting, usually the odds of the horse governed the bet, the shorter the price the bigger the bet. I know quite a few punters who do the same. I must admit I have had some good days betting in this way and also some disastrous days.

After reading the race card and the Racing Post it looked like the favourites were going to have a good day. I had a £20 placepot on the six favourites and £80 win on the first favourite Mr Auchterlonie at odds of 5/4. Everything was going well until he blundered and came down at the second last. I recovered in the second with £60 on Count Fosco which won at 5/2. I didn't back another winner all afternoon.

Angie who was betting with the Tote, and going to a different window for each race as she was handing them a handful of £2 coins each time also backed Count Fosco, she also got the forecast up in the third race.

Howden who is a fan of J. Howard Johnson backed Mr. Dude which won at 14/1.

Elaine backed Themanfromcarlisle, I think it was because she liked the name, but she claims to have really fancied its chances but that also won at 14/1.

Tam and Lisa had what you would call in betting terms a quiet day.

We said our farewells to Howden and Lisa, and were dropped off by Tam and Elaine at Waverley Station, everyone promising to meet up again soon. As we had quite a while to wait for our train we headed back to the station bar as our hangovers had long since subsided.

After reflecting on the weekend we started talking about holidays, and how in the past our daughter Hollie had looked after the dogs while we were away enjoying warmer climates. However, Hollie was planning on leaving home in the near future to move in with her boyfriend Michael, who is also from Dudley, but at that time was living and working in Edinburgh of all places. Although Grant was more than willing and more than capable of taking care of Cassie and Zak, two or three days would be his limit. We had always said we wouldn't put the dogs into boarding kennels, so holidays would be out of the question for the foreseeable future.

Even though we had seen quite a bit of Europe and even further afield neither of us had actually travelled a great deal round the UK. We were both keen race goers and we had both been to quite a few tracks, but there was a lot more we hadn't been to.

Seizing the opportunity to fulfil my secret ambition I came up with an idea; we would go racing to every track in the UK (59 at the time) maybe not a holiday but at least it would be giving us a break from our regular routines. I thought I would keep all the programmes as a memento starting with today's from Musselburgh.

Doing this we only had to leave the dogs in Grant's care for a day or two. We both agreed to go for it.

On the train journey home I suggested collecting our next programme from Sedgefield the following day.

Angie's verdict:

When I tell people I am a fan of horse racing and have visited all the tracks in the U.K. and Ireland I get a mixed reaction, some are intrigued and want to know all about it, and others are shocked as they think it is a male only pastime. However a survey that was carried out in 2000 on Britain's 59 racecourses revealed women accounted for 40% of race goers.

All racecourses are different and I can respect the management teams of each one are making the most of their available resources, and some doing their level best just to keep their heads above water, but this is no excuse for having poor facilities, and I am sure if this was made a priority, more tracks would benefit through bigger attendances.

Bearing in mind this is only my own personal view, I will give each racecourse a rating on how I found it on my visit. The majority of courses have private boxes, restaurants with waitress service and hospitality packages, for all of these I would advise you to book in advance. We are like most race goers and are mainly interested in the racing but we still like to know we can get a drink and a meal or a snack if we need one. On this basis, along with, cleanliness (especially the toilets) viewing and friendliness I will give my scoring. You must remember these are my own views and even Dave would score them differently. Or why not take the opportunity to go and score them all yourselves.

Since before Christmas I had been saving £2 coins, I had accumulated over £200. They were all bagged and ready to change into notes, unfortunately I forgot to go to the bank so I took them all with me; imagine the weight. Luckily I always carry a large handbag in which I usually carry binoculars, a water bottle (vodka), the Racing Post, or the bible as it is called in our house, along with all my personal items.

Even though I was slightly hung-over, I was ready for my day at the races. Although I don't like it too busy it's nice to see decent crowds at race meetings, even on a freezing cold day in February. Good crowds are what keep the racecourses going. Some people don't realise how much money it costs to stage a meeting. Musselburgh is a non-profit organisation, so everything they earn is invested back into the racecourse.

The general layout is good; it's not too small, nor too big so you're not walking all the time as everything is close to hand.

The facilities are nice and clean, and there are plenty of places to eat and drink. Staff are friendly and helpful, (just a shame they didn't hand out hot water bottles at the entrance).

It is quite a long walk from the car park to the entrance. Fair to say at this point ladies, 99% of car parks are fields, so wear either flats or wedges otherwise you'll be constantly cleaning mud from your heels!

Rating: Good ★★★★

How to get there:

To get there by road; satellite navigation maybe the in thing and
you may think we are dinosaurs but whenever we are driving
anywhere we use a copy of an AA route planner and a back up
road atlas. However Musselburgh is quite easy to find; both the
town and the racecourse are well sign posted coming off the A1.
Parking is free.

To get there by train; Wallyford is the closest station to
Musselburgh, trains run here from Edinburgh (Waverley). On
race days there is a courtesy bus which runs to the course,
returning after the last race.

Bus services 15 and 15a leaving from Edinburgh Princess Street
both run past the course.

Nearest airport is Edinburgh (17.6 miles)

Musselburgh itself has quite a few guesthouse and bed and
breakfast accommodation, which would be a lot more convenient
for the races than staying in Edinburgh, but Auld Reekie is a city
well worth a visit.

Monday 7 February 2005

Sedgefield Racecourse
Stockton on Tees
TS21 2HW
Tel: 01740 621925
www.sedgefield-racecourse.co.uk

Apart from the five Scottish tracks, which include Kelso as it is situated in the borders; Newcastle racecourse which is only 2 mile from our house is the most northerly track. We have two out to the west of us, Hexham and Carlisle. Heading south the nearest track is Sedgefield, which is approximately 40 miles. We can get there by car comfortably in an hour.

So getting ready to go to Sedgefield meant no rushing about, we had time to read the Racing Post over breakfast and take the dogs out for a walk before heading south to Sedgefield. The car we had at the time was a Citroen XM estate. A big car with a 2 litre engine, when I say big I mean long, as it was about 2 foot longer than any other estate car so had plenty room in the back for the dogs and its hydraulic suspension made it quite comfortable to travel in.

Anyway we arrived at the course in good time; real February weather had kicked in and it was bitter cold. Yes it is nice to get dressed up for the races, but Angie always says it makes more sense to dress for the weather.

We have been to Sedgefield on many occasions and it has always been quite a lucky track for us. I haven't seen him for a while now, but there used to be this old guy who would be greeting people as they were getting out of their cars, and offering to mark their race card for a couple of quid. I don't know whether he was getting information from the travelling lads as the horse boxes were pulling in or he was just a good judge, but letting him mark your card was usually a fiver well spent.

I decided to use the same tactics as I had the day before and put a £20 placepot on the six favourites. The first race was a hard race a beginners chase, I put £20 on Its Harry at 6/1 trained by Sue Smith, it finished last of the horses that completed the course but at least the favourite was second. The second and third races I had two £80 bets, both favourites, both won, Corlande, again trained by Sue Smith at 6/4 which returned 5/4 and top style at 2/1 which returned 15/8. If you go racing always look around the betting ring for the best odds for your chosen horse, even a quarter of a point makes a difference to your returns. No more winners but the first five favourites had been placed; my last horse in the placepot was Britesand 9/4 favourite and was pretty strong in the market. The race was a two mile bumper (national hunt flat race).Turning for home I pretty soon knew my fate, Britesand could only manage fourth. It so happens this was the only race Angie got a return in, she backed the second each way, The Wifes Sister at 33/1.

While heading for the exit we seen the strangest thing, there was this guy running around the area behind the grandstand like a headless chicken, every few seconds he would stop, raise his hand to his neck and make a slicing movement as if cutting his throat. It turned out his wallet had been stolen. Unfortunately where there are big crowds pickpockets will be operating, and because of the amount of money exchanged at the courses, racing is a prime target for these highly skilled thieves. I never take a wallet to the races; I wear trousers with buttoned back pockets, jackets with inside pockets and a shirt with a breast pocket. I always split my money up and put so much in each pocket. It might seem a little extreme, but better safe than sorry. It hadn't been a brilliant day betting wise but not as bad as the pickpocket's victim.

Angie's verdict:

I quite liked the idea of visiting all the racetracks, I'd already been to a few but not as many as Dave as he used to go racing even before I met him with his mates. I knew it was a bit of a secret ambition of his to see all the courses so I couldn't see any reason why he couldn't fulfil his dream and no reason why I shouldn't go along with him. Not exactly a holiday but at least the odd night staying in a hotel.

We have been to Sedgefield many times and one thing you can be guaranteed is a decent crowd and a very friendly atmosphere. We have always been given a complimentary race card at Sedgefield which I think is a nice touch, and it might not be much but it saves you a couple of quid.

There is a restaurant in the main stand and bars where as well as a wide selection of drinks you can purchase hot and cold snacks. There are usually one or two catering vans parked behind the grandstand selling fast food.

From the stands which overlook the parade ring you get an excellent view of the course.

There are ramps designed to give wheelchair users mobility around the enclosure. Everywhere is kept clean and the toilets are okay.

In the centre of the course is the family enclosure from where the best viewing is on the running rails. When Hollie and Grant were younger they enjoyed this enclosure as there were usually a few children's rides.

There is also a bar in the family enclosure which also offers hot and cold snacks.

Rating: Average ★★★

How to get there:

To get there by road; Sedgefield is one of the courses I would suggest driving to, it is easy to find being only five minutes from junction 60 off the A1 (M) from here the course is well signposted.

There is plenty free parking, although there is a £5 charge for paddock parking.

To get there by rail; the nearest mainline stations are Darlington and Durham, both about twenty minutes away by taxi. There are buses that run from both Newcastle and Middlesbrough to Sedgefield town, which is about a mile and a half from the course.

Nearest airport is Teesside (9 miles).

There is plenty accommodation in the Durham and Teesside areas. Finding hotels up and down the country is quite easy now with the help of the internet, and you can usually get a better rate by booking online.

Wednesday 9 February 2005

Carlisle Racecourse
Durdar Road
Carlisle
Cumbria
CA2 4TS
Tel: 01288 522973
www.carlisle-races.co.uk

More birthday celebrations, this time mine. 49 today, eight years older than Angie. We were up pretty early as we had planned to go to Carlisle races if the weather wasn't too bad. Angie and I getting up early didn't please the kids because Angie insisted everybody must be there while I opened my cards and presents. As usual I got some nice gifts plus a few quid cash which had been tucked away inside my cards. One of the presents Angie had bought me was called a gift experience which she had bought from Boots. The gift itself was a box containing a voucher for a one night stay in a hotel for two people, a brochure showing a choice of hotels and a disposable camera. Over the next week or so I pondered over the possible hotels which could be used for a racing trip, I eventually decided on Chester, but ideally two nights would have been better, and so to save the hassle of paying for one night by voucher and a second night by Visa I went to Boots and purchased a second gift experience, with these I booked a two night stay in Chester for a fixture in June.

With the present opening ceremonies over we had to make a decision, and although there was still a cold wind blowing it was quite bright outside, so Carlisle was to be my birthday destination. Hollie, who hadn't left home yet had agreed to look after the dogs for the day before making her way back to bed (Grant had already disappeared upstairs shortly after the last card had been opened).

I had every intention of having a drink on my birthday, so a taxi to Newcastle Central station and a train to Carlisle seemed the best option. Carlisle is only fifty miles from Newcastle, and a ride of about an hour and a half depending on how many stations the train calls at on the journey east to west. The line more or less follows the same route made by Emperor Hadrian while building the historic Roman wall.

Having made an early start we arrived in Carlisle with plenty time to spare, so we found a cafe where we enjoyed a full English breakfast before making our way to the taxi rank. We have found that if there is a queue at a taxi rank on race days, the chances are someone else in the queue is going racing, so don't be afraid to ask them. You will find most people are more than willing to share the cost of a cab. We found an elderly couple who were very happy to share and with who we had a great conversation on our way to the track.

I decided to bet £40 level stake in each race on the seven race fixture. I also picked out a £10 placepot of which I had four placed. Out of the rest of my bets I had the first winner Jorobaden at 6/4.The second winner Why The Big Paws at 7/2 and the fifth winner Corrib Lad at 9/4

Angie also backed Why The Big Paws and Corrib Lad along with two seconds and a third.

Keeping out of the cold wind we spent most of the afternoon in the bar under the grandstand, where we found two seats close to a television screen. This is where Angie's water bottle came into play as she had filled it with neat vodka. So after buying an initial round of vodka and lemonades in order to obtain two glasses, I only needed to buy lemonade to be used as a mixer. I know this a bit naughty but it does keep the costs down as vodka is never cheap at racecourses.

There were two other meetings on that afternoon, Ludlow and Lingfield which were both being televised on the tote television screen we were close to, so for a bit extra entertainment we took

18

turns at having a £5 tote bet on horses to be placed at both meetings. We didn't make a fortune but were quite successful. After racing we shared a taxi with two guys back to Carlisle where we had a few drinks in the bars near the station before our train ride back to Newcastle.

When we got to Newcastle Angie took me for an Indian meal to round off a very enjoyable birthday.

Angie's verdict:

As Dave says, we went for a drink. I feel I have to give this piece of advice early on, drinking and betting don't mix! If I know we're not going to any race meeting by car (which usually means we'll be drinking) I look at the Racing Post, get a good idea of my horses then when I've seen the race card mark down what I fancy, then we can start drinking. No matter how much money I win I never change my stake, and only change my horse if the one I've marked doesn't look right in the parade ring.

Carlisle Racecourse is a really nice course to visit. We have been there on a number of occasions as it is a convenient venue to meet up with Dave's sister Elaine and her husband Tam.

The grandstand is modern, clean and spacious with plenty of clean toilets. There is a restaurant in the County (member's) stand as well as bar facilities. From here the parade ring and winners enclosure are accessible and all other areas of the enclosures. The parade ring is actually a nice area to sit as it is usually sheltered from the wind.

The Tattersalls enclosure has bars and a variety of food to choose from. You also have access to the parade ring and winners enclosure.

Both enclosures have very good viewing though I would recommend you watch from the stands as a dip in the track a couple of furlongs out mean you lose sight of the action if watching from ground level. Facilities for the disabled include; parking, viewing platforms, toilets and lifts.

Rating: Good ★★★

Tip: Always wrap up well in the winter months, 3 hours is a long time to be outside in the cold. Also wear comfortable shoes as you might be on your feet all day.

How to get there:

To get there by road; take exit 42 off the M6 motorway and simply follow the signs to the course where there is plenty of free parking. Trackside parking costs £5 on weekdays and £7 on weekends.

To get there by train; Carlisle station is 2.3 miles from the course, there is a taxi rank just outside the station.

Nearest airport Newcastle (51 miles)

There are plenty hotels in the Carlisle area.

Saturday 19 March 2005

Newcastle Racecourse
High Gosforth Park
Newcastle upon Tyne
NE3 5HP
Tel: 0191 2362020
www.newcastleracecourse.

Newcastle, our local course is only a couple of miles from where we live. It is set in High Gosforth Park, an 800-acre woodland estate approximately 4 miles north of Newcastle city centre. We actually go to Gosforth Park four or five times a week, as there is some really good walks through the estate for the dogs.

Apart from the racecourse, the estate has two golf courses, a driving range, a huge wildlife reserve, a football complex (which is new), a garden centre and a scout camp, which I think is closed now. I have heard rumours it is going to be a caravan park. Also within the estate are The Gosforth Park (Marriot) Hotel and the Border Minstrel pub.

We used to go racing at Newcastle almost every time a fixture fell within my days off work, but since we started travelling round the rest of the courses we don't get there as much. However, one meeting we do try to get to every season is the Fighting Fifth hurdle which is held near the end of November. The reason this fixture is so special is it was where I took Angie on our first date.

When I first started going to Newcastle races there were three enclosures; the Member's enclosure, the Tattersalls and the Silver ring. The Silver ring being the cheapest, I think it was something like £3 or £4 entrance fee. When the Northumberland plate (pitman's derby) meeting was on in June, and the sun was shining, the Silver ring would be packed with working class families picnicking on the large grassy area adjacent the furlong pole. I don't know the reason why, but they closed the Silver ring turnstiles which made the paddock the cheapest admission and an expensive family day out.

The Northumberland Plate meeting still draws huge crowds, but the traditional pitman's derby family crowds have been lost in my opinion. A while ago while walking the dogs, we noticed construction work being carried out in the old Silver ring area. One of the old buildings had been demolished and a new building was being erected. I thought they were going to reopen the old family enclosure, but it turned out to be facilities for the new football complex.

We were in two minds whether to go racing on this day as it was a poor card which included a two horse race. But we had nothing better to do, so we went racing. This is something you must bear in mind when planning racing trips in advance, having booked hotels, travel tickets etc. the meeting you have chosen might have small fields of poor quality. When these occasions happen, you just have to make the most of it. A worse enemy is the British weather as we would find out in due time.

Because of the poor fields I didn't bother having a placepot, and decided only to bet £20 a race, missing out the two horse race altogether. It wasn't really cold outside but it was damp, so we thought we would just stay inside and place our bets on the tote. Amazingly we both backed the first winner Lady Past Times paying £10.50p on the tote.

Angie backed the second winner Torkingking which paid £4.10p a win.

In the rest of the races we didn't even get a run for our money. After racing we went into the Border minstrel for a couple of drinks, before getting a taxi to Brough Park (Newcastle greyhound stadium).

Angie's verdict:

The number of times we have been to Newcastle our local course is in 3 figures, so we could probably write a book on our experiences at Newcastle races alone.

The track in my opinion is one of the best in the country, unfortunately the back straight runs alongside woodland, which in the winter shades the track from the sun, and it won't be the first time our plans have been ruined due to the races being abandoned because of frost.

Change of owners and money invested has vastly improved the facilities at Newcastle though I think they still have a little way to go.

The Premier enclosure has a restaurant as well as bars and food outlets, one criticism I have is there isn't enough seats. This is also the case in the Grandstand and Paddock enclosure, where there is a self service restaurant as well as bars and fast food outlets.

In years past we have been to meetings that have had very poor attendances and we have more or less had the bar to ourselves. In recent times the average attendances are a lot better which is good, although Dave is always moaning about the size of the queues at the bar. In fact he says the only chance you have of getting served quickly is to go to the bar while a race is running.

Accompanied U16s are admitted free, but with there not being a family enclosure it can work out an expensive day. Newcastle does welcome kids however and often have a fun fair for their enjoyment. There are ramps, lifts and disabled facilities in both enclosures. The toilets are just average and hopefully will be the target for the next improvement.

Viewing is very good and Newcastle is well worth a visit, you will also meet one of the friendliest crowds in the country.
Rating: Average ★★★

How to get there:

To get there by car; the racecourse is well sign posted and just off both the A1 and the A19; there are acres of free parking.
To get there by rail; Newcastle Central station is easily reached from all directions, from here you can either get a taxi from outside the station, or catch a metro (regional train) from inside the Central station to either Regents centre or Four lane ends Metro stations, where there are free hopper buses to the track. These buses return up to one hour after the last race, but I would check with the driver on arrival the times of the return buses.
Bus services 42, 43, 44 and 45 leaving from Newcastle Haymarket bus station all stop outside the entrance to Gosforth Park. From here, walk through the entrance gates, then it is about a five minute walk until you come to the enclosures, just past the Border Minstrel pub on the right hand side.
Nearest airport is Newcastle (3 miles).
There is any amount of hotels in the area. Staying in Newcastle itself is a good option as it has a good variety of bars and restaurants, and was voted one of the five most popular destinations in the country for a night on the town.

Thursday 7 April 2005

Aintree Racecourse
Ormskirk Road
Aintree
Liverpool
L9 5AS
Tel: 0151 5222929.
www.aintree.co.uk

As a boy, I lived with my parents and my sister Elaine in a council flat on Longbenton Estate, which is on the outskirts of Newcastle. In those days, before computer games, the main interest for young lads was to play football. Every night after school we would have a kick around, but Saturdays were special. Every Saturday as soon as there were enough players we would start a match. The game would last all day. As more people came they would just join in, twenty a side wouldn't be unusual. Players would be called in by their parents at meal times, then join back in afterwards. There was only two things that stopped the game; the FA Cup final and the Grand National, everyone went indoors to watch them. It seemed that every parent, no matter how poor managed to put e/w bets on the Grand National for the whole family. It is still the bookmaker's busiest day of the year. Even from that early age I said that one day I would go and watch the race live.

I thought that day had come when we went on an organised Grand National coach trip run by our local newspaper. We would leave on Friday, stop in Blackpool overnight, racing Saturday then back to Blackpool for another night before returning to Newcastle on Sunday. Elaine and Tam also came on the trip, but instead of driving from Scotland to Newcastle, they drove straight to the hotel in Blackpool.

We hadn't backed a winner but were having a great day, three races gone, all won by big priced horses. Then the biggest

25

nightmare you could imagine happened. There was a lot of confusion going on, and then an announcement came over the public address system. The year was 1997, everyone was told to make their way to the centre of the course, and word got out there had been an I.R.A. bomb scare. After much chaos the rest of the meeting was abandoned. We stood for what seemed like hours, when someone told us they weren't letting the coaches' leave as they all had to be searched. It would be hard to describe what it was like, but thousands of people were stranded with no transport. The only logical thing to do was to start walking. We headed along Ormskirk road until we came to an Asda store where we called in for a welcoming warm drink. There was a massive queue at the public telephone box, with people desperate to find transport. What next? Head towards the motorway, we then had an unbelievable stroke of luck. We had just reached the roundabout on the entrance to the motorway where a taxi driver responded to us flagging him down, and he was more than willing to take a fare to Blackpool. We sat in the hotel bar for the rest of the evening, and even though we went to bed late, there were still people from our coach trip returning from their day at the races, each one with their own story to tell.

The next morning the coach driver had to go back to Aintree to retrieve our transport. Not knowing how long he would be, I asked someone to let him know we wouldn't be travelling back to Newcastle on the coach. Instead we got a lift with Tam and Elaine to Carlisle and caught a train home. Watching the news that night, it was announced that the big race would be run the next day. There would be one race only, the rest of the card cancelled. Not to be beat, Monday 7th April 1997, I drove to Aintree, parked the car in Asda car park and walked to the course. On arrival I was handed a race card with just the one race in it. Lord Gyllene won the Grand National, the horse I backed, Lo Stragone didn't finish, but at least I had fulfilled my boyhood ambition and seen the race live.

This time round we decided to go on the Thursday, the first day of the National meeting. I don't know if I was swayed by our earlier trip, but again I booked to stay in Blackpool, the Travel Inn, Blackpool central. We arrived on the Friday night and got a taxi down to the tower which was about two miles. Blackpool at the beginning of April is dead, most of the bars on the sea front were shut and the cold wind blowing in off the sea helped explain why there wasn't many folk around. We went one street back off the sea front, firstly to get some shelter and secondly to find a decent pub. We hadn't walked far when we found it, and I couldn't have given it a better name "The Lifeboat". A warm, friendly, bar with a good atmosphere and reasonably priced drinks. We stayed there for a couple of hours before moving on to Brannigans night club followed by an Indian restaurant. I must tell you at this point; we always eat late and when away from home nearly always Indian or Chinese food.

The next morning we had breakfast at our hotel before heading off on our 50 mile drive to Aintree. Once again we parked in Asda car park which is about a twenty minute walk from the course. Even though we got away with it, I wouldn't recommend to anyone to park there as they have a wheel clamping policy in operation. I think we only parked there because of what had happened on the last trip to Aintree when they weren't letting vehicles leave before being searched for explosives.

The strong wind that had swept Blackpool promenade the night before had eased, but was still blowing cold. When we arrived at the course there was a big queue, as security officers were thoroughly searching everyone before they entered (lessons learned). As far as the betting went, we had one of our better days. My plan was to bet £40 and Angie who had now run out of £2 coins was betting £20 a race, any profits to be carried forward to the next racing trip. There were seven races on the card, but we decided to leave after six and head back to the car before the mad rush.

Angie started the ball rolling by having £20 win on the first winner Monet's Garden at 11/2.

I had £40 on Grey Abbey at 11/4 which won the second

We both backed the next winner Faasel, both got 11/4, (£40 and £20)

Slightly away from plan I had £60 on the winner of the Foxhunters' chase Katarino at 100/30

Angie backed the fifth winner Fota Island for which she got 7/2

Nothing back in the sixth, after which we headed for the car and drove back to Newcastle, content with having showing a good profit on the day.

On the Saturday, Grand National day, we were taking Hollie and her belongings to Edinburgh as she was moving in with her boyfriend Michael. I stopped off at Ladbrokes en route and gave Angie £40 to have a bet in the big race. She had £20 e/w on Hedgehunter at 8/1. While travelling we were listening to the race on the car radio, we had more or less just pulled up at Michaels flat when Hedgehunter crossed the line, winner of the 2005 Grand National.

Angie's verdict:

I must say, I'm not a great lover of massive crowds, but to go to Aintree for the Grand National meeting is a must. We actually went on the first day of the festival which was a really cold, blustery day. I usually like to get dressed for race meetings but the weather told me smart but warm, so I opted for a pair of trousers and a long thick cardi. A lot of the ladies were dressed in flimsy dresses and hats, and even though they looked lovely it must have been a nightmare having one hand permanently on your hat and the other trying to stop your dress blowing up.

When the starter let the horses go for the first race the roar from the crowd was incredible; I got goose bumps all over. The atmosphere all day was electric. When you look around you can see the whole place is buzzing.

As you can probably imagine there are a number of enclosures at Aintree. The County stand which overlooks the winning post has bars and food catering on both levels. There is both seated viewing and rooftop standing in this enclosure, but being on the finishing line means badges sell out quickly for the County stand. Both the Princess Royal stand which is just before the winning post and the Queen mother stand which is just after the post have seated and rooftop standing viewing facilities. There are bars and food catering in both enclosures and again both stands are very popular.

By far the biggest enclosure and where we spent our afternoon is the Tattersalls which has bars, food outlets and catering vans throughout the enclosure. A huge marquee with bars, food and live music playing was also erected in the Tattersalls. The best viewing is from the Aintree mound where you can watch the horses running up the home straight, though if you can manage to find a space at the rails you can get a lot closer to the action.

All the mentioned enclosures have access to the parade ring and the winner's enclosure as well as the trade stands.

Disabled visitors will find the Princess Royal and Queen Mother Stands' are best equipped, but again I would advise you to book early.

On Grand National Saturday the No Nonsense enclosure is opened. This is the only enclosure where children get in free on National day. There is an open air seating platform, but apart from watching the National field pass a couple of times racing is viewed on big screens. A bar and food facilities are available in the stand.

Children are allowed in Tattersalls free on the Thursday and Friday of the National meeting if accompanied by an adult, but a better option might be to take them to family day in October when there is entertainment put on and you will be less likely to lose your offspring in the crowds.

Even though there was such a big crowd, the staff at Aintree was constantly making sure the enclosures were kept tidy. I only used the portaloos but they were spotlessly clean.

Rating: Excellent ★★★★★

How to get there:

To get there by car; from the north, leave the M6 at junction 26 and join the M58, you will pick up signs for the races from here. From the south, leave the M6 at junction 21A and join the M62 westbound, at junction 6 take the M57 signposted Southport; again you will pick up the racecourse signs.

There is a free car park from which they have a park and ride scheme, the car park is also well signposted.

To get there by rail; Liverpool Lime street is the nearest mainline station, a short walk brings you to Liverpool Central station. From here you catch the Ormskirk train which stops at Aintree. The station is opposite the racecourse entrance.

Nearest airport Liverpool (20 minutes) Manchester (40 minutes) Needless to say, with Liverpool being one of the biggest cities in the UK, finding accommodation is no problem, with a good selection of hotels within a few miles of the track.

Thursday 21 April 2005

Perth Racecourse
Scone Palace Park
Perth
PH2 6BB
Tel: 01738 551597
www.perth-races.co.uk

On previous visits we had booked accommodation in Perth but
this time we thought we would go back to Edinburgh after racing
and pay Hollie a surprise visit.
Grant was quite happy in his new role as dog sitter while we were
away though his rules were he would feed them and walk them
but he wasn't sitting in the house with them all day and all night.
Because it was going to be a surprise visit to Hollie we just told
Grant we were going racing and would be stopping away
overnight, and because he didn't ask where we were going we
didn't tell him. What we did tell him was if he encountered any
problems to ring Angie's mobile and if necessary we would come
straight home.
We had left in what we thought was good time for the races, but
we met traffic problems on both the A1 and the Edinburgh by
pass. By the time we reached the Forth road bridge we were
cutting it a bit tight, and what made it worse was, the clothes
Angie was travelling in were not the clothes she was going to
wear for the races, luckily the M90 north of the bridge was quiet.
We stopped for 5 minutes at Kinross services to allow Angie to
get changed before setting off for the last leg of the journey. It
was on this final stretch of road to Perth that the mobile phone
rang, expecting the worse Angie answered the phone. Luckily it
was Hollie making her daily phone call, she told Angie she was
looking for a job in Edinburgh which to us was a good sign that
she was settling into her new surroundings. After they had
finished exchanging their daily chit chat Angie told Hollie we

were on our way to Beverley races and Grant was Dog sitting. (If we had told her Perth she would have been expecting us).

We actually arrived at the course with a bit time to spare, but traffic is one thing you must take into consideration when travelling, especially travelling any distance. There have been times we have seen traffic jams over five miles long on motorways, though luckily they have always been going in the opposite direction to what we have been travelling. Not allowing enough time, and running into one of these tail backs could totally ruin your whole day.

I was betting £40 a race and Angie £20.We managed two winners each but unfortunately they were the same ones; Napolitan in the first and Commercial Flyer in the last, both at even money. Although it didn't rain while we were there the ground was wet and cars were finding it difficult to get off the car park with a tractor on stand by to tow anyone who couldn't make it to the road. Fortunately we did make it, though I must admit it was a struggle.

From Perth we drove fifty miles back to Edinburgh and found the hotel we had booked for the night, The Holiday Inn express, Edinburgh city centre. Parking in the city centre isn't the easiest, but the hotel had special rates for their guests in the N.C.P. near by.

After checking in we dumped our overnight bag in the room, and then went back to the main street from where we flagged down a taxi. Our destination was the Haymarket public bar which was Hollie and Michael's local. Angie and I still suited up looked a little bit out of place as we joined Michael and some of his workmates for drinks as they had came in after a days work on a building site

Angie made a phone call to Hollie to let her know where we were, and about four minutes later she came walking through the door. It had only been two weeks since we'd taken Hollie to Edinburgh, but it had seemed a lot longer. She was obviously happy in her new surroundings and acted as our personal guide as we enjoyed a night on the town.

Angie's verdict:

Perth racecourse and the surrounding area is very picturesque and if it hadn't been for the fact we were dropping in to see Hollie we would have definitely been staying there overnight.

When Dave said "we thought we had left in good time" what he really meant is he himself thought we had left in good time, and at one stage I thought I was going to the races in my jeans and T shirt.

Because we have always visited Perth races during the festival it has always been busy, but it has always been a real friendly atmosphere. With activities for the kids who get in free to every fixture if accompanied by an adult it can be a fun family day racing.

There is a range of bars and eating places throughout the enclosure as well as food vans and a few trade stands. One of the stands that day had a massive display of what a lot of parents in the Newcastle area would call rubbish: a range of sugary confectionary guaranteed to play havoc with your tooth enamel, Dave's sister would have been in heaven as I've never known anybody with such a sweet tooth.

The track is virtually flat which is great for viewing from the stands as you can see right round the course. We usually position ourselves close to the finishing line, but we watched a couple of races from the roof of a toilet block that is positioned close to the rails just past the winning post, from here we had a great head on view.

There are viewing ramps for the disabled, and with the area being so flat people in wheelchairs can easily manoeuvre round the enclosure.

Rating: Good ★★★

Both Hollie and I were very pleased to see each other, and even though nothing much had been going on in the two weeks since she had moved out we still found plenty to talk about, it was late into the night before we finally said our goodbyes.

How to get there:

To get there by car; from the South take the M90, leave at junction 11 onto the A85 where you follow the signs for Scone palace, these will take you to the course, from the north follow the A9.

Parking is free except for the picnic area which costs £15 per car (max. 4 adults)

To get there by rail, Perth has a mainline railway station which is about two and a half miles from the course; there is a free bus service from the town centre to the course.

Nearest airport Dundee (16 miles)

Perth is a very popular tourist destination; the Stone of Destiny, which was the throne on which the kings of Scotland were crowned, was once housed in Scone Castle.

Because of its popularity Perth has a wide range of value accommodation.

Saturday 23 April 2005

Ripon Racecourse
Boroughbridge Road
Ripon
North Yorkshire
HG4 1UG
Tel: 01675 602156
www.ripon-races.co.uk

If you are seriously considering visiting all the courses it is a good idea to try and fit more than one course into your trips especially if travelling long distances, if nothing else it saves on petrol money. Ripon and Wetherby are only an hour and a half from Newcastle but only 20 miles apart, so with them having racing on consecutive days we thought it a good plan to have a two day trip staying overnight in Yorkshire.

Because Grant wasn't working at the time there was no reason why he couldn't feed and exercise the dogs while we were away. In fact I think he quite enjoyed having the house to himself, especially when his mates came round as they could have the comfort of the living room instead of Grant's bedroom where they would normally sit.

On the Saturday morning I took Cassie and Zak to Gosforth Park (location of Newcastle Racecourse) for a good walk while Angie packed our case. Both dogs went very sulky when the suitcase came out, so it was best that I got them out the way while Angie was packing.

Setting off late morning we were rather surprised at how little traffic there was on the road, or there was until we reached a half mile from the course. It was here we joined the queue of traffic for the races, being a nice sunny day I think half of Yorkshire had decided to go racing. One consolation was the queue was moving and 15 minutes later we were guided by an attendant to line up among the hundreds of cars that had already been parked up.

With a bit time on our hands we had a walk around the enclosures before going for lunch in the self service restaurant. I have never tried a pint of John Smiths but it seemed to be becoming a very popular ale and the steak and John Smiths ale pie looked very nice so we both opted for that.

As we sat near the parade ring after lunch the sun was beating down and Angie told me to take my tie off and loosen my collar. This wasn't because I was hot but because it was covered in gravy from my steak pie. We sat for a while going through the card for Ripon and having a look at what was running at the rest of the days meetings, and as usual like most people are before racing we were quietly confident that we were in for a good day.

Studying the race card and the Racing Post didn't do us much good as I backed our only winner at Ripon that afternoon when I had £40 on Bow Bridge which won the third race at 3/1.

We did have another winner that afternoon however; 99% of the times we go racing we only bet on horses at the meeting we are at, but Angie fancied Well Chief which was running at Sandown that day and after looking at the race card I too thought it had a good chance, so we put £80 between us with the tote. Well Chief won paying £3.10p a win covering our expenses for the day.

After racing we drove to Harrogate where we had a room booked in the Moat House (I think it is now the Holiday Inn) and after an hour or two relaxing we had an enjoyable evening sampling Harrogate's nightlife.

Angie's verdict:

Being a sunny day made our trip to Ripon "the garden racecourse" even more pleasurable. There are three enclosures at Ripon Racecourse; Club, Tattersalls and Course, we did have a walk around the Tattersalls but spent most of the afternoon in the Club enclosure.

There is a wide variety of bars and restaurants in the two main enclosures as well as a few catering vans selling fast food and beverages. The Course enclosure also has a bar and a tea bar.

After we'd eaten lunch we managed to find a seat on the lawn at the back of the stands where we sat for half an hour reading through the card. Not far from where we were sitting a band was playing in the Victorian style bandstand, I can still picture the elderly conductor who was really into his role, and watching him you would have thought he was performing at the last night of the proms.

We were also sitting close to what I think is a really nice parade ring though we weren't sitting close enough to get a good look at the horses. There is no access to the parade ring from the Course enclosure.

Ripon was the first course to install a permanent big screen which is especially good for those watching from ground level, viewing from the grandstand is also very good.

Disabled racegoers will find the Club enclosure has the best access and also has viewing facilities.

Children are also well looked after, and Ripon can boast another first as they were the first to include a playground among their facilities. They now have 2, one on each side of the course, and another bonus for kids is in August when one of their fixtures is children's day which includes all kinds of activities. Everywhere including the toilets is kept very clean and tidy.

Rating: Good ★★★

How to get there:

To get there by road;   Ripon is another easy racecourse to get to by road, travelling either from the north or the south you leave the A1, and take the B6265 towards Ripon where you will pick up the signs for the course.

Parking is free; cars can be taken into the centre of the course at £12 per car (max. 4 adults)

To get there by rail; there is no railway station at Ripon, the nearest is Harrogate (11 miles) from where you can get a taxi. The nearest mainline station is York (25 miles).

Nearest airport Leeds and Bradford (21 miles)

There isn't a lot of accommodation close to the course, but a good selection in the surrounding areas.

Sunday 24 April 2005

Wetherby Racecourse
York Road
Wetherby
West Yorkshire
LS22 5EJ
Tel: 01937 588021
www.wetherby.co.uk

After a good nights' sleep, we got up with plenty of time on our hands as Wetherby is only a twenty minute drive away from Harrogate. So after a hearty breakfast Angie suggested we have a walk into town, I agreed even though I knew it really meant Angie wanted to look around the shops for bargains. There is one shop in particular that amazes me and that is Debenhams, for no matter where we are if Angie sees a Debenhams shop she insists on going in, and as far as I can remember she has never bought anything there, at least not while I've been with her. We did buy one or two bits and bobs on our stroll around town, including a book on betting systems for which you would have needed to be a mathematician to understand.

As the morning went on the day got warmer, and by lunchtime when we set off to the races it was red hot. The drive to Wetherby was only eleven miles but with it being so hot, it was a bit uncomfortable, especially with a collar and tie on (not my gravy stained tie, which I think ended up in the bin in our room in Harrogate), so as we came to Spofforth, a village en route I pulled into a pub car park, and we went in for a refreshing pint of shandy. There was only two other customers in the pub and the barman/manager looked quite excited when we walked in suited up. He asked us if a wedding party was coming in, and his excitement soon faded when we told him we were going racing and only increased his takings by the price of a shandy and a fruit juice.

Although it was Angie's first visit I had been to Wetherby on a few occasions and it had always been a lucky track for me, today was to be no exception. It didn't start too well however when my horse in the first Present Glory was beaten ½ a length, but things improved as the day went on. In the second I had £40 on the winner Mr. Bigglesworth at 13/2 which won pulling away. In the third £80 on Bob Ar Aghaid at 9/4 which was even an easier winner. In the fourth, £80 on Irish Blessing at 9/2, another winner.

In the fifth I had £80 on Jacka du Gord at 9/2 who looked like winning when taking up the running at the second last, but another one beaten ½ a length. In the sixth, £100 on Stan at 5/2, my fourth winner of the day.

Then in the last I had £100 on Notaproblem at 6/4, and then on my way back to find Angie I stopped at another bookie and had another £100 at the now 5/4. When I got back to where Angie was waiting, I told her what I had done, and she told me she had backed the same horse, and was looking for her fourth winner of the afternoon, she had already been successful with; Bob Ar Aghaid, Irish Blessing and Stan all to a £20 stake. As they jumped the last and approached the winning post there were three horses almost in a line, Notaproblem held on to win, winning distances ¾ length and a neck. If you are lucky enough to back the winner of the last race (often nicknamed the getting out stakes) don't hang around before collecting your money as bookies like to get away from the course and aren't obliged to stay more than 10 minutes after the weigh in.

As you can imagine, the drive back to Newcastle was a happy one, before we got in the car I had emptied my pockets into Angie's bag for her to count our winnings. We had just had a free weekend, and a nice few quid to put into our racing kitty.

Angie's verdict:

We had passed the signs for Wetherby racecourse on numerous occasions, and though I sometimes looked over from the car you can't see much from the A1. It was when we approached the car park and the grandstand was in view that I realised it was a lot bigger than I had imagined it was going to be.

Another hot day and another big crowd had turned out for what was becoming more and more popular "Sunday racing" a thing that had been frowned upon in the past, as a lot of people believed and some still do that gambling shouldn't be allowed on the Sabbath.

There are 3 enclosures at Wetherby; the Premier, the Paddock and the Course enclosure.

Although we had Premier badges we still had to pay £2 each for seats in the raised viewing area above the grandstand in the Paddock. Dave thought this was good value as it gives you a really good view, but I thought it was a rip off. I can understand having to pay to upgrade to a better enclosure but not to downgrade.

Both the Premier and the Paddock have a number of bars and eating places. Viewing from both stands is very good (still a rip off) and both are clean and tidy. There is disabled parking and toilets.

The course enclosure has a bar and a tea bar, but it might suit you better to take the kids and have a picnic, there is a playground in the course enclosure. Best viewing in the course enclosure is on the rails.

Rating: Good ★★★

How to get there:

To get there by road; Wetherby is on the B1224 York/ Wetherby road and is just off the A1, from the north take the first Wetherby exit and from the south take the second Wetherby exit, sign posted racecourse, turn right onto the B1224 towards York and the racecourse is about half a mile from here.
Parking; parking is free except for the centre of the course which costs £14 per car (max. 4 adults).
To get there by rail; Harrogate station is about nine miles, Leeds station twelve miles and York station
fourteen miles.
There are buses that run to Wetherby from both Leeds and York.
Nearest airport Leeds and Bradford (13 miles)
There are both hotels and guest houses in and around Wetherby.

Wednesday 27 April 2005

Kelso Racecourse
18-20 Glendale Road
Wooler
Northumberland
NE71 6DW
Tel: 01668 280800
www.kelso-races.co.uk

With Kelso only being 70 miles from our house, and the meeting
we were going to an evening fixture, we should have had ample
time to sort ourselves out, so we could set off with plenty of time
to spare. However that wasn't to be the case, we encountered all
kinds of setbacks that morning which needed sorting out before
we left, meaning we were running very tight for time.
Eventually we were ready to leave, approximately an hour after
our intended departure time. As we were getting into the car I
realised my lace was loose, and like everything else that had
happened that day, while fastening my lace I managed to snap it.
Angie had said she wanted to stop at the local shop for a bottle of
water so I took a gamble the local shop would sell shoelaces and
off we went. Thankfully my gamble paid off and Angie managed
to get my laces. The route from our house to Kelso isn't the best
for making up lost time so it was going to be tight whether we
made it for the first race.
I had only ever been to Kelso once before, and that had been a lot
of years earlier. The one thing that stands out in my memory of
Kelso is, it is the only place I have ever had a bet on the result of
a photo finish. The grandstand at Kelso brings you very close to
the action, and it was here I was standing, right on the finishing
line where I witnessed the horse I had backed win, in what was a
very tight finish (photo called). In the betting ring the bookies
were calling 2/5 on my horse getting the verdict, so I had £50 of
what was a lot of money to me then, on the outcome of the photo.

43

It seemed ages before the result was called, and as the minutes went on I was starting to have doubts in my mind, eventually the result came through, my horse had been beaten a short head. I have never had a bet on a photo since.

When we pulled up in the car park the horses were already leaving the parade ring and were making their way down to the start for the first race. Moving as fast as we could towards the entrance gates, me with my toes clenched to help keep my shoe on, we managed to get to a tote window just in time to back our fancied runners. I was having £40 stakes that evening and Angie £20. I would have been better off missing the start as my horse finished fifth, however Angie backed the winner Tandava which paid £3.10p a win.

With new laces now holding my shoes on, we were able to relax and enjoy the rest of the evening.

We both backed the second winner Tribal Dispute, I got 11/10, and Angie backed it on the tote which paid £1. 90p.

We both backed the last winner Ever Present for which we both got 13/8.

If the drive to Kelso had been a nightmare, the drive home was even worse. Like I said the road isn't the best and it was pitch black, and for some reason even though it wasn't foggy visibility was more or less non existent. We eventually made it home, and the next morning I went to check the car only to find a thick coating of mud covering the headlights.

Angie's verdict:

Because we only just made it to Kelso in time for the first race, I didn't have time for my usual pre-racing walk around. As it happens it wouldn't have taken me very long as Kelso is quite small and compact. The buildings are quite old and basic, but everywhere including the toilets is very clean.

There are two enclosures at Kelso, the Members and the Tattersalls both having bars and a variety of eating places. There is parking, toilets and viewing ramps for the disabled. With the grandstand being so close to the running rail the viewing is excellent, I can't think of any other that brings you so close to the action.

Children under 16 get in free if accompanied by an adult, though I have read that picnics are not allowed on the course at Kelso, which doesn't really encourage families to their meetings. I find this a strange decision from a place that is claiming to be Britain's friendliest racecourse.

Kelso is a real country course and definitely worth a visit.

Rating: Average ★★★

How to get there:

I would say driving is your best option for getting to Kelso. From the south take the A1 (m) pick up the A697 and A698. Once in Kelso take the A6089 to the course, which is just north of the town. From the west, come off the M6 at junction 44, and then follow the A7 and A698.

There is free parking at the course.

To get there by rail, the nearest mainline station is Berwick which is 22 miles away. There is a limited bus service from Berwick.

Nearest airport is Newcastle (63 miles)

There are about 100 available hotel rooms in Kelso itself, but there is other accommodation nearby in the Scottish borders.

Thursday 28 April 2005

Redcar Racecourse
Redcar
Cleveland
TS10 2BY
Tel: 01642 484 068
www.redcarracing.co.uk

Another easy course for us to get to by car, but we had decided to go by train this day as we intended on having a few drinks while we were there. Everything went smoothly that morning, we were up quite early, Angie had made us one of her full English specials to put a good lining on our stomachs, and I had time to take the dogs for a good walk before we set off. Grant had said he would see to the dog's needs for the rest of the day so everything was set.

We took a taxi to Newcastle Central station, from where we caught a train to Darlington for the connecting train going on to Redcar.

I was by now ordering our badges online through the British Horseracing Authority's website. This has to be done no later than two weeks before your intended meeting, but you will at least have your badges delivered before you go racing and sometimes at a discount price.

On arrival at the seaside town we started to walk the short distance from the railway station to the race track. We were only about 100 yards from the gates when we realised the couple who were walking behind us were not only trying to catch us up but were calling for our attention. He told us he had a couple of spare badges for the races, and we were welcome to have them, I replied we already had badges, but thanked him for his kindness. He then said the badges he had were owner's badges and would gain us access to more of the facilities on the course, so we thanked him and accepted his offer.

After introducing themselves as John and Elisabeth, he left us with the girl at the owner's entrance, telling her we were his guests, and telling us he would see us later.

The girl welcomed us as guests of Mr and Mrs Ranson, owners of Davy Crocket which was running in the third race. She handed us our badges and race cards, then wished us a nice day as we headed off for a drink in the owner's bar. As we were sitting there I told Angie I was just going to nip out to the entrance gate to give someone the badges I had already purchased online. I don't know whether people thought I was a ticket tout, but it took me nearly quarter of an hour to give the badges away.

By the time racing had started we had moved from the owner's bar to the member's bar in the grandstand. We were betting £40 and £20 and both decided to back the same horse in the first race. Angie said she wanted to go down to the betting ring so I gave her my £40. She came back saying she had £60 at 9/2 on Ryedale Ovation, which obliged by 2 lengths.

Nothing back in the second.

In the third race we again backed the same horse, £60 on Brace of Doves again at 9/2.

The race was just about to start when Mr Ranson turned up to stand right beside us to watch his horse Davy Crocket. We kept pretty quiet during the race. Davy Crocket finished a credible fourth. Brace of Doves won the race in a photo finish.

Although we didn't back any more winners that afternoon we still showed a profit. This wouldn't be the last time we would bump into Mr Ranson.

Angie's verdict:

You can't imagine what was going on in my head as the train was getting closer to Redcar. It was a dull miserable day, and as I looked out of the window at the rain falling over the steelworks I was not feeling in the best of fettles. However by the time we had got off the train the rain had stopped, and meeting Mr and Mrs Ranson put me in a better frame of mind.

Even though there was about a dozen people in the owner's bar you would have been able to hear a pin drop as they were all sitting in deadly silence. I would have thought it would have been buzzing; everyone should have been excited with the prospects of their horse giving a good performance, it seemed more like it was causing them anxiety. Or maybe they were like us and didn't own a racehorse.

There are three enclosures at Redcar; the Premier where we spent most of the afternoon as it had really good views over the course, and as well as its restaurants and bars there were plenty seats.

There is trackside parking for the disabled, as well as toilets in all enclosures and a viewing ramp close to the winning post.

The second enclosure is the Tattersalls which also has bars and a variety of hot and cold food on offer. Viewing from the Tattersalls is also very good.

The third enclosure is the Course enclosure which has both a bar and a cafe, the best viewing is from the running rail.

Rating: Good ★★★

How to get there:

To get to Redcar by road, whether travelling from north or south, come off the A1 (M) at junction 57, and then follow the A174. There is plenty of free parking.

To get there by rail, Darlington is the nearest mainline station. From here you can get a train to Redcar central station, from which it is only 5 minutes walk to the track.

Nearest airport is Teesside (16 miles).

With Redcar being a seaside town there is an abundance of hotel, guest house and bed and breakfast accommodation to choose from.

Saturday 7 May 2005

Beverley Racecourse
York Road
Beverley
East Yorkshire
HU17 8QZ
Tel: 01482 867488
www.beverley-racecourse.co.uk

When travelling what I would call medium distances, we don't always stop for a break, unless for fuel or if one of us is desperate for the toilet. On these occasions Angie usually makes a few sandwiches which we eat while travelling. Beverley being 136 miles fell into this medium distance category.

The day before travelling we went to our local shopping precinct to buy our favourite bread and sandwich fillings for the journey. While we were there I went into William Hill's to place a football bet on for a five man syndicate which I was part of along with my workmates. The bet was a £25 accumulator on eight teams which were playing on the Saturday. Because it was almost the end of the season and the bet looked good on paper I matched it with £25 of my own, making it a £50 accumulator with the potential winnings of just under £900 of which including my share of the syndicate money I stood to make over £500.

Leaving Grant in charge, we left early on the Saturday for East Yorkshire, our destination not Beverley but Hull which is less than 10 miles from Beverley and where we had booked our accommodation (Travel Inn) for the night. I booked accommodation in Hull because I'd heard the nightlife was very good but as things worked out I wasn't going to experience Hull's nightlife on this occasion. After a pretty quiet journey, sandwiches eaten, we arrived at our hotel at lunchtime; luckily our room was ready so we were able to check in early. After freshening ourselves up we ordered a taxi to take us to the races.

The weather forecast for the day was sunshine with heavy showers. On arrival we got out of the taxi and headed for the entrance gate right in the middle of one of the heavy showers (Angie was not amused).

Neither of us backed the first winner which returned at 50/1 Betting our usual stakes of £40 and £20, we both backed the second and third winners; Track attack at 6/4 and Philharmonic at 5/4.

We had started on the vodka out of Angie's water bottle quite early that day, and had found a nice little pitch out the way of the showers to spend the afternoon. I was on my way back from the confectionary stall behind the parade ring where I had been to replenish our lemonade stocks when I heard someone say Hello there; I turned to see Mr. Ranson standing behind me smiling and enjoying a large ice cream cone. He didn't have a horse running that day but he had been told Out After Dark would win the next race, the sprint handicap. When we had met him at Redcar he told me he didn't usually bet on horses as the prize money he could win give him enough of a buzz, however he was going to have a bet in this next race.

We both decided to back his tip, Angie gave me her £20 and I went down to the betting ring and had £100 on at 11/2.

Out After Dark seemed to come from last to first in the final two furlongs to win by nearly a length. We saw Mr. Ranson again after the race and he told us he had £2 on the winner. He also told us his horse Davy Crocket would be running at Newcastle on the 19th of May and after writing our names down he told us he would ensure badges were there for us to pick up. We went to Newcastle that day and the badges were there, but that is another story.

Nothing back in the fifth or sixth races but one of Angie's favourite jockeys Nina Carberry was riding in the last, so I gave her my £40 and she went down to put the bet on. I was quite surprised when she came back and told me that she had put £80 on at 3/1.

Blue Patrick ridden by Nina Carberry won pulling away inside the final furlong.

When we left, just outside the entrance gates there was a small queue of people getting onto a service bus which was going into Beverley, so we joined them and went into town for drinks. Having already finished the contents of Angie's water bottle and quite a few extra vodkas on top of that, Angie told me she couldn't drink any more and was ready to go back to the hotel and go to bed. Even though it was only half past eight I agreed we would go back after the next drink. During the afternoon I had been keeping an eye on the football scores and was sure seven of the eight teams we had backed had won and Man. United who were kicking off at tea time was the only result to come.

On the taxi ride back to the hotel I asked the driver if he knew how Man. Utd. had got on against West Brom. He told me he didn't know the final score but Manchester were winning 5-0 the last he heard.

I woke to the sound of people moving around in the corridor outside our room, thinking they were going down for breakfast I looked at the clock, only to see it was 23:40 and they weren't going for breakfast, but were coming in after their night out.

I lay awake most of that night. Angie didn't stir until nine o'clock the next morning. We decided not to have breakfast in the hotel but to stop somewhere on the way home. We stopped for breakfast at a Little Chef half way through our journey, where I bought a newspaper. Giving Angie the paper to check the results, I read out the rest of the teams, and sure enough they had all won. Instead of driving home I drove straight to William Hills and handed over my coupon only to be told there was nothing back, Man Utd had drawn 1-1 with West Brom.

I knew taxi drivers told a few porkpies just to keep a conversation going in the cab, but this one was a little bit over the top.

Angie's verdict:

Although I am a great believer in dressing for the occasion I got it wrong at Beverley. I knew there were showers forecast but it was sunny when we left the hotel and got into our taxi. By the time we got out of the taxi and made our way to the entrance gates the rain was bouncing off the ground. The trousers of my white wool blend trouser suit were covered in muddy, gritty splashes and the suit was ruined.

There are 4 enclosures at Beverley. The Club and Grandstand are the two main enclosures both have a number of bars and both offer a wide range of hot and cold food.

Both enclosures were very full the day we were there, especially the bars and eating areas. I don't know if this is the norm or if people were just staying inside away from the rain showers.

Viewing from both enclosures is very good; the Club grandstand overlooks the winning post. The "nice little pitch" which Dave mentioned did keep us out the way of the showers, but we were joined by an annoying 4-piece brass band that stood just a few yards from us. Thankfully they only played one or two tunes between races.

:he cost of entry is reduced for disabled racegoers for whom there is access to all areas, there is also a disabled viewing ramp.

There is also the Minster and Course enclosures, neither of which have access to the parade ring or winners enclosure. Both have bars and fast food outlets, and the Minster enclosure has a covered stand.

On a sunny day the Course enclosure which has a playground would be ideal for a family picnic. Accompanied under 18's get into all enclosures free of charge.

I would like to go back on a sunny day.
Rating: Average ★★★

How to get there:

To get to Beverley by road; from the north take the A1, A19 then the A1079.

From the south take the A1, M62 come off at junction37 and follow A614/A613 to Market Weighton, and then follow the A1079/A1035 to the course.

Parking is free except for the course enclosure which costs £4 per car and £3 per person

To get there by rail; from both York and Doncaster you can get connections to Beverley, which is on the main line to Hull.

Beverley station is just a mile from the course.

Buses run to Beverley from Hull, York and Leeds.

Nearest airport is Humberside (19 miles)

There are a few hotels and guesthouses in Beverley, Hull is also an option.

Saturday 28 May 2005

Cartmel Racecourse
Cartmel
Grange-over-Sands
Cumbria
LA11 6QF
Tel: 01539 536340
www.cartmel-steeplechases.co.uk

I have read that as far as crowds at national hunt festivals are concerned Cartmel comes third on the list behind Cheltenham and Aintree. I had only been there once before and that was on a Bank Holiday and can verify that the crowds were there in their thousands. A hot day, barbeques sparked up and a fun fair, all on top of a good days racing making it an excellent family day out. Hollie had found a job and had started work two weeks earlier for Greggs the bakers in Edinburgh, but had come home for the weekend so she was giving Grant a rest from dog sitting. Greggs is a Newcastle based company and just happens to be the baker of our favourite bread; The Stottie Cake, unfortunately they didn't sell them in Edinburgh so we had to buy some at our local Greggs so Angie could make the sandwiches for our journey. The meeting we were going to was an evening meeting, and the hotel we were staying at in Grange-over-Sands is only about three miles from the course, so a mid morning departure would get us there in good time. Normally if I was going across to the M6 I would head west out of Newcastle on the A69 towards Carlisle, which is a straight forward route to take. However the AA route planner came up with another route which was five mile shorter, or should have been. We headed down the A1, joined the A689 then the A688 to start our journey west. Everything was fine until we got through Barnard Castle: it was here we took a wrong turn and ended up in the middle of nowhere. Luckily we came across a house where a lady was doing a spot of gardening, and with her directions we followed a road that would have been better suited to a tractor but did eventually get us back on the right road. By the time we pulled up at our hotel we had done thirty mile more than we should have done. The Grange Hotel in Grange-over-Sands is considered to be one of the Lake Districts premier hotels, and I would recommend it to anyone looking for somewhere with a bit of grandeur. Dressed for the races and sitting in the hotel bar, the girl from the reception desk came to tell us there were only a couple of local taxis and they were fully booked. Luckily a group of four people who were also going to the races came into the bar; they had managed to book a seven seater earlier that afternoon and were happy to let us share. When we arrived at Cartmel the pubs were shut, the taxi driver told us the local constabulary closed the pubs when the races were on as they couldn't police both. I still don't know if this is true, or if it is just another taxi driver story. We were told if we wanted a taxi back 22:30 would be the last pick up, from where we were dropped off, and if we weren't there we would have to make our own way back to the hotel

Being a nice sunny evening and the fun fair in full swing another good crowd had gathered. Barbecues were in abundance in the family enclosure, we were quite content in the stands enjoying the racing and steadily making our way through the contents of Angie's water bottle.

Betting £40 and £20 it wasn't a brilliant night, but not a total disaster.

We backed two winners; Angie backed the first winner Dream Castle, £20 at 4/1, and we both backed the fourth winner, Sir Frosty £40 and £20 at 5/2.

After racing we had another couple of drinks on the course before heading for our taxi. Having had nothing to eat since the sandwiches Angie had made for our journey from Newcastle, and everywhere closing early I bought a couple of cheeseburgers from the burger van parked on the fun fair which was also ready to shut shop for the night.

The next morning after breakfast Angie had to rush back to our hotel room where she was sick. She blamed the cheeseburger from the night before; I think the vodka played its part.

Angie's verdict:

I wasn't impressed when we first got to Cartmel racecourse; I think this was due to Dave building it up so much that I was expecting a lot more than there actually was.

However as the night went on I got to like it more and more. The Paddock is the main enclosure at Cartmel; there is bar facilities, a restaurant as well as a snack bar and a few fast food outlets located around the enclosure.

I wasn't too keen on the viewing as the track actually runs out of sight round the back of the grandstand. The finishing straight however is where it matters and the grandstand is right on top of the finishing line. The stand is uncovered; luckily we were there on a sunny evening.

There was a lot of what I can only describe as eccentric country folk wandering around, dressed like they had just stepped out from an episode of Poirot. The buildings and toilet blocks in the Paddock were clean and well looked after.

Disabled facilities include a raised viewing platform. There is also disabled parking available, though I would book this in advance as Cartmel gets very busy (have your blue badge number handy when reserving your parking space).

The second enclosure is the Course where there is a bar and fast food outlets, though picnics and barbeques are very popular in this enclosure where as well as the racing to enjoy there is the traditional fun fair.

If you opt for the Paddock it will be well worth your while taking a look around the Course enclosure as there is a few trade stands situated there.

Best viewing is on the running rails opposite the Paddock stands.

Rating: Average ★★★

How to get there:

To get to Cartmel by road; exit the M6 at junction 36, take the A590 towards Barrow in Furness and follow the signs for Lindale roundabout.

There is free parking on the course.

Give yourself plenty time as the roads are always busy.

To get there by rail; there is a train service to Cark in Cartmel station, from where there is a bus service on race days.

Nearest airport is Blackpool (30 miles).

There is accommodation in the area, but you will find most of it at the higher end of the price range.

.

Monday 6 June 2005

Pontefract Park
33 Ropergate Street
Pontefract
West Yorkshire
WF8 1LE
Tel: 01977 781307
www.pontefract-races.co.

An evening meeting at Pontefract gave us a bit of time to walk
the dogs and get things sorted out before setting off on our trip.
Grant was back in charge and was pleased to hear we would be
back before lunchtime the following day as he knew we would
walk the dogs on our return saving him a job. Even though
Monday is one of the busiest times on the A1, we had a trouble
free trip to our hotel in Pontefract. We were stopping at the
Travel Inn, Pontefract North, which is less than three miles from
the course. On the way from the hotel to the races our taxi driver
had to drop us a little way short of the track because of traffic
congestion. This was partly to do with race traffic, and partly
because it was rush hour (whoever named it rush hour must have
been on drugs). We walked about a quarter of a mile to the
entrance gates on what was a red hot evening. I had seen
Pontefract racecourse a few times from the motorway, but I had
never actually been racing there. I don't know exactly what I was
expecting when I got in, but I was nicely surprised by the
standards of the facilities on offer. We watched the first two races
from the stands, none of our horses doing any good.
After the second race we had our usual walkabout to see what
was what. Behind the Paddock grandstand we spotted a small
marquee with one side opened up, and tables and chairs
positioned to catch the evening sunshine. It was here we parked
ourselves for the rest of the night. There was a tote window
opposite and a bar in the marquee, what more could a man ask

for? We spent the night sitting in the sunshine, betting on the tote and needless to say enjoying a few glasses of vodka.

Our racing kitty wasn't doing too badly and I can't remember how or why we'd started betting £40 and £20 stakes, but those were the stakes we again agreed on.

Angie had £20 on the third winner Sacranun which paid £3.80p a win on the tote,

She also had the fourth winner £20 on Red Bloom which paid £2.20p a win.

Even though I never backed a winner I really enjoyed my night at Pontefract races.

After racing we walked into town where we had a couple more drinks before going for an Indian meal. Leaving the restaurant we headed for a taxi office we had walked past earlier. When we got there we were greeted by what I can only describe as 'a fat lass', who was acting as some kind of bouncer. Anyway she ensured we got a taxi back to the hotel and was anything but shy of putting any young man who was brave enough to stand up to her in his place.

Angie's verdict:

One thing Pontefract proved to me was, places are never what you expect them to be. Although I had only seen clips of Pontefract the odd time on TV, I knew that West Yorkshire was an industrialised area and I imagined the racecourse to be pretty run down. I couldn't have been more mistaken, the facilities were of a very high standard, and the toilets, which I use as the first place to start judging anywhere, are among the cleanest and most modern. We started the night in the Club enclosure which is one of 4 enclosures at Pontefract. There are a couple of restaurants in the Club enclosure as well as a number of bars serving both food and drink. One thing that impressed me was even though it was quite busy we still had no problem finding a seat. I don't mind standing and at some courses you've got no choice, but when I can I like to find a seat as I'm sure a lot of people do even for a short while just to take the weight off your feet. There is a good view of the course from the stand and you are right on top of the winning post. The Paddock enclosure has a self service restaurant and also has a number of bars selling food as well as drink. Viewing from the Paddock stand is also quite good, and isn't too far from the finishing line. It was behind the Paddock that we set our stall out for the night sitting in the sunshine at a table in a marquee. People came and people went, and one or two even sat at our table for a while. Dave loves talking to people at the races and it is nearly always him that starts the conversation rolling but he found it hard work at Pontefract. People in Yorkshire are pleasant enough, but they seem to like to keep themselves to themselves, this we have noticed at one or two of the Yorkshire tracks.

Disabled facilities include toilets in all enclosures and designated viewing areas. There is step free access around the enclosures.

The Silver ring has four bars, one of which is a bar/restaurant. Viewing from the Silver ring is also pretty good.

The fourth enclosure is actually called the Third enclosure which also has a bar selling food and drink. There is a large play area in this enclosure and the viewing isn't too bad.

Rating: Good ★★★★

How to get there:

To get to Pontefract by road; the course is at junction 32 of the M62 motorway and is easy accessible from the A1, M1 and the M18.

There is plenty free parking. It costs £8 to park in the Third enclosure, which includes up to 4 adults.

To get there by rail; Baghill is the closest of Pontefract's three railway stations being only 1/3 of a mile from the course.

Nearest airport is Leeds and Bradford (19 miles)

There is a wide range of accommodation in Pontefract.

Saturday 25 June 2005

Chester Race Co. Ltd.
The Racecourse
Chester
CH1 2LY
Tel: 01244 304600
www.chester-races.co.uk

The trip to Chester had been planned back in February when I used the gift vouchers from my birthday to book two nights accommodation in Blossoms Hotel which is located right in the city centre. Hollie and Michael were coming to stay in Newcastle for the weekend as it was Michael's birthday on the Sunday, and they weren't planning on going back to Edinburgh until Monday afternoon. With them staying at our house we knew we didn't have to rush back, so I booked badges for Chester on the Saturday and for Uttoxeter on the Sunday. We were staying in Chester on Friday and Saturday night and with our house sitters not expected until Friday tea time we done everything that needed to be done; dog walking etc. in the morning and set off on our journey just after lunch. We did make a stop near the half way point as we had a three and a half hour drive from Newcastle, but still arrived in Chester before five o'clock. When we arrived we spotted our hotel more or less straight away, the only problem was we didn't know how to get to it. We were on a one way ring road and completed three or four laps before finally figuring out how to get to the car park. We were changed and back down stairs by about half six, ready for a good night out. Before hitting the town we went into the hotel bar from where I ordered two double vodkas with lemonade, glancing at the bar prices I was thinking I could buy a bottle of vodka cheaper than what the two drinks were going to cost. However we drank those and ordered two more before leaving. I just told the barman to put the drinks on our room bill. We spent the night sampling a few of

Chester's bars before tucking in to two sirloin steaks at an Italian restaurant.

The next morning after breakfast we went for a walk to see just how far it was to the racecourse from our hotel. It turned out to be not much of a walk as it was only about ten minutes away. It was Northumberland Plate day back in Newcastle and Angie fancied Sergeant Cecil to run a big race, so we looked for a bookies shop to see if we could get a guaranteed price as this is common practice where we live. The only bookmaker we could find was Ladbrokes who said they didn't need to give any special deals as they had no competitors in Chester to beat their prices, so Angie said she would just back it with one of the course bookies. We arrived about an hour before the first race, and already the stands were pretty full. Because of the big crowd and the sun beating down in all it's glory, we decided to make our way to the centre of the course where there wasn't as many people and more room to breathe.

Betting £40 and £20 Angie took the first prize again when she backed the first winner Indigo Nights £20 at 2/1

We both backed Ionian Spring which won the fifth at 1/1

Angie backed the last winner Handsome Cross £20 at 9/2

On top of this she had £5 e/w on the winner of the Northumberland plate, Sergeant Cecil at 14/1, which we watched on the big screen.

I saw something at Chester that I had never seen before at any other racecourse. The bookmakers in the centre of the course had orderly queues of people standing in lines waiting to place their bets. I got one or two angry looks as I was pushing straight to the front of the queue to ensure I got the best prices for my chosen horses. Not that it made much difference as I only had the one winner on the day and a horse that we'd both backed many times before, Ionian Spring. Angie used to be a member of the Elite Racing syndicate who owned Ionian Spring along with a number of other horses. So, naturally, we used to follow them, and even

though we had won money on some of the others, it was nowhere in comparison to what we had won on Ionian Spring.
When racing was finished we stayed in the centre of the course and had a drink while the bulk of the crowd were making their way out. Once again we had a night in the bars of Chester which because of the races being a lot busier than they had been on the previous night, we finished off the evening in an Indian restaurant.

Angie's verdict:

I was pleased we had a walk to the course that morning as we had a great view as we looked down from the city wall out over the racecourse. It looked very peaceful with only the odd peasant wandering around the Roman village that had been constructed in the centre of the course. It was a different story when we arrived that afternoon for the races, it was packed. In my opinion it was too busy, but apparently Chester always draws huge crowds.
There are restaurants, bars and fast food outlets in both the County and Tattersalls stands, but you might have to queue for a while. The best viewing is from the County stand. There are toilets and a viewing platform for the disabled in the paddock area.
We moved to the centre of the course where the viewing of the racing was poor, but at least we had some breathing space and a big screen to watch the racing. The people in the grandstand opposite were packed like sardines which had to be uncomfortable on such a hot day.
There is an under pass which takes you from the main stand through to the centre of the course, this is a great idea as it means you can cross the course at any time, not just in between races.
The litter pickers were working like ants in an attempt to keep the area tidy and even though I only used the portaloos of which there were plenty, they were clean and checked regularly. Apart

from the County stand, accompanied under 16's are admitted free. The whole set up is good even though it was too busy for my liking.
Rating: Good ★★★★

How to get there:

To get there by road; coming from the north or south take the M6, M56 and exit at junction14. It is well signposted from here. Car parking on the course costs £5 per car £10 per coach/ minibus.
To get there by rail; Chester has a mainline station which is only 1 mile from the course, there is a bus from the station to the track on race days.
Nearest airport: Liverpool John Lennon (10 miles).
With Chester being a popular tourist spot, there is a good selection of accommodation.

Sunday 26 June 2005

Uttoxeter Racecourse
Wood Lane
Uttoxeter
Staffordshire
ST14 88D
Tel: 01889 562561
www.uttoxeter-racecourse.co.uk

With it being less than 60 miles from Chester to Uttoxeter we were in no great hurry to get up that morning. We had planned to have a late breakfast before setting off to the Staffordshire track. There had been a big crowd at Chester races the day before, not only because of the racing, but it was Roman weekend and there had been gladiator fights and other crowd pulling events taking place in the centre of the course. I was sitting reading the Racing Post and Angie was in the shower when I heard a commotion out in the street. I looked out of the window to see a legion of Roman soldiers marching past the hotel, not something you see every Sunday morning. When we did go down for breakfast the dining area was almost empty as most people staying at the hotel had already eaten. We sat for quite a while without anyone coming to serve us even though one of the waitresses had looked our way on a couple of occasions. After about 15 minutes I caught the attention of who I took to be the head waitress and asked why no one had been to our table. She couldn't apologise enough and our breakfasts arrived less than 5 minutes later. On checking out of the hotel, the desk clerk again apologised for what had happened at the breakfast table, and told us there would be no charge for the extras on our room tab, which included the four over priced vodka and lemonades we had drunk on arrival.

The drive to Uttoxeter races should have taken an hour and a quarter, especially on a Sunday when the roads are normally quieter. Unfortunately this wasn't to be the case, we were still about a mile and a half from the course when we hit a traffic jam, and it was soon to become apparent that this was the queue for the races. It was an absolutely mad hot day, and even though I had all the windows down in the car it was very uncomfortable. Eventually we were getting close, so I took the lead from two cars in front of me and parked on an industrial estate not far from the course. I can't imagine Uttoxeter draws this many people for all its meetings, but a combination of the hot day and the staging of the Summer Grand National must have tempted them all from their armchairs.

We walked through the industrial estate which led us through to the course car park which was almost full. From the car park we crossed the railway lines where there was a guy selling racing tips for the afternoons action. I gave him a tenner for which he gave me an envelope, he also told me to leave the first race alone. Taking his advice I didn't have a bet in the first race which was won by Dewasentah at 10/1. Angie decided she was going to have a bet as she had already picked a horse out, and had £10 e/w with the tote on Keep On Moving which finished second paying £2.00 a place, which got her money back. Inside the envelope were the names of three horses. The first of the three horses Astronaut was running in the second race, I put £40 on at 11/4. There was about five minutes before the off when I had a horrible thought in my mind that I had left the back windows open in the car. Telling Angie I wouldn't be long I went back to check, only to find all the windows were closed (at least it put my mind at ease knowing for sure).

As I walked back to the track there were still cars trying to find parking spaces and there had already been two races ran. Angie gave me the bad news, Astronaut had finished third and she had backed it as well.

The second horse was running in the third race, Magic Sky for which I got 11/2, it was going well until it unshipped Ruby Walsh at the fourth last.

The third and final horse Comanche War Paint again ridden by
Ruby Walsh finished fifth at 4/1 in the fifth race.
We both managed to back the winner of the sixth, Stagecoach
Diamond £40 and £20 at 5/2.
Angie thought I was stupid paying for tips and looking back on it
I probably was, but people pay for tips all the time through phone
lines. It was a bit of fun and something different and I wouldn't
have done any better if I'd chosen my own horses so nothing
gained, nothing lost.
There was a seven race card that day, but we decided to leave
after the sixth to try and beat some of the traffic. Arriving home
at around nine o'clock we went to our local social club to have a
drink with Michael on his birthday.

Angie's verdict:

It must have been one of the hottest days of the year, perfect for a
picnic on the beach but uncomfortably hot amongst the huge
crowd that had come to watch the Summer National.
The two main enclosures: Premier and Grandstand & Paddock
have a number of restaurants and bars as well as outlets selling
hot and cold snacks.
I think the busiest outlet that day was the confectionery shop
which was selling ice creams.
Even though the enclosures were full we still managed to find a
place in the stands to watch the races. The viewing from here was
very good and would have been even better if our horses had
been a bit faster.
There is reserved parking on the rails, toilets and a viewing
platform for disabled racegoers.
The Family enclosure also has bars and fast food outlets though
there is no stand in this enclosure. Children under 16 are admitted
free when accompanied by an adult. There is a playground at

Uttoxeter and on bank holidays and big meetings there is a funfair.
Rating: Good ★★★

How to get there:

To get to there by road; from the north or south, come off the M6 and follow the signs for the A50 Stoke on Trent, then the A50 Uttoxeter.
Car parking is free.
To get there by rail; Uttoxeter railway station actually adjoins the course, you can get trains from Crewe or Stoke on Trent.
Nearest airport is East Midlands (22 miles)
There are plenty hotels, guest houses and bed and breakfasts in Uttoxeter and the surrounding area.

Wednesday 29 June 2005

Catterick Race Co Ltd
Catterick Bridge
Richmond
North Yorkshire
DL10 7PE
Tel: 01748 811478
www.catterickbridge.co.uk

Catterick is a course we have been to about half a dozen times and I think every time we have been it has rained; today was to be no exception. With it only being 60 miles down the A1, I think if we didn't already have our badges we would have taken a rain check. We had already been soaked once when we took the dogs out that morning, and although the weather forecast was for it to clear up in the afternoon, it was still raining quite heavily when we set off. As we were travelling down the road Angie was reading through the card for Catterick in the Racing Post when she noticed one of Mr Ranson's horses, Hiccups was down to run in the third race.

When we pulled up in the racecourse car park it had stopped raining, but everywhere was soaking wet. Luckily we got inside and had only just sat down for a cup of coffee when it started to rain again.

We had both picked out Confidential Lady for the first race, so Angie gave me her £20 and sent me out in the rain to place the bet, £60 at 5/6.

Confidential Lady led from start to finish, and although winning at short odds, the day started to look a little bit brighter.

We were still in the grandstand keeping out of the rain and finalising our selections for the second race when Mr Ranson spotted us. He came up and with a tone of excitement in his voice, he told us they thought Hiccups would run a big race, not only would the going be in his favour but the track would suit him and they had booked top jockey Jamie Spencer for the ride. After watching our horses finish well down the field in the second race, it was time for Hiccups to earn his keep. The rain had stopped by this time so Angie said she would go to back it herself. We met back in the grandstand and had both taken 7/2, me for £100 and Angie for £40.

After the race we joined the crowd and applauded Mr Ranson as he collected his trophy as winning owner.

Nothing back in the fourth, but we both backed the fifth winner, Alabama Twist, £40 and £20 at 6/4.

I also backed the last winner Hilltime again ridden by Jamie Spencer £40 at 4/1.

So we ended up quite a few quid in profit, and to think if we hadn't already purchased our badges, we probably wouldn't have gone.

That night we went for a couple of drinks at our local social club, where a friend of ours Dennis, who actually owns the club told us he had a quarter share in a nice two year old filly trained by Mick Channon. She was going to have her first run at Nottingham on Saturday night, and they were expecting a good run from her.

Angie's verdict:

We have been to Catterick racecourse a few times over the years and although it is not one of my favourite tracks, I have noticed some big improvements to the facilities.

There are three enclosures at Catterick; the Club which has a bar and food area selling a range of hot and cold food and drinks, you can usually find a seat alright especially at the midweek fixtures.

The best views are from the Club grandstand which overlooks the winning post.

The Tattersalls has bars, a self service cafe and usually one or two vans selling fast food. The Tattersalls also has a grandstand from where the viewing is quite good. The toilets in both enclosures are clean and well kept.

There is parking, toilets and dedicated viewing for disabled racegoers.

The third enclosure is the Course where there is a bar area serving drinks and snacks. There is no stand in the Course enclosure.

I don't know if it is just me but I find the crowds at Catterick to be cliquish, and although there is a good racing atmosphere at Catterick, I don't think it is a very friendly one.

Rating: Average ★★★

How to get there:

To get to there by car; follow the A1 and come off at the sign for Catterick, the course is just on the outskirts of the village.

Car parking is free

To get there by rail; Darlington is the nearest mainline station which is 13 miles away, there are frequent bus services from the station. There is also a station at Northallerton which is 9 miles away.

Nearest airport is Teesside (12 miles)

There aren't many hotels close to the course, but North Yorkshire and Durham have plenty on offer.

Saturday 2 July 2005

Nottingham Racecourse
Colwick Park
Nottingham
NG2 4BE
Tel: 0115 9580620
www.nottinghamracecourse.co.uk

We hadn't planned on going to Nottingham on this particular day, but with our friend Dennis telling us that his horse Crabadabadoo was making her first racecourse appearance that evening, it seemed a nice idea. We already had flights booked for the following Monday from Newcastle to Heathrow as we were going to a meeting at Windsor on the Monday night. Because of this Angie wasn't sure about going to Nottingham as she didn't want to leave the dogs too long. I told her we could leave Saturday lunchtime, we would be back on Sunday, Leave again on Monday morning and be back on Tuesday. Grant was happy with these arrangements, so Angie agreed.

So I set to work on the Internet, I booked a room at the Travel Inn, Nottingham city centre, printed a copy of the route planner, then while looking for the time of the first race I realised Market Rasen was holding a meeting on the Sunday and being only 57 miles from Nottingham, I convinced Angie it would make economical sense to go to both meetings.

Leaving at lunchtime Saturday, we had another trouble free journey and reached our hotel at about 4 o'clock. This gave us time to relax for a while before getting our taxi to the races, as the first race wasn't due off until 6:50 pm.

We had decided on the way down that we would only bet £40 a race instead of £60 at the two meetings, and instead of both betting in every race we would alternate. Angie decided she would take the first race as Dennis's horse was running in the second and she was leaving that race to me. She made a wise

73

decision, as she had £40 on Piddies Pride which won the first at 4/1.

I would have liked to have seen Dennis before I put my bet on the next race, but I wanted to get an early price. The bookmakers opened up at 12/1, so I had £20 at 12's. We took a walk to the parade ring where I managed to catch Dennis's attention. He told me the trainer was expecting no worse than a place, so with this information I went back to the betting ring. The word must have been out, Crabadabado was now trading at 11/2, so with the price gone I put a £20 place bet on with the tote. Even with Angie's binoculars we couldn't see exactly what was happening at the 6 furlong start, it seemed a horse had gone down in the stalls. It was Crabadabadoo, the stalls handlers managed to get her out and she was given the ok to race and was put back in her stall.

The gates opened and Crabadabadoo came out last, her jockey Ted Durcan didn't even put her in the race and she was tailed off. On his return to the unsaddling enclosure he told the owners she shouldn't have been allowed to race. Further checks found she had cuts to one of her legs and a damaged hoof, she has never raced since.

Nothing back in the third, or fourth races.

Angie backed the winner of the fifth Bureaucrat £40 at Evens, and I backed another loser in the last.

After racing we got a taxi to take us straight to an Indian restaurant where we had our normal late meal before going back to the hotel.

Angie's verdict:

Summer is definitely my favourite time of the year, and I just love being outside on summer evenings, whether it be at a race meeting or simply sitting on our patio having a drink and a barbeque. The night we were at Nottingham races it was a little bit overcast, but it was a lovely warm summers evening.

Both of Nottingham's enclosures are very good. Apart from the rooftop restaurant, the Premier enclosure has a couple of bars one of which sells a selection of hot and cold food. Although we didn't watch any of the races from there we went into the grandstand which is quite spacious and got an excellent view over the course.

The Grandstand also has a number of bars offering a full range of drinks and a variety of foods. This enclosure also has a good grandstand looking out over the course. Everywhere including the toilets are very clean and seem quite new.

There are viewing ramps for the disabled at the parade ring and trackside, both enclosures have lifts.

Accompanied children under 16 get in free; there is an adventure playground and additional entertainment at weekend fixtures.

We had a lovely spot by the rails, with a table under the canopy of a long gazebo, the people we met were all friendly, especially the three young couples who we shared a table with. They were really interested in our plan to visit every racecourse and in between races they wanted us to tell them about the courses we had already done.

Rating: Good ★★★

How to get there:

To get there by road: from the north and south, come off the M1 signposted Nottingham and pick up the A60.From the east and west follow the A52.

Once in Nottingham, follow the brown tourist board and park and ride signs to the course.

Car parking is free.

Bus service 44 will take you there from King Street in the City centre.

To get there by rail; Nottingham Midland station is just 2 miles from the course, there is a taxi rank at the station.
Nearest airport East Midlands (14 miles)
Again, with Nottingham being a city, there are plenty hotels to choose from. The course is just 2 miles from the city centre.

Sunday 3 July 2005

Market Rasen Racecourse
Legsby Road
Market Rasen
Lincolnshire
LN8 3EA
Tel: 01673 843434
www.marketrasenraces.co.uk

I woke up at about seven o'clock that morning, made myself a coffee, and pulled a chair up to the hotel room window. I watched as three anglers were setting up their rods to try to outsmart the fish in the canal below. As I sat I was thinking back to the racing the night before, it had been a total nightmare for Dennis and his partners, and the worst thing was the horse wouldn't run again, but they didn't know that at the time. Luckily I only staked £40, and thanks to Angie we didn't lose at the meeting.
Angie woke at about eight thirty, and by this time I was getting bored with the anglers who hadn't even bagged one fish between them. We went down for breakfast, and then returned to our room, we were going to check out last minute as our drive to Market Rasen was just over an hour. Market Rasen is the only course in Lincolnshire, though I have heard there have been thoughts of reopening Lincoln Racecourse although I haven't seen this documented anywhere, it was probably a taxi driver that told me.
It was a day early, but the theme for the day was Independence Day, with majorettes, skateboard demonstrations and line dancing all part of the entertainment. I amused myself with a different type of line (not drugs). Before the first race we had been sitting on the stone stairs of the grandstand which were marked with yellow lines, when we got up Angie had a yellow line across her butt which between us we managed to almost wipe off. I spent

the time between races literally looking at bums; I bet I saw at least thirty people with a yellow line across their backside.
Angie went first again with the betting, and although she said it had nothing to do with the name, she had £20 e/w with the tote on the first winner, Angie's Double which paid £5.30p a win and £1.70p a place.
I had £40 on the second winner Enhancer at evens.
Angie keeping up the good work had £40 on the third winner Touch Closer at 2/1
Nothing back in the fourth, or the fifth.
The last race was delayed as there had been a bad fall in the fifth race, and the jockey had been taken away by ambulance. For safety reasons we had to wait for the ambulance to return to the course before the last race could be run.
The horse I backed in the last pulled up, but again we hadn't lost anything.
We drove straight home after racing, where we had a couple of drinks to wind down before going to bed.

Angie's verdict:

Before our trip to Lincolnshire, I wasn't even sure where Market Rasen was. The hours ride from Nottingham was a delight, as we passed nothing but countryside and it was a lovely sunny summer's day. We had arrived pretty early and found some nice seats in the member's bar where we sat and had a coffee while studying the form for the days racing.
As well as the member's restaurant there are a few bars and food outlets in this enclosure. There is good viewing over the course and parade ring.
The Tattersalls enclosure is also quite nice; there are a couple of bars one of which has a hot and cold buffet. Viewing is pretty good from the stand, but finding a place right on the running rail

isn't too easy because of the parade ring and the hedge that runs along it.

The facilities in both enclosures are clean and there was a nice, almost relaxing atmosphere. There are toilets and a viewing area for the disabled.

The Independence Day entertainment seemed to go down quite well with the crowds.

The Silver ring or family enclosure also has a bar and food on offer though I always think that family enclosures are ideal for taking your own picnic. There is a play area in this enclosure and accompanied under 16's are admitted free in all enclosures.

I wasn't amused by the yellow lines painted on the grandstand steps. I'm sure they were painted on with the public's safety in mind, but surely a permanent paint would have been the sensible thing to use.

Rating: Good ★★★

How to get there:

To get there by road; the course is just off the A46, next to the A631.

From the north, A1, M62, M18, M180 link to A15 and then the A631.

From the south, A1 to the A46.

The parking is free except for the picnic area which is £4.50p a car.

To get there by rail; Newark is the nearest mainline station.

Market Rasen station which is only a mile from the course is on the Newark to Cleethorpes line.

Nearest airport is Humberside (14 miles)

Although there are one or two closer, Lincoln is a good option for accommodation as it is only twelve mile away.

Monday 4 July 2005

The Racecourse
Maidenhead Road
Windsor
Berkshire
SL4 5JJ
Tel: 0870 2200024
www.windsor-racecourse.co.uk

We had made up our minds we were going to do this one in style, flights were booked to Heathrow and we had booked a room at The Oakley Court Hotel, a Neo-Gothic mansion just outside of Windsor with 35 acres of land and overlooking the Thames. I believe it has been the setting for quite a few films; including Dracula and the St Trinian's films.

We took a taxi to Newcastle airport, checked in then headed for the departure lounge. Angie went to order two coffees while I headed for WH Smiths to buy our Racing Post. I was shocked when I saw the front page of the paper. The young jockey, Tom Halliday who had been taken to hospital after his fall at Market Rasen the day before, had died of his injuries. I don't think people really appreciate the risks these young men take day in and day out, just for our enjoyment. Angie was also deeply shocked when she saw the headlines, I don't know if it was because we had been there at the time, but it was certainly hard to swallow.

The flight to Heathrow took under an hour, and after collecting our case and Angie's brolly, which had been bent to the state of being unusable, we went to get an airport taxi dumping the brolly on the way. There was a guy with a clip board coordinating the taxis, when he asked us where we were going I said Windsor, which I knew was less than 8 miles. He said it was a fixed price of £48 and showed me a printed price list, and sure enough that was the price. Angie wanted to find another means of transport, but I told her we had planned to do the trip in style and having over 2 grand distributed among my pockets I said we would take the cab. I told the taxi driver on the way I would give him £30 for himself rather than pay the £48, but he told me he couldn't as the guy with the clip board would have his destination logged.

The hotel which was built in the style of a French chateau looked very impressive as the taxi turned into the drive. After checking in and sorting our room out, we went for a walk down to the river through the garden of the hotel which looked even more impressive from the back.

On the way to the races I told our taxi driver what we had been charged from Heathrow to our hotel. Seizing the opportunity to get himself a nice little earner, he said he wasn't working the next day but he would pick us up and take us to the airport for £25. (The deal was done) We told him we would be going into Windsor for a drink after the races, so he gave us his mobile number and said he would make himself available to pick us up when we were ready to go back to the hotel.

When we got inside the course we went into the bar for drinks where we got talking to this fellow who had been to 54 of the 59 tracks, with only 5 of the northern tracks to visit. With us only being on 19, we still had a long way to go. After another drink at the bar we went outside, keeping hold of the glasses for drinking the contents of Angie's water bottle.

Before racing started a minutes silence was held for Tom Halliday

As far as betting went, we had a pretty good evening. We were back to our £40 and £20 bets.

We both backed the first winner, Art Market £40 at 5/4 and £20 at 11/10.

We stood in the stand to watch our horses finish nowhere in the second. By this time it had started to rain, and even though we were just under the cover of the stand we were still getting wet. Angie was cursing the airport baggage handlers for breaking her brolly.

We both backed the third winner Without a Trace £40 and £20 at 7/4

Still raining we found a nice sheltered spot under a canopy where we got talking to 3 young lads, who because of my size nicknamed me the bear. There was also an Australian girl, who had made it obvious she had taken a fancy to me and was trying to get into our company. But Angie showing her Alpha female instincts chased her off. While we were having a good laugh with these lads we lost track of time, and I heard the commentator say the horses were down at the start for the fourth race. Angie gave me her £20 and leaving her with our new found friends I dashed out in the rain and had £60 on One To Win, which did win at 3/1. By the time of the fifth race the rain had eased a bit, I had £40 on Shared Dreams at 6/4, Angie who still didn't fancy going out in the wet put £20 on Almost Innocent with the tote.

Almost Innocent beat Shared Dreams by a short head paying £5.90p a win.

Nothing back in the last, but not a bad evenings work.

Windsor racecourse being right on the river has its own jetty, from which we boarded the river bus to take us into Windsor. We had a couple more drinks in town before contacting our taxi driver to come and pick us up. When he dropped us off we arranged a time for him to pick us up for the airport the next morning.

Having not had a proper meal that evening, we decided to call room service and were told that because of the time, sandwiches were all that was available. We ordered three rounds of sandwiches; ham, chicken and cheese. While waiting I dozed off sitting in a big comfy armchair. Angie woke me to tell me the sandwiches had arrived and there had been a power cut. I looked on the table to see three of the biggest trays of sandwiches you could imagine, not even managing to get halfway through them, we'd had our fill and went to bed. The next morning on checking out there was no reference to the sandwiches on the bill; they mustn't have managed to get them onto their computer due to the power cut. Our driver arrived bang on time, and took us to Heathrow for our flight home. We had done Windsor in style and the Windsor bookies had paid for most of it.

Angie's verdict:

This really was style; I couldn't believe how grand the hotel was. It sort of took my mind off my broken brolly, my pride and joy Toon Army golfing brolly (and the rip off taxi fare). When we first got to the racecourse I was drawn to the sound of a Caribbean steel band, which was a great improvement to the brass band that seemed to have followed us around the past few Yorkshire courses.

There are plenty bars and eating places to choose from in the Club and Tattersalls enclosures, including quite a few fast food outlets selling a good variety of snacks. I think Dave went to the stall selling shellfish three times.

Viewing from the stands is very good, but the cover could do with being extended a bit as we were still getting wet even though standing under it.

Disabled facilities include lifts, toilets, parking and a viewing stand. The facilities are good, and the toilets are very nice. I would love to go back on a sunny evening though when you're winning almost any weather is bearable.

The group of lads we were talking to were really funny; because we'd flown down and were staying at Oakley Court they asked if we were millionaires one even asked (in fun) if we had a daughter, to which I replied: yes and she is spoken for, we kept them guessing whether we were rich or not.

There is a third enclosure, the Silver ring where the viewing is okay but away from the winning post. Facilities in the Silver ring include a cafe and an adventure playground.

Rating: Very Good ★★★★

How to get there:

To get there by road; the course is on the A308 between Windsor and Maidenhead, from the north the M25, M4 then the A308. From the south the M3 then theA332 to Windsor and from the east or west leave the M4 at junction 6.
Parking is free except for the member's car park and the silver ring picnic area which both cost £5.
To get there by rail; there are frequent trains from both Paddington and Waterloo to Windsor Central and Windsor and Eaton Riverside stations, from here you can try an alternative type of transport, as there is a river bus which will drop you at the racecourse jetty.
Nearest airport is Heathrow (7.6 miles)
Windsor is one of England's most popular tourist attractions because of Windsor castle and the royal connection, and because of this there is plenty of accommodation on offer.

Thursday 7 July 2005

Doncaster Racecourse
The Grandstand
Leger Way
Doncaster
DN2 6BB
Tel: 01302 304200
www.doncaster-racecourse.com

After Newcastle, Doncaster was the second racetrack I had ever been to, it was on a day trip from work to the 200th St. Leger meeting in 1976. Although I didn't back Crow which won the big race, I had 3 winners on the card. It wasn't entirely down to the St. Leger trip I got myself hooked on racing, but it certainly played its part. We have both been to Doncaster a couple of times since then.

After our success at Windsor on the Monday night, I booked a room at Doncaster Lakeside Travel Inn for another evening fixture. The hotel being just off the motorway and less than 3 miles from the course was in an ideal location. Doncaster is only 130 miles from our house which meant we could leave mid afternoon for the races, then leave just after breakfast the next day and be home before lunch. Arriving at the hotel just before five, we got changed and took a taxi the short journey to the track where we bought members badges then made our way to the members bar. We had a couple of drinks in the bar while studying the racecard, then took a drink outside with us to the seats in the grandstand where we sat for the rest of the night. There was extra room in Angie's bag for her water bottle as she had lost her binoculars; she thinks she left them in the Indian restaurant we went to after racing at Nottingham. Even without the bins we had a good view, not only of the course but of the fight which had broken out between two young lads on the grass just below us. I

85

don't know if they were thrown out, but security took them off somewhere. I have seen 3 fights while at the races and all in Yorkshire; this one and 2 on different days at York. The 2 at York were both in the betting ring, and both between bookie and punter, obviously over money.

Three races had gone and not 1 winner. It was just after the third race that Angie spotted Mr. Ranson walking towards the bottom of the grandstand. I managed to catch his attention and went down for a chat about the prospects of Hiccups which was running in the last. He certainly didn't have the same confidence about his horse as he did when it ran at Catterick. He said a 6lbs penalty after his last win meant he was carrying top weight, and he had heard whispers that a couple of horses further down the handicap were fancied to run well, one of them was Yorkshire Blue which was nearly a stone and a half better off in the weights.

Nothing back in the fourth, or the fifth race.

Not happy with our losing streak, I wanted to plunge on the last race, but Angie said I'd had too much to drink to make sensible decisions and had to stick to our planned stakes. To make sure I did she came with me to the betting ring.

Hiccups opened up favourite at 100/30; Yorkshire Blue was trading at around 6/1. We eventually made up our minds and decided to back Yorkshire Blue each way which by then was down to 5/1.

Yorkshire Blue won the race, we had £30 e/w at 5/1 and Hiccups finished down the field. It was about a year later at Newcastle races the next time we saw Mr. Ranson, and it was here that he told us he had sold up everything including his horses and was now living in Malta. He was only in England to attend a business meeting, so he thought he would have a day at the races while he was over here. Mr and Mrs Ranson were certainly two of the nicest people we have met on our travels.

After racing we were walking across the car park, and as we were passing a mini bus which was being boarded by four middle aged

couples I asked them if there was room for two more. Telling them we were just going into town they willingly gave us a lift. Once in town we went through our normal routine; a few drinks followed by an Indian meal.
Angie's verdict:

We weren't in the taxi long before pulling up at the racecourse which is on town moor, a green belt area among the suburbs of Doncaster. Because we arrived shortly after the gates had opened we sat alone with our vodkas and racecards in the very comfortable member's bar. However, by the time we had read through the form for the evening's entertainment a few more folk had arrived and a very pleasant atmosphere was developing. Apart from reading the race card I also read the interesting fact that Doncaster is not only home to the St. Leger, the oldest of the five U.K. classics, it also stages the opening and closing fixtures of the turf flat season.
The enclosures at Doncaster are big, and the grandstand, where we sat most of the evening is huge. There are plenty of bars and restaurants to suit all tastes. The view from the grandstand is excellent with plenty of seating available, I think more courses should have seats available even if they are called stands. All areas are clean and well maintained. Persons in wheelchairs along with one carer are admitted free of charge.
As well as the Members and the Grandstand enclosures there is the family enclosure which also has bars and food outlets. Viewing from here is also quite good though further from the winning line.
Rating: Very Good ★★★★

How to get there:

To get there by road; from the north or south, A1, M1, M18, there are signposts to the races from the motorways.
All car parks are free.

To get there by rail; Doncaster Central is a mainline station and is only 1.5 miles from the course. From here you can either get a taxi or a service bus. Buses 55,170 and 171 leave from just outside the station, and drop off not too far from the course. Nearest airport is Humberside (31 miles).

Doncaster has plenty of accommodation to choose from.

Saturday 9 July 2005

Hamilton Park Racecourse
Bothwell Road
Hamilton
ML3 0DW
Tel: 01698 283806
www.hamilton-park.co.uk

To buy tickets online, you must order them not less than two weeks before the date of the meeting you wish to attend. Even though Hamilton had been planned in for a while I didn't order badges, this was because I was told Hamilton was all one enclosure. I had however booked our hotel, a room for one night at the Travel Inn Hamilton, which is just off the motorway and only a mile and a half from the racecourse.

My preference is national hunt racing, especially the winter jumping season, however as far as our lifestyle and domestic commitments are concerned summer racing; and even more so evening meetings suit us better. The meeting we were going to at Hamilton was an evening meeting.

Trivia- Hamilton was the first U.K. course to hold an evening meeting.

Angie, after sorting things out with Grant and before our departure told me she hadn't filled her water bottle as she needed a new one. Instead she had put a 1 litre bottle of vodka in our overnight bag, and would buy a bottle of water on our journey. Having left Newcastle at lunchtime on a hot Saturday, the road west towards Carlisle was really busy. A lot of people from the north east tend to head for the Lake District when the sun comes out. Once we reached the M6 and started north on the motorway it was still quite congested but at least we kept moving, and the further north we got, the quieter it got. Deciding to stop for a coffee and to buy our new water bottle, we pulled in at

Annandale Water service station which is on the A74 (M). The bottle of water we bought, the coffees we didn't, I have never seen so many people in a service station, the whole building was crammed with massive queues for everything, so we just bought the water and left.

We checked in to our hotel at about half three, and were told by the girl on the desk, Hamilton was the only unlicensed Travel Inn in the whole of the U.K. Luckily, even after filling the water bottle there was still enough vodka left in the litre bottle to have a drink in our room while getting changed for the races. I went to the nearby services and bought a cold bottle of Sprite, and as we dressed for the races we had a couple of drinks, which we drank out of two plastic glasses Angie had found in one of our cupboards at home and had packed along with the vodka.

We shared a taxi the short journey from the hotel to the track with a young couple who were also going racing. They had travelled down from somewhere north of Glasgow to what was their local track; I wouldn't have liked to use their home as a base for travelling around all the courses. When we arrived at the course I was surprised to find there were actually two enclosures. We went into the club enclosure, while our companions wished us luck and headed into the grandstand enclosure.

Because it was a poor card with some small fields, we had agreed while driving up the motorway to use the same system we had used the week before; £40 a race with alternative picks (Angie wanted to go first).

In the first race she had £20 e/w on Victoria Park, which won at 4/1.

In the second I went down to back Give Me The Night which was 4/6 so I put £20 to the £40 I had, and put £60 on at 4/6. Angie said I wasn't sticking to what I'd agreed, but the horse won so she said no more.

After the second race we went for a stroll round the back of the stands, where there was a large grassy area with tables laid out, and the whole area was covered with families picnicking, barbequing and generally enjoying the summer evening. We managed to find a spot at one of the tables, and it was there we stayed for the rest of the night.

I kept our table while Angie went down to bet her horse for the third race, she said she wanted to see the betting as she couldn't make her mind up between two. Luckily she decided on the right one and backed the winner Amprior £40 at 9/4.

I found myself in the same situation in the next race, where I was undecided between two, so I ended up backing them both, £20 on Hula Ballew at 4/1 which finished second, and £20 on Jordans End at 7/2 which finished fifth.

Angie had £40 on the favourite in the fifth One Great Idea which won at 11/10.

And even though my horse finished last in the sixth race we were showing a profit.

After racing I asked a policeman who was directing traffic onto the main road how far it was into town, he told me it was a five minute walk. We walked for nearly half an hour on that very warm night before we reached our destination. By that time we were both uncomfortably hot, and even going into bars for a drink we just couldn't seem to cool down, so we decided to get a taxi back to the hotel. Before getting the taxi we called in to a fish and chip shop for a carry out. Angie ordered mince pie and chips which she ended up throwing in the bin as she said it was disgusting, and I ordered three pieces of what turned out to be the best southern fried chicken I have ever had. Because Angie's supper was in the bin next to the empty vodka bottle I offered her some of my chicken, but she refused as she can't eat chicken off the bone (what a shame).

I have told Angie I would like to go back to Hamilton one day, for both the races and to visit the fish and chip shop.

Angie's verdict:

We picked a good night to go to Hamilton, not only was it red hot, it was family night sponsored by the Sunday Mail, and even though there was a big crowd we had plenty of space. There was loads of entertainment on for the kids, with bouncy castle, merry go rounds, face painting etc. they even held a fancy dress competition.
Both the Club and Grandstand enclosures have plenty bars and eating places and there is a good friendly atmosphere. The toilets were okay though they were a bit messy, but this was probably due to the number of kids that were using them. There is disabled parking, toilets and a dedicated viewing area.   Viewing from both enclosures is very good.
One meeting I am really looking forward to going to is the Saints and Sinners charity meeting which is held yearly in early summer. Dave's sister, Elaine, and husband Tam often attend this fixture and say the atmosphere is great.
Rating Good ★★★

How to get there:

To get there by road; from the south take the A74 and M74 and exit at junction 5.
From the north take the M74 and exit junction 5. Coming from Edinburgh take the M8 to junction 6 and then the A723.
Parking is free in the main public car park.
To get there by rail; Glasgow Central is the nearest mainline station, from here get a connection to Hamilton West station which is less than a mile from the course.
Nearest airport is Glasgow (15.8 miles).
You will find accommodation in Hamilton itself, but Glasgow being only 10 miles away is another option.

Saturday 16 July 2005

Newmarket Racecourses
Westfield House
The Links
Newmarket
Suffolk
CB8 0TG
Tel: 01638 675500
www.newmarketracecourses.co.uk

Newmarket, headquarters of British flat racing was one of the courses I had really been looking forward to visiting, and what should theoretically have been one of our best trips turned out to be a bit of a nightmare.

Grant by now was getting used to the routine and was happy enough to be left dog sitting for one night. We were driving down to Huntingdon on Friday afternoon where we had a room booked for one night at The Premier Travel Inn. From there we were going to Newmarket on the Saturday and driving home after the races.

We arrived at our hotel in Huntingdon late afternoon and not wasting much time after checking in we ordered a taxi which took us into town, the driver giving us a bit of a guided tour on the way. I think he went a little bit off the direct route just to show us where Oliver Cromwell had attended school. Having asked him to drop us off near some decent pubs he pulled up outside a bar with a beer garden, which was ideal as it was a glorious summers evening. Before he drove off he pointed up the street to two bars which were pretty close to each other and told us we would be wise to steer well clear of the two of them. After a couple of quiet drinks in the beer garden we took a stroll up the street and headed for the pubs we had been warned off from. Just as we had suspected they turned out to be two lively pubs with great atmospheres, and it was back and forward between the two we spent our night. (Strange guys taxi drivers).

We drove to Newmarket the next morning, and even though we stopped at Cambridge service station for breakfast we arrived a few hours early. We parked up in the town and had a stroll down the high street stopping only at the chemist to buy a pack of Imodium to settle my stomach which was fighting with my breakfast.

Tip. This kind of medication is handy to take on your travels, as even the slight change in the water throughout the British Isles can upset ones stomach.

After parking up and approaching the enclosure something was telling me all was not right. This didn't look the same as what I could remember from TV. The whole place was buzzing. Champagne was flowing, ladies in their summer dresses and gentleman in their short sleeved shirts all gave the place a sort of garden party atmosphere. We went into a bar at the back of the grandstand and ordered two glasses of orange with ice and sat at a table near a free standing electric fan which helped to get our blood temperatures down to somewhere near normal. I took out the Racing Post and asked Angie to pass me my specs which she always carried in her bag for me on our trips. I haven't got them was her reply, and no matter how hard I tried it was impossible to get the newspaper print into focus, so I said I would just back the favourites for the day.

Feeling refreshed we went out onto the grandstand to take a look at the course, and even though I knew there was the July course and the Rowley mile it took a while before I realised there must be two grandstands.

I was staking £40 a race and Angie £20, and after the first five races we hadn't had a return. £300 down we decided to cut our losses and leave early for our 250 mile drive home. As it happens the sixth favourite won at 10/11, but that wouldn't have even covered the bet for the seventh race where the favourite finished nowhere.

While driving home I told Angie we would have to come back to Newmarket when racing was being held on the Rowley course before we could tick Newmarket off our list. She agreed.

Angie's verdict:

Things you read about places plant a picture in your mind of how they would look, and the one I had of Newmarket was one of a town over run by vertically challenged people, as I had read that the streets of Newmarket were full of ex jockeys and stable lads. As we walked down the main street I soon realised this wasn't the case, and Newmarket looked pretty much like any other town on a busy Saturday morning.

I must have also had some kind of picture built in my mind of what the racecourse was going to be like, and just like the town, the racecourse was not what I was expecting.

There were already quite a few cars in the car park when we pulled up, and about one in ten of them had their boot open being used as a serving hatch as people were enjoying picnics in the sunshine.

I thought the parade ring was really nice, and I enjoyed watching a couple of races from the head on stand.

The Member's and Grandstand & Paddock enclosures were alright, but I thought they could have done with a facelift, though I have read that improvement plans are being considered.

If you are more interested in food and drink rather than racing, you won't be disappointed as there is a big range of both eating places and bars, including a couple which are open aired which were very popular that day as people were taking advantage of the weather.

Viewing from the stands is very good, and one thing I really did like was the bench cushions that were scattered about in the stands which enabled you to take the weight off your feet without the worry of ruining your clothes. I think more courses should follow this example as I'm sure there is more than me that likes to sit down now and then, and this is a lot cheaper option than having seats fitted.

There are toilets and a good viewing area for disabled racegoers The Family enclosure has a temporary stand for viewing. Fast foods and drinks are available in this enclosure which also has a playground. Sensible shoes are a must in the Family enclosure as there is a lot of grassy areas. Like all other family enclosures there is no access to the parade ring or winners enclosure.

Backing a winner would definitely have made the day better.

Rating: Good ★★★

How to get there:

To get there by road; from the north, A1 (M), then A14 and A1304. From the south A11, M11 to junction 9 then the A1304. From the east and west the A14 then the A1304.
There is free car parking. Day member's car park costs £5.
To get there by rail; Trains run from both Liverpool St. and King's Cross to Cambridge from where you can get a courtesy bus to the track. There is a limited service train that goes from Cambridge to Newmarket station which is 1.1 miles from the course.
Nearest airport is Cambridge (9 miles)
There is an abundance of accommodation in the area within a good price range.

Saturday 6 August 2005

Ayr Racecourse
2 Whittlets Road
Ayr
KA8 0JE
Tel: 01292 264179
www.ayr-racecourse.co.uk

I had telephoned my sister Elaine earlier that week for a general chit chat, and just happened to mention we had badges for Saturday night at Ayr races. She told me she wouldn't have minded going, but wasn't sure of what her and Tam had planned. On the Friday morning she rang me back and told me they were going to the races along with Howden and Lisa. Angie and I had a room booked for one night at The Travel Inn, Ayr, which is about six miles from the course. Elaine however said they wouldn't be stopping over, so she wouldn't be drinking as she was the nominated driver.

Because it was an evening meeting, we left Dudley at eleven thirty for our three and a half hour drive. There didn't seem to be any serious delays on our journey, but a few small delays cost us time and it actually took us four and a half hours, which meant we arrived at our hotel only two hours before the first race was due off. We checked in and asked the girl on the desk if she could order us a taxi to take us to the races, and we would be back down in five minutes. After getting ready in near record time we were back down after about fifteen minutes, but there was no sign of the taxi. The girl on the desk phoned again and was told the taxi driver was on his way. It actually took fifty five minutes from the original phone call for the taxi to arrive. During this time Elaine who was already at the track had phoned Angie and told her where we had to meet them; in the Champagne bar. With no real apology, but with a multitude of reasons why he was late the driver took us to the track. As we approached the enclosure I realised I had made a mistake ordering our badges online, it was ladies night and women were being admitted free of charge.

We soon found the Champagne bar, it was a lovely evening and Elaine and Lisa had kept a seat for Angie at the table they were sitting at out on the lawn. We declined Tam's offer of a glass of bubbly and said we would stick to vodka.

£40 a race taking turns was the "intended" betting system for the night, with Angie to pick the first, but because of her talking and not much time before the race she asked me to go first. I had £40 at 7/4 on Diablerette which won, returning at 9/4.

Nothing back in the second, or third.

Angie sent me down to put £40 on Mystic Man for her in the fourth which won at 7/4.

I thought the favourite Annibale Cairo looked a real good thing in the fifth, and probably influenced by the vodka which we had been drinking at a fair pace; I had £150 at 4/6.

I was pretty confident before the race, but even more confident as they turned for home. The second favourite Pearls a Singer slipped and fell on the bend, sending jockey Robert Winston crashing through the running rails. Three other horses were brought down and two others badly hampered in the incident, Annibale Cairo was eased down at the finish to win by 12 lengths.

The rest of the meeting was abandoned due to unsafe ground, and jockey Robert Winston who had been a leading contender for the jockey's title was taken to hospital with multiple fractures to his jaw.

Instead of going into Ayr we decided to go to Prestwick for a drink after racing, Elaine said she would have to ferry us as there wasn't enough room in the car. She took Angie and me first while Tam, Howden and Lisa were finishing off their sixth bottle, and dropped us off outside Flanagan's, the pub where we were supposed to meet them. We went in, turned around and walked straight back out, there was that many people in the bar it would have been almost impossible to get served.

We found a quieter bar and only had one drink; food seemed a better option at this point, so we found an Indian restaurant and sat down for a feast. We had almost finished our meals when Elaine came in and sat down beside us, she had been looking all over for us and had seen us through the window of the restaurant. We told her we'd had enough to drink, so she phoned Tam to say she wouldn't be long and gave us a lift back to our hotel.

Angie's verdict:

I usually dress for the races anyway, as Dave nearly always wears a suit and tie, so being ladies night I didn't have to put much more effort into my choice of clothes, only to make sure Dave's tie matched my outfit. I wasn't amused standing around in the hotel car park waiting for our taxi, so was glad of the seat Elaine had kept for me in the champagne bar. We actually went into the marquee next to the champagne bar first, where they sold vodka which enabled us to acquire two glasses for the bottle I had in my bag. While we were in there we sat at a table next to a couple who were convinced we had travelled to Ayr to back one horse. Even though we promised them we hadn't, they just wouldn't believe us and went away looking rather dejected because we hadn't supplied them with some winning information.

The facilities at Ayr are very good; there are two enclosures, the Club and the Grandstand both of which are quite big. The track itself reminds me pretty much of Newcastle's.

Both enclosures have a number of bars offering a wide range of drinks and the restaurants and food outlets serve a variety of foods to suit everyone's taste. Views over the course from both stands are very good and both have access to the parade ring. There are viewing ramps and toilets in both enclosures for the disabled.

Rating: Good ★★★

I felt really sorry for Robert Winston that night; I had been following him through the season and thought he had an excellent chance of finishing leading jockey.

How to get there:

To get there by road; from the south take A74, A70, A713 then the A77 into Ayr.
From Glasgow take the M8 then the A77.
All parking is free.
To get there by rail; Ayr has a mainline station, from where there are buses to the course which is a mile away.
Nearest airport is Glasgow Prestwick (3 miles).
Ayr is a popular seaside town and has a good range of accommodation.

Wednesday 17 August 2005

York Racecourse
The Racecourse
York
YO23 1EX
Tel: 01904 620911
www.yorkracecourse.co.uk

If someone asked me to choose which flat racing course was my
favourite, I would have to say York. Not just because it is a
northern track, but it really is splendid and with some of the best
horses from the south travelling up to compete with the best from
the north you are almost guaranteed quality racing.
We have been to York races quite a few times and nearly always
by train, and although we have had overnight stays in hotels at
York we have never stayed on a race day. We were sitting that
morning having a coffee and watching the news when the phone
rang. It was Darren a friend of mine from work, he told me that
he and his wife Jane were going to York for the Ebor, and there
was room in the car for me and Angie if we wanted to go. Caught
a bit off guard, I told Darren we had a few things to do but if he
rang back in half an hour I would let him know for definite.
Darren once worked in a racing stable and still gets the odd bit of
information. At one time he was well into the horses, but now
he's more into poker which he mainly plays online and is
showing a nice little profit from. He still likes the odd bet
however, and the occasional trip to the races.
As I said we have been to York races quite a few times, and most
of them to the Ebor meeting which is a popular fixture for a lot of
racing fans here in the north east. For those of you who don't
already know it Ebor is short for the Latin name for York,
Eboracum.

It didn't take long before we'd decided the few things we had to do could wait, and by the time Darren rang back we were already getting dressed for the races.

Darren and Jane picked us up at eleven and we set off on our two hour drive to York. It was the first time Angie and Jane had met, but you could tell by their conversation they had hit it off, and we were all set for a great day.

We parked in a residential area about half a mile from the course where Darren had to change into his suit standing on the roadside. After escaping arrest for indecent exposure we walked the short distance to the course. With soaring temperatures and the massive crowd, standing was a bit uncomfortable so we found a spot in the shade where we spent most of the time between races.

Because it was a trip we hadn't been expecting we decided to only bet £20 a race alternative picks. Luckily we did as we managed to back seven losers.

Darren backed one winner Punctilious for which he got 7/1.

Although Angie and I hadn't backed a winner we'd had a great day out, Darren hadn't won a fortune but he'd covered his day, Jane hadn't been betting but they too said they'd had a great day. Darren was driving but said it would be a shame to go straight home, so he suggested we stayed in York for an hour or so and go for a drink, he himself being happy just to a have a couple of glasses of shandy. We'd had a real good laugh in the afternoon at the races and it continued into the early evening, so much so that when they finally dropped us off at home it had been decided by the girls that Darren and I had to arrange another trip away, and preferably for a weekend.

Angie's verdict:

I can do nothing else but give York a very high rating, but in the same breath York just isn't my cup of tea. The reason being no matter when we have been there I have found the people to be very snobby.
York is without doubt the most impressive course in the north, and probably rates among the top half dozen in the country.
The grandstands have been well planned and give an excellent view over the track.
There is a wide variety of food on offer throughout the enclosures, and plenty of bars for those wishing to quench their thirsts. The buildings are a mixture of old and new, and even though the toilets were very busy they were clean and tidy.
There is parking for the disabled (car park C) as well as toilets throughout the enclosures and designated viewing areas.

One thing that does stick in my mind about York is the number of ticket touts on the approach to the course. My advice is to avoid the temptation of trying to save a couple of quid through buying cheap tickets from these guys. A while ago we were going to the races with my mam (Daisy) and her partner Joe. I couldn't find our badges which I thought were in my hand bag, so I went straight to the racecourse reception and explained my situation to one of the receptionists. She looked up my name, and without hesitation gave me new badges. She told me she had cancelled the original badges and if anyone presented them for entry into the races, their systems would automatically reject them. So be very wary of buying tickets when you don't know where they have come from.
I actually quite enjoyed that day at York, but I think that was down to the company we were in.

Rating: Very Good ★★★★

How to get there:

To get there by road; from the north take the A1 then the A59, then the York ring road which avoids the city centre. From all other directions take the A64 and A1036 once you get near the city.
There is plenty of free parking.
To get there by rail; York has a mainline station which is only 1 mile from the course. There is a regular bus link to the course from outside the station.
Nearest airport Leeds and Bradford (24 miles).
Although York has a vast amount of accommodation on offer, you can sometimes find it difficult to get booked up when there is a big meeting on.

Thursday 25 August 2005

Lingfield Racecourse
Racecourse Road
Lingfield
Surrey
RH7 6PQ
Tel: 0870 2200022
www.lingfield-racecourse.co.uk

Although she wasn't totally convinced, I told Angie we could
quite comfortably travel to Lingfield and back in one day using
the railway as our transport. I booked everything online; the rail
tickets, which arrived in good time and the badges for the races
which hadn't arrived with Wednesday's post which was the day
before we were travelling. I phoned the course explaining we
would be leaving before the post arrived the next day, so they
arranged for badges to be left at the racecourse office for us to
pick up on arrival.

We got up at six o'clock and had coffee before getting ready for
our taxi which was picking us up at ten to seven. The journey to
Lingfield meant getting three trains; Newcastle to King's Cross, a
tube train from King's Cross to Victoria followed by a train from
Victoria to Lingfield.

Angie had packed some sandwiches for our journey, and had our
vodka supply in her trusty water bottle, safely stored in her bag
for later in the day.

We walked the short distance from the railway station to the
course and collected our badges. With there being a mixed bag of
weather that day, we spent half the time sitting in the sunshine
and the other half indoors sheltering from the rain. While sitting
outside we got talking to some guys from up north who were
showing an interest in our quest to visit all 59 U.K. racecourses.
They too had been to quite a few, including some of the Irish

courses. We told them we had discussed the possibility of visiting the Irish tracks, but would probably finish the U.K. first. They all agreed that we would probably enjoy the Irish racing better.

My great grandfather moved from Ireland to Newcastle when he was a young man, and found employment in the then thriving shipyards on Tyneside. Neither Angie nor I had ever been to the emerald isle but that would all change.

We didn't have a bad day as far as betting was concerned, we were still betting alternative races but upped our stake back to £40, me to go first this time.

We had nothing back in the first three races.

Angie backed the winner in the fourth, £40 on Time For Life at 2/1.

I had £40 on the fifth winner Renderoc, for which I took 3/1 Nothing back in the sixth.

I finished the day off by backing the last winner South O'The Border £40 at 7/2.

We waited over half an hour for our train to Victoria which arrived late, meaning we had missed our connection. So with a bit time to kill we had a couple of drinks sitting outside in the shade at a pub near Victoria station watching the hustle and bustle of the London traffic. I don't know what route it goes but what we noticed was every third bus that went past seemed to be a number 38. Eventually we got the tube to King's Cross and caught the nine o'clock train which arrived at Newcastle at quarter to one in the morning, and by the time the taxi dropped us off at home it was nearly one thirty.

So yes I was right, we could travel to Lingfield and back by train in one day, but I wouldn't recommend it to anyone as we were both wrecked.

Hollie came home later that day as it was bank holiday weekend. Before she went back to Edinburgh on the Monday tea time she told us she was pregnant.

Angie's verdict:

Why I let Dave talk me into travelling to Lingfield and back in one day I will never know, we should definitely have booked an overnight stay at a hotel.

The short walk from the railway station to the course was really lovely, and thankfully we made it before the rain started.

There are bars and a wide variety of food on offer in both the Member's and Grandstand enclosures. The members bar looked like it had just been refurbished as everything looked new, even a brand new carpet had been laid and the toilets were spotlessly clean. There is parking, toilets and viewing areas for the disabled. We actually spent most of the afternoon dodging the showers in the grandstand where everyone we spoke to was very friendly and the viewing was very good. At weekend meetings they have a children's play area.

Rating: Good ★★★

How to get there:

To get there by road; Lingfield is best reached from the M25 coming off at junction 6 onto the A22 and then the B2028.
There is free parking at the course.
To get there by rail; Lingfield station is only half a mile from the course.
Nearest airport is Gatwick (9 miles).
Being only 9 miles from Gatwick airport there is accommodation to be found all within easy reach of Lingfield. London is another option as it is only 20 mile away.

Saturday 3 September 2005

Folkestone Racecourse
Stone Street
Westenhanger
Kent
CT21 4HX
Tel: 01303 266407
www.folkestone-racecourse.co.uk

Angie reckons I sometimes have some crazy ideas and probably one of the craziest was when I planned the trip to Folkestone races. Folkestone racecourse is the only racecourse in Kent, 350 miles and a 6 hour drive from our house. The sensible thing would have been to wait until we could have fit Folkestone in with another meeting or even two and visited them all in one trip. Unfortunately the racing fixtures that week didn't go well with my days off, and wanting to go somewhere we'd never yet been to Folkestone was the only choice.
We travelled down on the Friday night as far as Thurrock, where I had booked a room for the night at Thurrock East Travel Inn. This meant we would only have 56 miles to drive to Folkestone the next morning.
We stayed in our hotel room on the Friday night, watching TV, while checking Teletext for the following days racing we found out that the first race at Folkestone was 11:30.and the last 14:05 which at least meant we would get an early start for our drive home.
What the Teletext didn't tell us was the meeting at Folkestone was banded racing also known as regional racing. Banded or regional racing was introduced to cater for horses of poor quality with a rating of less than 45. But on the bright side there were six races so there had to be six winners, we just had to find them. Unfortunately we didn't find any of them, and even though we

108

nearly changed our minds to drop to £20 a race, we stuck with £40.

The interesting thing about banded racing is, it was starting to become quite popular with everyone except the bookies who were struggling to get the market right, especially with some of the older horses which once showed a bit of form but had dropped down to the lowest of grades. The races were run off level weights and were often ridden by apprentices with a weight allowance, so you can imagine what kind of problems the bookies were facing. Most banded meetings were run on the all weather but there was a few on the turf including a couple of national hunt fixtures. I believe that the British Horseracing Authority put an end to banded racing in 2007.

We were well on our way home when Angie's mobile phone rang; it was Tappy, a lad who was on my shift at work. He wanted to know if we were at he races as he had just received a call from someone in Folkestone saying they had found a pair of spectacles. I must have left my specs on the seats next to the fish pond behind the grandstand. We had been sitting there most of the afternoon enjoying the sunshine, luckily I had Tappy's number written on a post it note tucked away inside my glasses case.

Quiet roads, and only stopping once for fuel, meant we arrived home in less than 5 hours which was pretty good going. We had just completed a 700 mile round trip highlighted by watching some of the lowest rated racehorses in the country trying to earn their keep. On top of that we had done our money in, the good thing was we were going to Goodwood the following week with no fears of having to watch banded racing.

As it was Saturday and the night was still quite young we went to our local social club where we stayed until chucking out time.

I spoke to someone at Folkestone racecourse the next day, and gave them my name and address. The postman delivered my specs two days later.

Angie's verdict:

The first thing I thought was nice about Folkestone was there was only one admission charge giving access to all areas. When we first arrived at the course we bought coffees and sat outside the pavilion bar which has tables and chairs on the lawn among the trees. There are a number of food and drink outlets, but I must admit the food we had that day wasn't to our liking.
There are toilet facilities for the disabled on the ground floor of the grandstand, and the upper level can be reached by a lift.
From the grandstand you get a good view of the finishing straight, and even though we didn't have a winner I enjoyed our day at Folkestone.
Behind the grandstand is lovely lawned area very well looked after and we spent quite a lot of the afternoon sitting in the sun in front of a fish pond built into in a nice grassy area which the kids also seemed to enjoy. Entertainment is put on for kids on race days held during the summer holidays.
Rating: Average ★★★

How to get there:

To get there by car; from the north take the B2068 from Canterbury,
From the south the A259 from Hastings, and from the east or west take the M20 coming off at junction 11.
There is free car parking. To park in the picnic area costs £5 a car and £5 per occupant.
To get there by rail; Westenhanger railway station is very close to the course. Special raceday trains run to Westenhanger from both Charing Cross and Waterloo East.
Nearest airport is London Manston (22 miles)
There are quite a few hotels and guest houses in the Hythe area which is just a few miles from the racecourse.

Saturday 10 September 2005

Goodwood Racecourse Ltd
Goodwood
Chichester
West Sussex
PO18 0PS
Tel: 01243 755022
www.gloriousgoodwood.co.uk

Goodwood was another course I had been really looking forward to visiting. Our friend Dorothy who along with her husband Billy had already been to all the tracks said it was probably her favourite course, and T.V. commentators were always commenting on how spectacular Goodwood was. One thing I did know was we were guaranteed good racing.
Hollie was home again that weekend, so we had no worries; as we knew the dogs were in good hands.
We set off Friday lunchtime for another 350 mile drive; our destination was The Travel Inn, Bognor Regis, where we had a room booked for two nights. Bognor because it is only nine miles from Goodwood racecourse, and two nights because the fixture list was a bit kinder to us that week, and we were going to Stratford races on the way home on the Sunday.
The journey to Bognor took us a lot longer than planned, we stopped 3 times on the way down, the third stop happened to be a service station with a Ladbrokes betting shop. I gave Angie £20 to have a go on the roulette machine while I had a couple of bets on the greyhounds, after four bets I was about £30 up, Angie by this time was doing quite well on the machine. Because the time was getting on I suggested she cashed in and we got back on the road. So after about another quarter of an hour she collected her win voucher and cashed it in collecting £275. We also hit traffic problems on the M25 which cost us quite a bit of time, and we

eventually arrived after nine o'clock at our hotel, where we had a couple of drinks before going to bed reasonably early.

With the sun shining and us feeling quite fresh, we drove into Bognor on the Saturday morning, and went for a stroll along the promenade before finding a cafe where we had breakfast. We sat for a while reading the Racing Post, and both feeling quite confident of having a few winners we drove back to the hotel and got suited up for the races.

Twenty minutes after leaving our hotel we were in the Goodwood estate, I was surprised there wasn't more traffic on the approach to the car park, but when we got there the car park was already packed as most people must have set off early. Even for a Saturday I would say this was a very big attendance, I can't imagine how full it would be when the Glorious Goodwood festival is on. Once inside the Enclosure and looking out over the course it was plain to see why Goodwood is to many the most picturesque racecourse in the UK.

The few quid we'd taken off Ladbrokes the previous afternoon had given us a nice start and betting £40 and £20 we were hoping to add a few more quid to our kitty.

I started the day backing the first winner Punta Galera, £40 at 2/1

Angie backed the second winner Serre Chevalier £20 at 5/2

Angie backed the third winner True Cause £20 at 9/4

Nothing back in the fourth

Our horses dead heated for first place in the fifth race, I had £40 on Ashdown Express at 2/1, and Angie had Moss Vale £20 at 5/2

We both backed The Nawab which won the sixth, and both took 5/2Nothing back in the last.

On the way back to the hotel we were discussing the days racing, we had backed the winners of 5 races, and were only showing a profit of £140, but in the same breath getting paid £140 for enjoying yourself isn't bad, and adding it to the money we'd won the previous day we were having a pretty good weekend. When we got back to the Travel Inn we stayed in the hotel bar for a couple of drinks, and then went back to our room where we had a bottle of vodka waiting for us.

Angie's verdict:

Even though our friends Dorothy and Billy had told us how much they had enjoyed Goodwood, it still surprised me to see just how splendid it really was.

Goodwood has three enclosures; the Richmond, the Gordon and the Lennox and all are a lot more modern than I somehow expected them to be.
We spent most of the day in the Richmond enclosure, which during the Glorious Goodwood meeting is only open to annual members, their guests and private parties. The facilities in the Richmond enclosure are really good, numerous bars and eating places offer a wide range of drinks and a good variety of hot and cold food. There is an excellent view from the grandstand, and the parade ring is one of the nicest I've seen. There were a good number of bench seats on the lawn in front of the running rails. The facilities in the Gordon and Lennox enclosures are also of a very high standard, and again both these enclosures have a number of bars and no shortage of food outlets. Both the Gordon and Lennox stands have good views of the finishing straight. All three enclosures are well maintained, and the toilets are spotlessly clean. There are extensive facilities for the disabled at Goodwood racecourse.
A nice thing about Goodwood is, they have a racecourse club for 10-16 year olds, but I believe there is a maximum number of 200 members allowed.

Because of its setting alone I would put Goodwood in my top three flat racing venues.

Rating: Very Good ★★★★★

How to get there:

To get there by road; from the north take the A3 then the A286. From the east the A27 then A285, and from the west the A27 then A286.
There is free car parking available. There are other car parks that do have a charge, but these need to be booked in advance.
To get there by rail; you can get trains from Victoria and Waterloo to Chichester station which is four and a half miles from the course. From here you can either get a taxi or the shuttle bus which runs on race days.
Nearest airport is Southampton (27 miles).
There are a few hotels within a five mile radius of the course, Bognor is also an option.

Sunday 11 September 2005

Stratford Upon Avon Racecourse
Luddington Road
Stratford-on-Avon
Warwickshire
CV37 9SE
Tel. 01789 267949
www.stratfordracecourse.net

Although Stratford isn't on a direct route from Bognor Regis to Newcastle, it was 155 miles in a northerly direction which made it too tempting an opportunity to miss on our journey home. The trip was going to take about three hours, so we decided we were going to stop somewhere about half way for breakfast. Unfortunately things don't always go to plan. We had turned off the M3 and had travelled about 10 miles down the A34 when the engine high temperature alarm signalled on the dash board. I drove another couple of miles and turned into a service station. There was no use panicking, so we had breakfast while the engine was cooling. Luckily I was carrying 2 five litre water bottles in the boot, one which was used for topping up the radiator and the windscreen wash, the other we used for dog's drinking water after we'd been walking on hot days. I filled the radiator and expected to see a leak at the water pump, but nothing happened. I turned on the engine and waited, and after a couple of minutes spotted a leak on one of the hoses. Not having the gear to repair it, and not being dressed for messing on with engines, I had an idea. Making sure both water containers were full we drove towards Stratford making note of how many miles we could drive before the warning light came back on, we managed 47 miles. I pulled over onto the hard shoulder of the M40 and filled the radiator, I reckoned as long as the leak didn't get any worse we should make it to the races without having to top up again, my calculation was right.

So we pulled into the car park and walked away from the car still being able to hear the hissing under the bonnet. Angie was showing concern about driving home in the dark as we would obviously have to make a few stops, but we were there to have a days racing so I said we would decide what to do about the car later and we headed for the enclosure.

After a lengthy discussion over a coffee we had came to a decision; we were going to bet £40 a race, I was going to pick a horse in the first three races, and Angie to pick in the last three.

In the first race I backed the winner Star Member, £40 at 9/4.

My horse in the second race Phar From Frosty finished second.

My horse in the third race Beauchamp Prince pulled up at the second last.

Even though she'd had loads of time to pick her first horse, Angie was sitting on a bench seat near the grandstand flicking between the racecard and the Racing Post, finally having made up her mind she had £40 on Glengarra at 7/2.

We then went down to the winning post, I was standing between the running rail and the parade ring and Angie was sitting on the rail of the parade ring, from here we watched Glengarra win by a distance.

Collecting her winnings on the way, she returned to the same bench seat where she chose her horse before we went back via the betting ring to the same position from where we had watched the previous race. Again we watched Angie's horse Mister Moussac win easily, and again she took 7/2.

Following the same routine as the last two races; she made it three in a row with £40 on Fourty Acers at 4/1.

Before leaving I filled the radiator and both water carriers, Angie also bought two bottles of water from one of the racecourse caterers as back up. We made it home having made six stops, including twice at service stations where we filled our water carriers.

The next morning it cost me under £5 for a length of hose and a bottle of anti-freeze, and after a quick repair the car was ready for our next trip.

Angie's verdict:

When we pulled up in the car park at Stratford racecourse I had a headache, with my eyes switching from route planner to road signs to temperature gauge and worrying about our journey home it was a relief just to stop, if only to give my brain a rest.
There are three enclosures at Stratford, the Members and the Tattersalls are the two main enclosures, and though not very big they have a good atmosphere. Both these enclosures have ample bars and food outlets, including a number of catering vans selling fast food.
Viewing from the grandstands is quite good, the Member's stand overlooking the finishing post and the Tattersalls a bit further down the finishing straight. I quite enjoyed my lucky spot watching from the rail. Both enclosures are clean and everywhere, including the toilets, are well maintained
There is parking for the disabled as well as toilets and a viewing area, the disabled parking is next to the viewing area.
The third enclosure is the course enclosure, which also has bars serving hot and cold snacks as well as drinks. The course enclosure is ideal for picnics; there is no stand in this enclosure so the best viewing is from the rail.
There is a playground for the kids; and speaking of kids, I watched Robert Thornton refuse to autograph a young boy's race card on his way to the parade ring. I know he has a job of work to do, but every little helps when encouraging the younger generation to come racing.

It seemed ages for the fourth race to come around and me have my first bet, but three winners in a row wasn't bad going,
Rating: Good ★★★

How to get there:

To get there by road; from the north M42, M40 coming off at junction 15 then the A46.
From the south take the M40 followed by the A46.
If you are coming off the M5 take junction 7 then take A44, A46 and B439.
There is plenty free parking, but the main car park costs £2
To get there by rail; Stratford-on-Avon railway station is under a mile from the course.
Nearest airport is Birmingham (19 miles)
Because of its Shakespeare connection Stratford is a popular tourist attraction, I believe only London has more visitors. So a good range of accommodation is available close to the course.

Saturday 17 September 2005

Warwick Racecourse Company Ltd
Hampton Street
Warwick
CV34 6HN
Tel: 01926 491553
www.warwickracecourse.co.uk

It took some time, but I eventually managed to get Angie to start believing me when I told her the repairs to the car were fine, and we would be alright to take a day trip to Warwick races. So with Grant left in charge of domestic duties we set off on our journey. I had filled both water bottles and put some extra tools in the boot, but I hadn't told Angie as I didn't want to cast any doubt in her mind.

We had set off pretty early that morning, and by the time we had reached Trowell service area on the M1 where we stopped for breakfast, Angie was starting to feel more relaxed, she had been keeping her eye on the temperature gauge for over a hundred miles.The rest of our journey went smoothly, but one thing I had started to notice was the number of cars that were broken down and pulled over to the side of the road.

On arrival we made our way into the main enclosure and had our usual tour before heading for a snack.

We sat indoors enjoying soup and a sandwich while looking through the racecard; we had no difficulty finding seats as most people had been drawn outside to watch a jousting competition that was going on in front of the stands.

Even though we'd been successful at Stratford the previous week, Angie said it was no fun her having to wait until the fourth race before having a bet. Angie was proving to be a better judge than me, so I suggested we both bet £40 a race, but she said she was quite happy for me to bet £40 and her to bet £20.

119

I'd been reading an article on each way betting which made sense, so our new tactics were; if we were betting a horse under 7/2 we would back it to win, and if it was 7/2 or greater we would back it each way.

Fair enough if I'm betting £40 on a 7/2 chance and it wins I'm going to collect £180, but if it is second or third I have lost my money.

If I bet £20 e/w on a 7/2 and it wins I am still collecting £124, £90 for the win and £34 for the place (worked at 1/5th odds).

The fact is, if my horse is second or third I will still collect £34, which means I'm only losing £6 instead of £40.

There was an eight race card scheduled, but we had decided to only stay for seven so we could beat the traffic, six if the bookies were beating us.

Although it was odds on we both backed the first winner Military Cross and both took 4/5

Angie had £10 e/w at 5/1 on Blue Grouse which finished second in the second race.

Angie backed the winner of the third Count Treviso £20 at 11/4

We both backed the winner of the fourth race, Willhego, £20e/w at 5/1, and £10e/w at 9/2.

Nothing back in the fifth, or sixth.

We weren't doing too badly but we decided to call it a day and make our way home.

The repairs to the car had stood up to the trip to Warwick but it had still been a bit of a worry, and I had been surprised at just how many broken down cars we had passed on our journey. We still had quite a few courses to visit, and apart from Hexham they were all a good distance away. I thought it would be wise to have some kind of back up, so I joined the A.A.

Angie's verdict:

Dave gets some funny ideas in his head, and after our recent
experience coming home from Stratford, I thought driving to
Warwick and back in a day was one of them. But he assured me
the car was alright, and he didn't mind driving the eight hour
round trip, so off we went.
I wasn't expecting Warwick racecourse to be anything special,
but it was quite pleasant. The facilities are basic but very nice,
and the grandstand gives you a good view of the course.
There are a number of food and drink outlets selling both hot and
cold food, and everywhere is nice and clean. There is a raised
stand, easy access ramps and toilet facilities for disabled
racegoers.
One thing Warwick Racecourse didn't have was cash machines,
and I personally think they should be barred from all racecourses.
When I have seen cash dispensers at courses they have always
had a big queue waiting to use them, and normally after three or
four races have been run. I know some cases are genuine, but I
am willing to bet at least two thirds of the queue have lost their
money, have had a drink and are trying to win their money back.
The chances are they will lose even more, so for their sakes I
think cash machines at racecourses should be a no no.
Rating Good ★★★

How to get there:

To get there by car; from the north take the M6 to junction 4
followed by the M42, M40 and A46.
From the south, the M40 to junction 15 then the A46.
There is plenty free parking. Non members can park in the
member's car park for a charge.
To get there by rail; there are hourly trains from London to
Warwick railway station which is less than a mile from the
course.

Nearest airport is Birmingham (14 miles)
There are quite a number of hotels within a few miles of the course.

Thursday 6 October 2005

Southwell Racecourse
Rolleston
Nottinghamshire
NG25
Tel: 01636 814481
www.southwell-racecourse.co.uk

Although all weather racing isn't our favourite form of entertainment we do sometimes have a bet when watching it on television, and to be perfectly honest we do no better or no worse than when we're betting on the turf. A friend of mine bets on nothing else but all weather racing as he reckons the form is a lot easier to follow and he claims to be well in profit, but I'll take that with a pinch of salt as I can't remember him having any big wins.

I'd walked the dogs early that morning while Angie was making sandwiches to have on our journey down to Nottinghamshire, as we didn't plan on making any stops.

We set off at ten o'clock for the three hour drive and were just talking about things in general when Angie just out of the blue said "I think I'll write a book." I have heard people half heartedly say they could write a book about things that have happened in their lives, but I knew by the way Angie said it that she meant it. She then went on to tell me that the books she had read on racecourses were probably written by people who hadn't even been to them, and she thought a woman's point of view would make a good book.

I knew she was pretty serious, but there is a difference between saying you are going to write a book and actually sitting down to put pen to paper. We talked about it for the rest of the journey, and although I was trying to encourage her to go ahead with it, one or two negative comments that I made seemed to put her off the idea a little. At least the conversation made the journey time pass a bit quicker as well as planting a seed in my head. When we arrived at the course the sun was shining but being October it was a bit chilly, so we went inside for a warm drink and a sit down while we read through the racecards.

We changed our betting strategy again for Southwell, this time we were betting £40 a race, alternative picks and e/w on anything 7/2 or bigger. Angie went first.

Nothing back in the first two races.

Angie backed the winner of the third race, Prince Vettori, £20 e/w at 4/1.

I had £40 on Brave Chief, which won the fourth race at 9/4.

Nothing back in the fifth, or sixth.

Not a brilliant day but we hadn't lost. On the way home, although we didn't talk about it I was thinking about the conversation we'd had about the idea of writing a book earlier that day.

Angie's verdict:

"I should write a book" is what I really said. Because we were planning to go to all the courses Dave had bought a racecourse guide, and to be perfectly honest it was a little bit misleading. One or two of the courses were nothing like they were described in the guide which seemed to concentrate mainly on things like corporate facilities and group hospitality bookings. There was little or nothing about facilities for the everyday racegoer.So for that reason I thought it would be a good idea to write a guide for the average punter.

It's a lot less stressful if you are sitting down while reading through your racing paper, as keeping it intact reading it while you are standing is virtually impossible. So as we arrived at Southwell we made our way for a coffee and a nice seat. The coffee was pretty standard, but the seat we got was one of the many very comfy plush leather settees that were arranged around the tables in the member's bar (very nice touch).

I had watched Southwell races many times on TV, and to me it always looked grey and drab, and there never seemed to be many people there. The image on TV had been deceiving as Southwell racecourse is actually quite nice and is set in a scenic location. The numbers of people I saw on TV however mustn't have been a deception, and we were there amongst what I would consider a poor attendance.

One group of people who had turned up were a bunch of school kids who looked about 14 year old. They must have been on some kind of educational trip accompanied by a couple of teachers who were turning a blind eye to them smoking and even taking their money to go and place bets with the bookies for them. At least they seemed to be having a good time.

There are two enclosures at Southwell; the Member's enclosure and the Tattersalls, both of which have ample bars and food outlets. All areas of the enclosures are well kept and the toilet facilities are of a good standard. Viewing at Southwell is also very good, with the Member's stand best located at the finishing line.

There are toilet facilities for the disabled as well as viewing platforms; there is also a lift to the first floor.

Young children can enjoy a supervised play area.

Rating: Average ★★

How to get there:

To get there by road; from the north the best route is the A1 followed by the A46 then A617.

From the south take the M1 to junction 25, and then take the A52, then A46.

From the east the A17, and from the west the A617.

There is plenty free parking.

To get there by rail; trains run from Nottingham to Rolleston railway station which is only half a mile from the course.

Nearest airport is Nottingham (12 miles)

There isn't a lot of accommodation close to the track, but there is plenty within a 15 mile radius.

Thursday 13 October 2005

Newmarket Racecourses (Rowley)
Westfield House
The Links
Newmarket
Suffolk
CB8 0TG
Tel: 01638 675500
www.newmarketracecourses.co.uk

Although we had already been to Newmarket when we went to the July meeting, we weren't ticking it off our list until we had visited the Rowley mile course
Why Newmarket is classed as one of 59 courses beats me, I know you could argue that courses that have both national hunt and flat tracks have two courses, but Newmarket is different as it has two grandstands, one for each course.
After giving Grant his instructions on Wednesday night, we were up early on Thursday morning to drive the 250 miles to Newmarket. We stopped at Blyth service station for breakfast and to refuel before continuing our journey to the races.
It was while we were sitting having breakfast I asked Angie if she'd had any more thoughts on writing the book. She told me she hadn't really put much more thought into it, I told her I had. I actually told her I'd been thinking about it since she first mentioned it and suggested we write it together. At first she wasn't too keen, but when I told her what I thought might be a reasonable format she started to show more interest.
The racecourse guide we had read was all to do with what big races were held at each course, along with corporate facilities, private boxes and waitress service restaurants. These things are all very nice, but not what your average racegoer is looking for, so I suggested we tackled it from a different approach.

A short piece on our day including our bets for the day, which luckily I had kept record of in one of the two programmes we had bought at each meeting. "I'll think about it" was her final response, but I know when Angie says she'll think about something she invariably means yes.

We didn't talk about it any more that day, but over the few weeks following we finally started to put a few notes together and the book was started.

When we arrived at the course we were both in good moods, but that was more down to the prospects of a good day racing rather than the possibility of becoming budding authors. I had been a bit disappointed when we went to the July course as it wasn't what I'd been expecting, but this time things were different the Rowley mile enclosures looked magnificent and was exactly what I'd been expecting.

We had no happy memories of the July course as we had done our brains in, but never the less we were both looking forward to our return to Newmarket where we would hopefully make amends for our previously disastrous days betting.

We were betting £40 and £20 and sticking to our e/w betting system

I backed the first winner Scandal Keeper £40 at evens, Angie backed the second You Call That Art £10 e/w at 5/1

I had the second winner Ebtikaar £20 e/w at 4/1

Angie had £10 e/w on Royal Alchemist which finished second in the third race at 8/1

I backed the winner of the fourth Bold Crusader, £40 at 11/4 and Angie backed the second Baskerville £10 e/w at 6/1

Nothing back in the fifth

Angie had the winner of the sixth, Gramm, £10 e/w at 6/1. My horse Munnings dead heated for second, £20 e/w at 5/1

We also had £10 e/w on our namesake, Conroy, which had been running earlier in the afternoon at Ludlow. He put up a bold show leading at the last only to be beaten on the run in, finishing second at 14/1.

Even though we were only driving as far as Grantham where we had a room booked for the night we left before the last race. Firstly to beat the traffic, and secondly to get as far north as we could before it got dark. Thankfully we'd had a much more successful day than on our first visit to Newmarket.

Angie's verdict:

As we'd been to Newmarket just a few months before, my job as navigator was pretty much redundant as Dave more or less knew where he was going. I thought the July course was okay even though it was a bit old fashioned, and it went through my mind a few times that the facilities in the Rowley mile enclosures would probably be the same. I couldn't have been more wrong. We were there early so had plenty time to have a look around, and right from walking through the turnstiles I was amazed at the comparison, there was so much to take in.

There are three enclosures at the Rowley Mile course; the Member's, where as well as restaurant facilities there are bars and an area where you can buy teas, coffees and light snacks. There is excellent viewing from this enclosure.

The Grandstand and Paddock enclosure also has a number of bars and eating places, including the Paddock food court where mobile catering units offer a variety of foods and are positioned around a nice seating area.

This enclosure also has very good viewing; there is a balcony at the back of the grandstand looking over the parade ring.

We had a walk round the Gift shop and shopping stalls outside, and although Dave kept telling me to buy a souvenir nothing really caught my eye.

The toilets and facilities are of a high standard and exceptionally clean and there are plenty seats to be found.

Disabled racegoers can enjoy access to all areas; there is designated parking, toilets and specially designed viewing platforms.

The third enclosure is the Rowley enclosure (family enclosure) there is a children's playground in this enclosure and picnics are allowed. There are also mobile caterers offering hot and cold drinks and snacks.

Viewing from this enclosure is okay but it is away from the finishing line.

Rating: Excellent ★★★★★

How to get there:

To get there by road; from the north A1(M) then A14 and A1304, from the south A11,M11 to junction 9 then the A1304.. From the east and west the A14 and A1304.

There is free parking. Day member's car park costs £5.

To get there by rail; Trains run from both Liverpool St. and King's Cross to Cambridge from where you can get a courtesy bus to the track. There is a limited service train that runs from Cambridge to Newmarket station which is 1.1 mile from the course.

Nearest airport is Cambridge (9 miles)

There is a good choice of accommodation in the area within a good price range.

Saturday 12 November 2005

Wolverhampton Racecourse
Dunstall Park Centre
Dunstall Park
Wolverhampton
WV6 0PE
Tel: 0870 2202442
www.dunstallpark.co.uk

Hollie and Michael were coming home and stopping at our house for the weekend, so with their agreement I went online and booked two nights away for our last trip of the year. Our first stop was to be Wolverhampton, the member's badges we had for the Saturday night fixture also entitled us to watch the live band who were performing after racing. The following day we were heading for Cheltenham where we were hoping to end the year on a high note.

We set off mid-morning on our four hour drive to The Best Western Connaught Hotel, Wolverhampton where we had a room booked for one night. We had originally tried to book a room at The Holiday Inn which is in Dunstall Park, but there were no rooms available.

Although not a great fan of the all weather tracks, I was looking forward to my first experience of floodlit racing. We arrived at our hotel late afternoon, which gave us plenty of time to get ready for the races.

On our short taxi ride from the hotel to the course the driver gave us a piece of advice; He told us that under no circumstances should we walk back from the track to our hotel as we would be 99% sure to become the victims of muggers. It didn't look any different to any other city we had been to, but I thought this could be one taxi driver worth believing.

We showed our badges as we went in and were shown to a lift and told to get out on the first floor. The lift was actually the same one used by the hotel guests. We went into the bar, ordered a couple of vodkas and sat at a table not far from where there was a small stage set up with a couple of microphones. Naturally we thought this is where the band would be performing after racing. We had decided to back just one horse a race for the two days we were away; £40 stake, alternative bets and sticking to our e/w rule. Angie went first on the six race fixture.

Unfortunately the only return we had was in the fourth race when I had £20 e/w with the tote on After The Show, which finished second paying £4 a place.

We had both commented on how few people were going outside from the bar to watch the racing and how there was a lack of a racing atmosphere. We also noticed how full the bar was getting and decided to give up our seats and stand as we were getting sick of having to move our seats to let people pass.

We were also wrong about where the band was performing, as an announcement came over the P.A. system saying anyone with members badges who wished to see the live band should leave through the doors at the back of the room. We followed the flow of people downstairs and eventually arrived at a huge entertainment hall with a full size stage. The room was set out with rows of tables that would sit 10 to 12 and almost every table was full with people who had obviously been there all night. Whether they had been watching the racing on TV screens from here I don't know, but it seemed more like a social club than a race track. We had long since finished the contents of Angie's water bottle, so I went to the bar and ordered a couple of drinks. We stood drinking them at the back of the room while listening to the bands attempt at a couple of soul classics.

Deciding we'd had enough we went outside where there was a taxi standing and asked him to take us to a good Indian restaurant. Once inside we ordered drinks and our meals and were asked the strangest question you could possibly be asked in a restaurant; the waiter asked us if we would like plates. Naturally we said yes, we did however notice some student types who were eating their food out of what looked like small woks, so I presume this must have been the alternative.

After our meals we took a taxi back to our hotel where we would have a good night's sleep and a better day to look forward to on the Sunday.

Angie's verdict:

I didn't know exactly what to expect when we got to Wolverhampton races, but I certainly didn't expect what we got. The whole place including the course reminded me more of a greyhound stadium except with not as much atmosphere.

The groups of people in the member's bar seemed more like they were out for a normal Saturday night on the booze, in fact one group of eight young men were standing quite close to our table, and not one of them had a racing paper or even a racecard, which I thought was very unusual.

There are restaurants with panoramic views over the course, but these need to be pre-booked. The views from the grandstand are also very good, though the night we were there we more or less had the stand to ourselves.

There are bars selling both drinks and food in both of Wolverhampton's enclosures. The parade ring looked quite nice as it as well as the course was all lit up.

Carers for the disabled are admitted free of charge, disabled facilities include; parking, toilets and lifts to the upper level. There is a children's playground close to the parade ring.

Rating; Average ★★

How to get there:

To get there by road; from the north take the M6 to junction 12 then the A5 and A449. From the south take the M6 to junction 10A, then the M54 and A449.

From the east and west the M54 and A449.

There is free car parking available.

To get there by rail; Wolverhampton railway station is only a mile from the course.

Nearest airport is Birmingham (28 miles)

The most obvious is The Holiday Inn at Dunstall Park, but I think it will be hard to get a room on race days. There is however plenty other accommodation to choose from in Wolverhampton.

Sunday 13 November 2005

Cheltenham Racecourse
Prestbury Park
Cheltenham
Gloucestershire
GL50 4SH
Tel: 01242 513014
www.cheltenham.co.uk

With only an hour to drive from Wolverhampton to Cheltenham, we had plenty time for breakfast before getting ready for our trip to my favourite racecourse. Although I had been before, this was going to be Angie's first of her visits to Cheltenham, and I knew once she had been it would become her favourite as well. After a disappointing visit to Wolverhampton, we were hoping for a better time in Cheltenham. We had a room booked at The Travel Inn, Cheltenham Central for the night, but drove straight to the course, as I wanted Angie to have a good look round before racing started.

We parked up and made our way to the enclosures, and once inside I took Angie straight out onto the grandstand so she could look down the finishing straight and get her first look at the famous Cheltenham hill. After having a look around the club enclosure we spent half an hour browsing around the tented village before having a bite to eat and a read of our racecards. We were betting the same system as we had been the night before at Wolverhampton; £40 a race, alternate picks and each way on anything 7/2 or over, and because it was our last meeting of the year we decided to have a placepot. We had to pick a horse each in every race, whoever was picking the main bet in each race would have first pick in that particular leg of the placepot. We were only staking 50p which came to a total of £32, Angie was picking first.

In the first race Angie had £40 on Neptune Collonges at 5/2, which finished fourth, but I had the third Massini's Maguire in the placepot.

In the second race I had £20 e/w on Nippy Des Mottes, which was going well when it fell at the second last. Angie put the winner Hordago in the placepot.

Angie backed the third winner Accordion Etoile, £40 at 5/2, which she also put in the placepot.

The bookie she had put her bet on with wasn't in the main betting ring; his pitch was at the back of the grandstand not far from the parade ring. He paid her out and made some crack about Geordies.

Before the next race Angie said she needed something to eat, and said she would just go and get a sandwich somewhere and meet me back near the statue of Golden Miller, which was our pre arranged meeting place and not far from the bookie she had just collected from.

Tip- It is a good idea when you first arrive at a course and you are in company to agree on a meeting place that everyone will remember, this way you will be unlikely to lose any of your party.

I stood for a while watching the bookies as they were putting up their prices for the fourth race. The bookie Angie had just been paid by had the horse I had picked for the next race Lingo priced at 9/1 so I had £20 e/w at nines.

By the time the race had started Lingo's price had dropped to 5/1 and he proved worthy of the confidence in the betting ring winning by three and a half lengths.

I gave Angie the winning ticket and she went to the bookie who gave her the winnings accompanied with another pop at the Geordies. As he already had his prices up for the next race she put £40 on her fancy Bannow Strand at 6/4, and we watched our third winner in a row win by eight lengths plus we were still in the placepot with one leg to go.

We decided to keep the same routine for the last, Angie picked the money up from a not so cocky bookie and she put £40 on my fancy, Leading Contender at 2/1.

Leading Contender won the bumper, the bookie paid Angie for the fourth race in a row and said she would more than likely feature in his nightmares, and we had the placepot up but only for 50p.

It is more or less impossible to try and guess what a placepot dividend will be, but we thought even if we won enough to pay our hotel bill it would be a bonus. We seemed to be waiting ages, but eventually the dividend was announced and it paid £476 to a £1 stake this meant we collected £238 which just topped the day off fine.

We drove the couple of miles to our hotel, checked in, freshened up then went out for the night. We started in TGI Fridays which adjoins the hotel where we sat having a few vodkas while watching a wannabe cocktail waiter dropping bottles (which were fortunately empty) on each of his routines. From here we took a taxi to the Montpellier district which was recommended to us by the girl on the hotel reception. The bars were pretty quiet, all except one which was an Irish bar and where we had a good night in the company of a group of lads from the emerald isle.

We finished our evening in an Indian restaurant, where for some reason we got talking across tables to a couple of ladies on one side, and a couple of guys on the other, the topic was racing and how Lingo had landed a gamble in the fourth race.

It was when someone mentioned it might have a chance in the Champion Hurdle that one of two fellows who were sitting a few tables away turned around, and in a strong Irish accent said Brave Inca will win the Champion Hurdle, he then turned back to continue with his meal.

We took our time driving home the next day. It was a few weeks later when I went into Ladbrokes and put £80 e/w on Brave Inca to win the Champion Hurdle 9/2 anti post.

Angie's verdict:

Cheltenham is the one racecourse I would absolutely recommend any racing fan to visit, and if national hunt is your preference Cheltenham is the ultimate in jump racing.

Admission prices are very reasonable; especially when you see what you get once you are inside. You can pay the same price or even more at other courses around the country and don't get half as much for your money. There is no dress code at Cheltenham, so both gentlemen and ladies are mainly dressed casual but smart. There is food and drink throughout all four of the enclosures to suit everyone's palate and pocket. I have read that there is almost a hundred catering outlets present during the festival in March, when there are attendances of up to 50,000 a day.

I haven't actually been there for the festival, which has been described as the Olympics of national hunt racing. However I have been a couple of times to the Open meetings in November, which also attract large crowds. The open is also popular with the Irish who come over in numbers, helping to make an atmosphere that has to be experienced to appreciate.

Unless you can get a position on the rails or you are very tall, viewing from ground level is almost impossible because of the crowds, try to get a into the grandstand where the view is overwhelming. We have also been in the centre of the course during a cross-country race, fair enough you don't get to see much but you get really close to the action.

There is viewing facilities in all enclosures for the disabled, and also an area overlooking the parade ring. Accompanied children less than 16 years are admitted free into all enclosures, except for the festival meeting when full charges apply.

Another thing I must mention is the tented village where you could spend a full day just browsing round the stalls, and if you are like me you will more than likely end up buying something. Everyone was really friendly, even the bookies when they were paying out.

Cheltenham is definitely my favourite racecourse.
Rating: Excellent ★★★★★★

How to get there:

To get there by road; from the north M5 to junctions 9, 10 then
theA435. From the south M5 to junctions 10, 11. From the east
the A40 and from the west the A40 followed by the M4 to
junction 20, then the M5 to junctions 10, 11.
The routes in are well signposted by the A.A.
There is loads of free parking except on festival days when there
is a charge.
To get there by rail; Cheltenham Spa railway station is 2 miles
away and is served by direct trains from both London and
Birmingham. There is a bus link on race days to the course.
Nearest airport is Birmingham (39 miles)
There is a lot of accommodation in the area, however if you are
looking for somewhere to stay during the Festival you will find it
a bit harder; as hotels and guest houses are usually booked up a
year in advance by people who go year after year. It is worth
looking a bit further afield.

2005 had come to an end and we had been to 32 tracks, which
wasn't bad going. The only problem was; apart from Hexham
which is only twenty miles along the Tyne valley from where we
live and Thirsk in North Yorkshire, the nearest course we still
had to visit was Leicester, which is 180 miles from Newcastle.

We decided to buy a new car before the start of the next years travelling, and thought it would be a good idea to buy a 4x4 as most racecourse car parks are fields. We ended up buying a 3 litre Toyota Hilux Surf (Japanese import 4x4) which was ideal for racing, and there was loads of room in the back for the dogs.

With Hollie being pregnant she had decided to move back to Newcastle and would live with us until she could find a house of her own. Michael was also going to quit his job in Edinburgh and find employment in the Newcastle area. He too was moving in with us, the advantage this had was we could book trips for more than just a couple of days at a time in the coming year.

As part of our wedding anniversary present in October 2005, I had adopted in Angie's name an ex drug addict chimpanzee called Charlie who was housed in Monkey World, an ape rescue centre in Wareham near Poole in Dorset. Monkey world had its own television series of which Angie used to watch every programme and knew most of the apes by sight, Charlie being one of her favourites. We agreed we would visit Monkey World when we were down the south coast.

Although we'd had a few really bad days betting in 2005, we had managed to get at least one return at most meetings and had one or two really good days.

One bit of news that had come out was the building of a new course which was going to open at Great Leighs near Chelmsford in Essex.

Wednesday 15 March 2006

Huntingdon Racecourse
Brampton
Huntingdon
Cambridgeshire
PE28 4NL
Tel. 01480 453373
www.huntingdon-racecourse.co.uk

This was actually our second attempt of having a day at
Huntingdon races; the first was in January 2006. It was still in the
middle of winter, and quite a few meetings had been lost due to
heavy frosts. I'd just had a stroke of luck winning £1400 on the
Irish lottery and £280 on a midweek football bet, both on the
same night, and because I was on a seventeen day break from
work it seemed a good idea to go racing.
We were still in the proceeds of buying our new car and didn't
fancy a long winter journey in the Citroen, so we decided to go to
Huntingdon by rail. We booked our train tickets online through
G.N.E.R. and just had to pick them up at Newcastle Central
station on the day we were travelling (25/01/06).
The weather up north hadn't been too bad, but parts of the
country were still suffering freezing cold nights, including
Huntingdon who were holding an inspection that morning. Before
our taxi arrived to take us to the Central station I phoned
Huntingdon racecourse and was told by a secretary that the
groundsmen were out walking the course and they were quite
confident racing would go ahead, and on these words we set off
on our journey.
We were on the train well on our way south when Angie phoned
Hollie who was back living at home by this time, and asked her
to check the teletext to see if there was any news on the

inspection at Huntingdon. A few minutes later Hollie rang back to tell us the meeting had been abandoned. It was pointless staying on the train so we got off at Doncaster and not to waste our day rang Hollie back to find out if the meeting at Catterick was going ahead. After she confirmed it was, we bought tickets to travel back up the line to Darlington from where we got a taxi to Catterick races.

Having nothing to lose I wrote a letter to G.N.E.R. and enclosed the Huntingdon rail tickets (used and unused), and told them we had to get off the train at Doncaster due to unforeseen circumstances. I was quite surprised a week later when a letter arrived from G.N.E.R. they explained in their letter that it wasn't their policy to refund fares, but they sent me rail vouchers to the full value of our original purchase.

By March the winter was all but gone, we had our new car, a Toyota Surf 4x4, and we were ready to rock and roll, and with pregnant Hollie being back at home it made the planning of racing trips a lot easier. We decided to drive straight to Huntingdon, then after racing drive back to Grantham, where we had booked a room for the night at the Travel Inn.

It was the second day of the Cheltenham festival and my anti post bet had come good the previous day when Brave Inca won the Champion Hurdle. Huntingdon were showing the races from the festival on the big screen, and because we'd arrived early we managed to get one of the few free Cheltenham programmes they had to give away. Although we did have a couple of losing bets at Cheltenham, we concentrated on the meeting we were at, and having not thought of a better system we were staying with our £40 and £20 stakes.

Nothing back in the first three races.

We put our money together in the fourth and had our £60 on Picot de Say which won at 5/6.

I backed the next winner Ocean Tide, £20 e/w at 5/1.

Angie had £20 on the sixth winner Clouding Over at 2/1.

We didn't stop for the last race, but we hadn't lost much.

Angie's verdict:

Dave knew that I'd always fancied owning a 4x4, and although he obviously wanted a car that was comfortable to drive, he more or less left it up me to choose which one to buy when we were looking round the showrooms. We had already had a trip to north Wales in our new car and as navigator I found it was much easier to read the road signs than it was in the Citroen as we weren't as low down.

We'd had a good day in one of our local pubs watching the racing from Cheltenham the previous day, so were ready for some live action when we travelled down to Huntingdon. Being March the worst of the winter had passed, but it was still quite cold so we got wrapped up for the day.

The main enclosure at Huntingdon isn't very big but is clean and well maintained. There are a few bars and a selection of hot food and snacks can be found at the various food outlets. Although there isn't a huge amount of seating, we managed to find one without any problem.

Viewing from the stand is very good, and we had the added enjoyment of watching Cheltenham on the big screen. There is a viewing ramp for the disabled as well as toilets in all areas. Huntingdon also has the Picnic enclosure which isn't open for all meetings. As its name suggests this is ideal for a family picnic, there is no children's entertainment in this enclosure and on meetings where kid's entertainment is provided it will take place in the main enclosure.

There is a bar in the Picnic enclosure where you can get both food and drink, but this will not be available at evening meetings.

Rating: Good ★★★

How to get there:

To get there by road; the course is quite close to the A1, from the A1 take the A141.
From the east and west take the A14.
Parking is free.
To get there by rail; Huntingdon station is just two miles from the course, from here you can catch the race day shuttle bus which starts two hours before the first race. The last bus back to the station runs half an hour after the last race.
Nearest airport is Cambridge (20 miles)
Although there isn't a great deal of accommodation in Huntingdon itself, there are plenty within a ten mile radius.

Saturday 25 March 2006

The Racecourse
Bangor-on-Dee
Wrexham
LL13 0DA
Tel. 01978 780323
www.bangordee.co.uk

Bangor-on-Dee is another course we had two attempts at; the first
was at the beginning of March 2006. We had just got our new car
and were pretty keen to try it out, so we booked a three day trip
taking in two meetings. The first was to be Bangor on Sunday 5th
March followed by Hereford on Monday the 6th.There had been
snow in parts of the country but nothing much to worry about,
however it was a slight concern that they were forecasting Wales
and the west of England to see the worst of it. Our plan was to
leave on the Saturday afternoon, stay at the Travel Inn Wrexham
Saturday night, racing at Bangor on Sunday, then after racing
drive to the Travel Inn Hereford ready for racing on the Monday.
 Before we left I phoned the racecourse to find out the state of
play, I was told the course had a slight covering of snow which
was thawing nicely, and providing they didn't have any more
snow racing was 95% sure of going ahead, but there would still
be an inspection on the Sunday morning. We decided to go for it,
and even though we did drive through one or two snow showers
on our way to Wrexham, they were nothing to shout about and
the snow wasn't lying.
We woke up the following morning to brilliant sunshine, and
when I looked out of the window the snow except for a few small
patches that were in the shade had gone. Looking forward to our
days racing I put the television on and checked the teletext only
to see the meeting had been abandoned. We then checked the
going for the following days racing at Hereford which read;

Hereford- snow, racing unlikely, inspection am.
Because of this we decided to cut our losses and go home. The
girl who checked us out of our hotel phoned the Travel Inn
Hereford and cancelled our room and we started our journey
north. As we were driving up the M6 feeling a bit deflated, Angie
rang Elaine and Tam to see what their plans for the day were, and
as they weren't doing anything special they agreed to meet us for
lunch in Dumfries. At home the following morning I put on the
TV only to see Hereford had passed its inspection and racing was
going ahead.
So three weeks later we set off again on our four hour drive to
Bangor-on-Dee. This time however we were setting off on the
morning of the races and driving straight to the course. After
racing we were again staying at the Travel Inn Wrexham, which
is actually in Gresford, near Wrexham and about nine miles from
the course.
The weather was quite nice when we first got there, and a good
crowd were already gathered. This was partly due to the theme of
the day being country day and various displays were being held
before racing began.
Sticking to our £40 and £20 a race, we'd had better days.
In the first two races our horses were both well beaten.
I had £20 e/w on the third winner Ross Comm at 4/1.
The weather started to change by now and it started to rain, so we
found the best shelter we could close to the enclosure buildings
but in view of the course, only to watch our horses lose in the
next three races.
It was raining pretty heavy by the time of the seventh race which
luckily we decided to stay for as we both backed the winner
Closed shop, £40 and £20 at 7/4.
After racing we drove to Wrexham's Travel Inn for our second
stay in three weeks. We didn't bother having a drink that night as
we drove to a nearby Chinese takeaway later in the evening for a
meal that we took back to our room.

Angie's verdict:

It was a nice sunny afternoon when we first arrived at Bangor racecourse, and the first thing we did was join a crowd of people that were gathered around the rails of the parade ring to watch a falconry display. This was the first time I'd seen such a display and was totally fascinated by it all.

There are two enclosures at Bangor; the Paddock enclosure and the Course enclosure, and if you are like us you will probably spend your time in both. This is because there is no grandstand at Bangor, and from the Paddock enclosure you only get a head on view of the course. If you want to be side on at the finishing straight you need to get a pass out and transfer into the Course enclosure.

There is parking for the disabled, toilets and a viewing platform in the Paddock enclosure.

The facilities are clean and modern, but unfortunately there just wasn't enough room for everyone to get inside to shelter from the rain. Apart from the main restaurant there is a rather nice carvery and a number of bars and fast food outlets.

Rating: Average ★★

How to get there:

To get there by road; from the north take the M6 to junction 9, then the M56, M53 and A483.From the south take the M6 to junction 15 then the A483.

From the east the A525, and from the west the A5 followed by the A483 and B5424. Parking is free.

To get there by rail; Wrexham station is just less than 5 miles away, from here there is a free bus service which runs an hour and a half before the first race, and returns after racing.

(Check the return times with the driver)

Nearest airport is Liverpool John Lennon (24 miles)

There is plenty accommodation around the border areas of England and North Wales.

Saturday 1 April 2006

Fontwell Park Racecourse
Fontwell
Arundel, Nr. Hythe
West Sussex
BN18 0SX
Tel: 01243 543335
www.fontwellpark.co.uk

Our plan was to visit four tracks in the south in one trip; Fontwell, Newton Abbott, Exeter and Taunton, with a trip to Monkey World also included in the agenda. Hollie's baby wasn't due for another 3 weeks, but nature can be a funny thing so we told her if need be we would come home at short notice.

First stop Fontwell; we booked a room for two nights at the Travel Inn, Bognor Regis, knowing this wasn't far from Fontwell Park as we'd passed Fontwell racecourse back in September on our way from Bognor Regis to Goodwood.

We left Dudley midday Friday and arrived at Bognor Regis late evening where we had a couple of drinks in the hotel bar. While we were there Angie thought she would order herself something light to eat and decided on a B.L.T. club sandwich. When it was served it actually looked quite tasty and well presented. Luckily she didn't take a bite, she lifted the top off her sandwich to add a sprinkle of pepper, but instead of adding the seasoning she immediately caught the attention of the manager who was making his way round his customers ensuring all was well with their food. He came over, and the look of shock on his face was a picture as again Angie lifted the top off her sandwich to reveal three raw bacon rashers garnished with lettuce and tomato. He told us the chef was new and said he would take the sandwich away and bring back another, Angie who was feeling a bit less peckish by now declined his offer. A bit later in the evening, the manager came back over to our table and explained how the person he had earlier called chef but was now calling kitchen worker was foreign, and thought that was how bacon was served. He also told us that someone had stored the bacon on the top shelf of the fridge among the cooked meats. We did accept his feeble explanation as an apology, but I bet he didn't dispose of the rest of the now possibly contaminated cooked meats.

The next morning we drove to the seaside where we had breakfast (with cooked bacon) and a stroll along the promenade, before returning to our room to get changed for our afternoons racing. The drive from the hotel to Fontwell Park is only three and a half miles.

Saturday meetings are usually popular wherever you go, and with Fontwell putting on one or two added attractions that day it really was busy.

As for the betting we decided to stick to our usual £40 and £20 stakes.

Angie got the show on the road by backing the first winner; Love Of Classics, £20 at 5/2.

Nothing back in the second or third.

We put our money together in the fourth, and Angie went to the betting ring and put our £60 on the winning favourite Lewis Island for which she took 10/11.

Another winner for Angie in the fifth £20 on Sesame Rambler at 3/1.

Nothing in the sixth.

I had £20 e/w on the last winner Supreme Cara at 4/1.

We drove the short journey back to our hotel where we had a couple of drinks in the bar before going to our room to watch some TV before going to bed. We were both looking forward to Newton Abbott the next day.

Angie's verdict;

The first thing that caught my eye as we went into the races were two beautiful shire horses that were standing harnessed to a dray. We spent a few minutes admiring them before heading into the Premier Grandstand. We had a good walk round and I thought the whole set up was lovely. There are plenty of places to eat and drink, and everywhere including the toilets are nice and clean. There is parking for disabled racegoers who must display their badges, and toilet facilities in both enclosures.

Fun fair rides and children's entertainers are a regular feature at weekends, bank holidays and fixtures held during school holidays.

I had phoned Hollie that morning and she told me everything was fine, but while I was in the toilet at the races my phone rang. It was Hollie, and I knew by the tone of her voice something was wrong. At first I feared the worst, but she hadn't phoned to tell me my grandchild was on the way. When she did tell me what was wrong I thought it was an April fool prank. She told me Michael was locked in the bedroom as the door handle had snapped internally, and she didn't know how to get him out without breaking the door. I told her I was in the toilet and would get Dave to ring her back, and eventually with Dave's instructions, the help of Grant and a couple of screwdrivers they released the prisoner.

Before racing we joined a crowd of punters and listened to a tipping forum that was being held behind the stands, after which we spent the afternoon between both the Premier and Grandstand enclosures.

We watched a couple of races from the grandstand from where you get a really good view of the course. The rest of the afternoon we spent mainly in the seated area on the lawn by the running rail, though we did venture upstairs in the grandstand to watch a couple of games of darts as Andy Fordham and Trina

Gulliver were there for the afternoon playing 301 challenge
matches against members of the public.
Rating: Good ★★★

How to get there:

To get there by road; from the north and south take the A29
which runs from Billinghurst to Bognor Regis. From the east and
west take the A27 which runs from Brighton to Chichester. The
course is just off the roundabout where the two roads cross.
Parking is free unless you want to park in the centre of the course
or the trackside picnicking area where the charges are £5 a car
and £11 per person into the enclosure.
To get there by rail; Barnham station is less than two miles from
the course, from here there is a shuttle bus on racedays which
starts two hours before the first race and stops running
immediately after the last. (Don't forget to check the times with
the driver).
Barnham can be reached from London Victoria, Portsmouth,
Brighton, Southampton and Winchester.
Nearest airport is Gatwick (28 miles).
There are quite a few hotels within a ten mile radius of Fontwell
Park. A night near the seaside at Bognor Regis is also an option.

Sunday 2 April 2006

Kempton Park Racecourse
Staines Road East
Sunbury-on- Thames
TW16 5AQ
Tel: 01932 782292
www.kempton.co.uk

After both having a good nights sleep, we were fresh and ready
for whatever the world had to throw at us, or should I say almost
anything. We were having a coffee in our room, Angie was
starting to put a few things into the suitcase, and I, while sitting
on the edge of the bed decided to switch on the TV and check the
teletext to find out the going for the days racing. I couldn't
believe what I saw on the screen in front of me; Newton Abbott
had been abandoned due to a waterlogged course. Hexham had
also been lost due to the weather that day, and the only surviving
meeting was an all weather fixture at Kempton. So we had a
decision to make, a day at the seaside or a trip to Kempton, the
seaside lost by two votes. Luckily all our accommodation was
booked at Travel Inns that week, so with the help of the hotel
receptionist I booked an extra night at Bognor Regis, and making
a couple of phone calls the receptionist managed to reshuffle our
accommodation to suit our new schedule.
    The drive to Kempton was only 60 miles which we broke up by
stopping on the way for breakfast. The disappointing thing was it
was an all weather meeting we were going to, which wasn't the
type of racing I would have planned to see at Kempton, but there
again even all weather racing was a better option than a day at the
seaside.
    We arrived early, and although the gates were open there was
something missing, there was no one outside selling the Racing
Post. There was a man inside dressed in a suit and obviously

153

coordinating things with the aid of a walkie talkie and he assured me someone would turn up with the papers. Ten minutes later he came over and said he had been looking for us, the Racing Posts were now on sale at the turnstiles.

Kempton had only just started staging all weather racing the week before, and even though the jockeys were saying it was a fair racing track there had been teething problems. The first race on the opening day had been delayed almost half an hour, as officials had to walk the course removing stones that had somehow found their way onto the polytrack. Apparently some of them were quite large and were an obvious danger if kicked back by a horse during a race.

Because it was polytrack and the official going soft, we decided to only back one horse a race at £40 with alternate picks, Angie as usual went first.

In the first race Angie had £40 win on Nice Tune at 3/1. The horses were put in their stalls and came under orders, it was at this point that Kempton's teething problems continued; the stalls failed to open, and after a lot of confusion at the start the horses were taken out of the starting stalls.

The stewards then decided to use a starting tape, again they came under orders and the horses were let go, all except one Obrigado. They decided it was a false start and the horses recalled. So they tried again and this time Obrigado went with them and won the race beating Angie's horse Nice Tune into second. I thought Angie was unlucky; as some starters would have let the first tape start go declaring Obrigado as refusing to race.

Maybe the Kempton stewards were just in a very embarrassing situation for the second week in a row.

Starting stalls now working, nothing back in any of the next three races.

Angie broke the duck in the fifth race when she backed Polish Power £40 at 9/4.

I got our money back for the day when I had £40 with the tote on the last winner Trans Sonic which paid £3 a win.

When we got back to our hotel we took a taxi into Bognor Regis, where we tried a couple of their drinking establishments before finding an Indian restaurant.

Angie's verdict:

I have lots of positives to tell you about Kempton, the first is the car park, not a field but a proper tarmac car park, so even you girls who think high heeled shoes are appropriate footwear for a day at the races will probably get away with wearing them for Kempton.

Kempton's main grandstand has two floors, the lower floor being the Paddock enclosure and the first floor the Premier suite. When we first arrived we sat in the ground floor of the grandstand (which is big enough to hold hundreds of people) having a coffee. Unfortunately the table we were sitting at had a wobble, and Dave leaning on the table top spilled the drinks, within seconds a young man was on the scene and quickly mopped up the mess. We were then approached by the guy with the radio who told Dave the Racing Posts had arrived. The only time I can remember having service like this at the races was when we were the guests of Mr. Ranson in the owner's bar at Newcastle. Just before racing started we moved upstairs into the Premier enclosure where we spent the rest of the afternoon, mainly indoors as it was very windy.

Both enclosures have various bars and catering facilities including a large food hall on the lower floor. Because we'd had breakfast on our way to the races we only had a snack from one of the mobile catering units while we were there. Dave had a cheese and onion toastie, which he said was the best toastie he had ever eaten. Even to this day he still mentions it now and then (sad man).

The parade ring at Kempton is very nice and viewing from the stands is excellent, especially of the jumps course which is closest to the enclosures.

There are toilet facilities for the disabled as well as a viewing area at the front of the main stand, the annual member's lift can be used to access the first floor.

Another enclosure at Kempton is the Family enclosure which also has food and drink facilities, but this is only open on selected race days.

There is a playground at Kempton and each year there are a number of family fun days where the kids can enjoy a host of free entertainment.

Rating: Very Good ★★★★★

How to get there:

To get there by car: The best route to get to Kempton is from the M25 to junction 12 where you join the M3 to junction 1 and then turn onto the A308. Kempton is about a mile from here.

There is free parking, parking costs £5 in the member's car park.

To get there by rail: Kempton Park has its own railway station. Trains to Kempton leave from Waterloo.

Nearest airport Heathrow (4 miles)

With Kempton being so close to London finding accommodation is no problem.

Wednesday 5 April 2006

Exeter Racecourse
Kennford
Exeter
Devon
EX6 7XS
Tel: 01392 832599
www.exeter-racecourse.co.uk

Monday morning, in Bognor Regis, and two days until our next race meeting at Exeter. This gave us plenty time and an ideal opportunity to meet Angie's adopted chimpanzee Charlie for the first time. After breakfast and a leisurely morning, we left Bognor and drove the two hours to Wareham, arriving at Monkey World early afternoon. We spent the rest of the day there before driving to our next hotel, the Travel Inn, Poole Centre.
Monkey World was the idea of an American, Jim Cronin, who set the centre up as a sanctuary for abused Spanish beach chimps. Charlie was one of these Spanish chimps, born in 1980 he had been used as a photographers prop. When he arrived at the centre he was a drug addict, he had a broken jaw, cataracts and only four teeth. But he was quite happy in his new home, a large purpose built enclosure with friends of his own kind.
We spent the night in Poole and were setting off for Exeter the next day and because we had another free day we decided to stop and call into Monkey World again to say goodbye to our adopted son.
Monkey World now works with governments around the world trying to stop the illegal smuggling of primates. They now house not only rescued beach chimps, but have chimps that have been used and abused in laboratories, and even exotic pets who have grown too big to handle. Sadly since our visit both Charlie and

Jim Cronin have passed away, but the centre still carries on doing its good work.

We arrived at the Travel Inn, Exeter where we had a room booked for two nights, had a meal and a couple of drinks in the hotel bar before retiring to our room to watch some television.

Wednesday morning, raceday, I went out and bought a Racing Post, and as we only had six miles to drive to the course we had plenty time to sort the form out before setting off to the course.

We arrived about an hour before the first race, the sun was shining, it was a little bit breezy but nothing like the strong winds we'd been having since Sunday, and even though the winds had helped dry things out, the official going for the day was good to soft, soft in places.

We had already decided while reading the Racing Post back in our hotel room to again only back one horse a race. Again taking turns and again Angie first, this turned out to be a good decision.

Angie backed the first winner Domeys Will, £20 e/w at 9/2

I backed the second winner In Accord £20 e/w at 5/1.

Angie's horse Holy Joe finished runner up in the third race, £20 e/w at 8/1

Another winner in the fourth, Chilling Place, £40 at 6/4.

Nothing back in the fifth, but I backed the last winner Lorient Express £40 at 6/4

Happy with our day's work we spent the whole night in our hotel room watching TV and feasting on the nibbles we had bought on the way back from the races.

Angie's verdict:

One of our local courses Hexham stands high on a hill and invariably it is cold and windy, so when I read that Exeter is the highest racecourse in the country I was half expecting similar conditions, especially after the strong winds we'd been experiencing over the previous couple of days. But that wasn't to be the case; the strong winds had died down to a gentle breeze which was actually quite pleasant as we looked out over a course that is set in one of the most scenic locations in England.

The enclosures at Exeter aren't very big but are comfortable and well maintained. They do however have everything there to meet the regular racegoers needs, and all close to hand.

There are a few bars and eating places offering a good variety of food ranging from restaurant meals to light snacks.

Whether you decide to watch the racing from the stand or the rails you will find the viewing is very good.

There are toilets and viewing ramps for the disabled, and a lift gives access to the upper floor of the grandstand.

Clip clops, which I think is a lovely name is Exeter's play area for the under 5's. There isn't much for older children, but I think they should be enjoying the racing with their parents anyway.

Rating: Good ★★★

Although I really enjoy racing and we were having a lovely time at the tracks we were visiting that week, the highlight of the trip for me was our visits to Monkey World. I had watched all the television programmes and I'd been following the progress of the rescued apes and seeing them all live was like meeting long lost friends.

How to get there.

To get there by road; Take the M5, which is fed from both the M4 and M6, from the end of the M5 motorway take the A38 which runs right past the course.

There is plenty of free car parking.

To get there by rail; St.Davids, Exeter is the best option from where you can get a free bus to take you the 8 miles to the course. Trains run to St. Davids from London, Paddington.

Nearest airport is Exeter (9 miles)

With Devon being a popular holiday destination, it is quite easy finding nearby accommodation.

Thursday 6 April 2006

Taunton Racecourse
Orchard Portman
Taunton
Somerset
TA3 7BL
Tel. 01823 337172
www.tauntonracecourse.co.uk

We had a late breakfast and just took our time packing the cases
for our journey from the Travel Inn Exeter to the Travel Inn
Taunton Central, a distance of 35 miles. Being the last of our four
days racing, we thought we would splash out, so were leaving the
car at the hotel and took a taxi to the races. When we got to the
hotel our room wasn't ready, so we just said we would check in
later that night, and asked the girl on reception if she could order
us a taxi to take us to the racecourse. I had more or less just put
our luggage back in the car when our taxi pulled up. We arrived
at the course really early; in fact the gates had only just opened,
so we had nearly two hours to kill before the first race.
Going back to £40 and £20 a race, Angie was going to stick with
the system we had been using; backing anything 7/2 or more e/w.
I was going to try something different. I had been reading some
statistics in a book I had taken away with me stating on average
nearly 40% of national hunt races are won by the favourite, 26%
the second favourite and 34% the rest. And even though
Taunton's stats were a bit lower than this I was going to have £40
win on the seven favourites. I wrote the bet out and put it on in
the course betting office, Taunton FAV'S 7 X £40 WIN.

I couldn't believe my luck and thought I was in for a cracking
day when Le Forezien won the first race 7/1 favourite. I was £40
up on my £280 staked and still had six races to go.

Angie backed the second winner Vingis Park, £20 at 11/4
Another winning favourite in the third, Traprain at 5/4, Angie also backed the winner, £20 at 11/8.
Angie had the second in the fourth race, Magico, £10 e/w at 5/1. Nothing back in the fifth or sixth.
The favourite, Kelv won the last, but because there were 10 non runners it went off at odds of 1/2 in the now 4 runner field. Angie put her £20 on the favourite to beat the second favourite Gandy Dancer in a straight forecast. Gandy Dancer did finish second, the forecast paying £2.11p.
Even though I had three winners I was a bit disappointed after having such a good start. We spent the end of the afternoon in the bar above the grandstand, which looks out over the course. While we were in the bar we got into conversation with a man and his teenage son. They had a taxi booked to take them back into Taunton, and they agreed to let us share their cab. While we were waiting by the roadside waiting for our cab to turn up both Angie and I commented on what a lovely evening it was. The two of them looked at us in astonishment and the pair of them said they were freezing; a couple of days in Northumberland with the wind blowing in off the North Sea would soon toughen them up.
We had a few more drinks in the bars of Taunton before heading for an Indian restaurant at around eight thirty. Early to bed early to rise for our 345 mile journey home the next day.

Angie's verdict:

The final leg of a really enjoyable trip, and although I wouldn't class it as a holiday it was the nearest thing we'd had to one for almost 2 years. At least we were in the south of the country where the temperatures are nearly guaranteed to be a few degrees warmer than back home. When we got out of the taxi at the racecourse it was a lovely sunny day, but again there was a slight breeze.Taunton at the time was Britain's newest racecourse having its first race in 1927, a race won by Baalbek

Taunton, just like Exeter is another racecourse I would class as small but having adequate facilities, just like the Devon track Taunton racecourse is set in a lovely location with fabulous views.

There are two enclosures at Taunton, the Portman Grandstand and the Tattersalls both of which have bar facilities and a range of food on offer. We really enjoyed our lunch at Taunton and were served by some of the friendliest staff we have met at any racecourse.

We watched most of the races from the Portman stand and a couple from the bar above the stand and the viewing from both is very good.

All areas of the enclosures have good access for the disabled; other facilities for the disabled include toilets and a viewing area.

Rating: Good ★★★

How to get there:

To get there by road; the course is close to junction 25 of the M5, come off the motorway and follow the signs for the racecourse which is off the B3170.

Parking is free.

To get there by rail; Taunton railway station is 3 miles from the track, taxi's are available from here. Trains to Taunton leave from Paddington station.

Nearest airport is Bristol (31 miles).

There are quite a few nice hotels in Taunton.

Wednesday 10 May 2006

The Racecourse
Fakenham
Norfolk
NR21 7NY
Tel: 01328 862388
www.fakenhamracecourse.co.uk

On the 2nd of May 2006 and two weeks late, Alex James Stanley was born. Hollie was actually in Newcastle registering his birth the day we set off for Fakenham.

The trip was over four days and without encountering any unforeseen problems we were visiting three tracks. Fakenham on the Wednesday, Yarmouth on the Thursday, then the long drive across the country for an evening meeting at Wincanton on the Friday before coming home Saturday morning.

Us going away for four days at this particular time actually suited everyone, as not only did we get a chance to have three days racing, it gave Hollie, Michael and Alex a bit of time on their own to play happy families.

We were however going to miss a couple of good days in Newcastle, as it was Alan Shearer's testimonial that night, and on the Friday it was black and white day in the toon (Newcastle town centre) where the majority of the shops in the city were having a black and white theme day, black and white being the standard colours of Newcastle United's football strip. Baby Alex only a week old already had two Newcastle strips as his proud dad Michael is what you would call a Newcastle United fanatic, and he was going to make every effort to ensure his newborn son was going to follow in his footsteps.

We'd had the customary wetting of the baby's head twice already, but everyone was so happy to welcome the new addition

163

to the family it was quite a while after when the celebrations ended.

We had to set off early on the Wednesday morning as we were driving straight to Fakenham racecourse and only planned to stop for breakfast and for fuel on our five hour journey.

As we were driving through Norfolk towards our destination, there were two things that stood out; firstly and most obviously was the mile after mile of agricultural farming that was going. Secondly and what we both found most intriguing was just about every mile or so down the road there was someone in a lay-by selling asparagus. There must have been dozens of them and as far as I can remember we didn't see anyone who had pulled over to buy their produce, so surely they couldn't all be making money out of it.

Even after our stops we had been making pretty good time, but with agriculture comes farm vehicles and a few times we joined queues of traffic behind heavy machinery, and although this did slow us down a bit we still arrived at the course well before the first race.

We were sticking to £40 and £20 a race, and even though I had showed a profit betting the seven favourites at Taunton, I wasn't trying it again at Fakenham.

Nothing back in the first.

Angie backed Chain, which finished 3rd in the second race, £10 e/w at 9/2.

We didn't have a bet in the third race which was won by the favourite Marycross at 4/11.

We put our money together in the fourth race and backed Ryders Storm, which won £60 at 4/6.

Again putting our money together we backed the fifth winner Montys Tag, taking evens.

We put our money together once more in the last race, only to watch our horse Reverse Swing finish down the field.

After racing we had a 46 mile drive to the Ryecroft Guest House in Great Yarmouth, where we had a room booked for two nights. We arrived at about seven o'clock, checked in, and then went to check out what Yarmouth had to offer.

Angie's verdict:

Fakenham is another small course set in a nice location. There are three enclosures at Fakenham all of which are well equipped to cater for their public.

The Member's and Grandstand enclosures both have bars and a selection of food; although we ourselves didn't try one, hog roast sandwiches seemed to be very popular that day.

There was a good atmosphere in the grandstand, from where there is an excellent view over the course. The toilets were clean but a little old fashioned, there were even showers in there. I presume these were put there for female jockeys to use. There is reserved parking, toilet facilities and a viewing stand for the disabled.

The third enclosure is the Course enclosure which has a small stand. Food and drink is also available in the Course enclosure.

I found the people were quite friendly, though one thing sticks in my mind about Fakenham; we were standing at the parade ring, and there was this young lady who joined two other girls and a young man, all of who looked about the same age. She obviously knew someone who worked in a racing stable and she was making sure everyone within 20 yards of her were going to hear what she had to say, most of it was rubbish, and her friends, if they were her friends were obviously embarrassed by her big mouth. The three of them must have had a very depressing day as I saw them on a couple of occasions that afternoon, and big mouth was still tagging along, and still going on about her alleged knowledge of everything that was going on in the world of horseracing.

Rating: Good ★★★

How to get there:

To get there by road; driving is probably your best option to get to Fakenham; from the north take the A1, A17 then the A148. From the south, take the A1065, from the west the A148 and from the east theA1067.
Apart from the member's car park which costs £8, all parking is free.
To get there by rail; the nearest railway station is King's Lynn and this is 22 miles away.
Nearest airport is Norwich (21 miles)
Norfolk, home of the Norfolk Broads is a very popular tourist area and has a lot of varied accommodation on offer.

Thursday 11 May 2006

Great Yarmouth Racecourse
Jellicoe Road
Great Yarmouth
Norfolk
NR30 4AU
Tel: 01493 842527
www.greatyarmouthracecourse.co.uk

When we booked the Ryecroft Guest House for our two night
stay in Great Yarmouth, it was described as a friendly hotel run
by racing enthusiasts. The hotel boasted a bar set with a racing
theme having its walls covered in horse racing memorabilia.
When we arrived this wasn't the case, the old proprietors had
sold up and moved on, and the bar which they had stripped of its
racing souvenirs before they left wasn't even open for business.
This was mainly due to the fact that the male partner of the new
man and wife owners had just went through heart surgery so had
to take it easy, leaving his wife to run the show.
During breakfast on the Thursday morning, I asked the landlady
how far and which direction it was to the racecourse. To my
surprise she said she didn't know, and told me they had just
recently moved from the London area to Yarmouth, and with her
husbands' condition and herself spending nearly all her time
trying to put the guest house the way she wanted it, they just
hadn't had time to familiarise themselves with their new
surroundings.
After breakfast I went out to find a newsagent to buy a Racing
Post, and with it being a nice sunny morning I thought I would
take a walk in the direction I believed the racecourse to be. Ten
minutes later I was standing on the side of a road looking at the
gates of Yarmouth racecourse on the opposite side; it was less
than a mile from our hotel. When I got back with my Racing

Post, the landlady was delighted to hear how close they were to the racecourse, and said she would use their proximity when advertising the hotel. A couple of hours later I went for the same walk, this time with Angie as we made our way to the races. Yarmouth racecourse is very popular with holiday makers, but being a nice sunny day there was a good crowd even though Yarmouth's holiday season wasn't yet into full swing. We were both quite thirsty after our walk so we went into the bar situated at the grandstand for a thirst quencher. Being too early for vodka and lemonade Angie opted for a fruit juice and I ordered a pint of lager. Sitting down at a table to enjoy our drinks and sort out the runners for the afternoon's action I took a mouthful of what turned out to be a mixture of lager and the cleaning fluid they use to flush out the lines. Needless to say when they offered me a replacement I refused and asked for my money back. Not a good start to my day at Yarmouth.

My day didn't get much better. We decided to go £40 a race alternative picks, Angie going first as usual

Angie backed the first and third winners, Duty at 8/11 and Stage Gift at 6/4, and they were the only two returns we had.

After racing the sun was still shining so we walked from the course to the town centre, stopping at a couple of waterholes on the way. The route we walked didn't exactly take us off the beaten track, but it did take us through an area where the pubs we called into were pretty rough. Although we were fine with the almost hostile surroundings not everyone would feel comfortable in such establishments.

I had never been to Great Yarmouth before, but Angie had been on holiday there once before with her parents when she was young, so her memories were that of seaside and sand and merry-go-rounds, but seeing it again through adult's eyes I think was a bit disappointing for her.

When we reached the town centre we tried one or two more bars which I must admit also looked a bit rough and ready, but once we had broken the ice with them we found the natives weren't that hostile after all. We finished our night in a nice Indian restaurant.

Having been able to visit both Norfolk tracks on consecutive days had certainly been a big bonus, and although we had a long drive the next day we were both looking forward to the next leg of our trip.

Angie's verdict:

Dave should practice what he preaches; I have often heard him tell people not to buy draught beer until a few pints have been pulled through the pumps, so with him buying the first draught lager to be served that day the outcome was inevitable.

There are two enclosures at Yarmouth, the Premier enclosure and the Grandstand and Paddock enclosure, although we did spend a little time in the Premier enclosure we spent most of the afternoon enjoying the sunshine in the Grandstand.

Both enclosures have bars and a good variety of food on offer, including what Dave said was his only winner of the day when he found a stall selling shellfish.

Viewing from the Premier enclosure is much better as you can set yourself right on the finishing line, but we still enjoyed watching from the grandstand where the viewing is okay.

There is good access throughout the enclosures for disabled racegoers, as well as toilet facilities and viewing platforms.

Yarmouth is an ideal place to spend a family outing; like most other courses accompanied under 16's are admitted free, there is a picnic area and a nice playground with a nearby tea room. During the school summer holidays there is extra children's entertainment for your kids to enjoy.

Rating: Average ★★

Although I agree with Dave that it was a bit rough, I will always have some happy childhood memories of Great Yarmouth.

How to get there:

To get there by road; from the north take the A1, A49 then the A149. From the south, the M11, A11 and A47. Coming from the west take the A47.
Parking costs £2.
To get there by rail; Great Yarmouth station, which is on the Norwich line is only a mile from the course.
There are taxis at the station and a regular bus service from the town centre.
Nearest airport is Norwich (19 miles)
There is an abundance of accommodation to choose from in Great Yarmouth.

Friday 12 May 2006

Wincanton Racecourse
Wincanton
Somerset
BA9 8BJ
Tel: 01963 32344
www.winantonracecourse.co.uk

Under normal circumstances I wouldn't even have considered including the Somerset track in the same trip as that of the two Norfolk courses, but I did have my reasons. First of all it was the last meeting of the season for Wincanton, and our plan was to have all the courses in the south west completed by the end of summer 2006. Secondly it was an evening meeting so we had plenty time to get there, and even though it was a 260 mile drive from Great Yarmouth, it was still 80 miles shorter than what the drive from Newcastle to Wincanton would have been.

It was another hot day and the roads were very busy making the journey to our hotel take a little bit longer than we'd anticipated. We were stopping for one night at Holbrook House, an upmarket Georgian country house which is set in a woodland estate. The room we were allocated was really nice, and I think we could have both done with an hour or two just relaxing in our new surroundings, but time was against us and all we had time for was a quick shower before getting ready for the races.

Another good point about Holbrook House is it is less than three mile from the racecourse, we had asked the girl on reception to order us a taxi when we first arrived at the hotel which thankfully was waiting for us when we came out into the hotel's car park. A short time later we were at the course though we couldn't have cut it much finer as there were only twenty minutes to spare before the start of the first race for which the runners were in the parade ring.

171

There was a good attendance for what was promising to be a very good night to go racing. It was Wincanton's closing fixture of the season, the sun was shining, it was Friday night and there was live entertainment after racing.

Although we'd enjoyed our two days racing at the Norfolk tracks we hadn't been too successful as far as betting was concerned. Between us we had found a couple of winners but being short prices we were showing a loss. The card at Wincanton looked promising and we were quietly confident of backing a few winners and recovering the money we had lost on the previous two days.

We watched a couple of races from the stands, but both feeling a little tired after our long day we thought it would be nice to find somewhere to sit. We were walking between the two main enclosures and couldn't have timed it better; there was an open sided marquee, almost identical to the one we had found in Pontefract and just as we reached it a table became vacant. So we parked our bums and it was there we spent the rest of the night sitting in the sun, only one of us leaving the table at any one time to ensure we didn't lose it.

We just carried on with £40 a race, as we had done at Yarmouth the previous day. Angie went first.

A good start, Angie had £40 on the first winner Ameeq at 2/1.

And that was the end of the season at Wincanton, or it was as far as we were concerned as we never backed another winner all night.

After the last race we were still sitting with full glasses, we sat watching as the crowds started to position themselves in front of the stage ready for the band to come on, we actually had a decent view from where we were sitting. The group that was playing that night was a 60s tribute band who called themselves the Rolling Clones. We listened to their first two songs, weren't impressed, so walked from the course into town where we finished our evening with an Indian meal.

Angie's verdict:

Still feeling tired after our night on the town in Yarmouth, I didn't enjoy the long journey to Wincanton. I couldn't even close my eyes to rest them for a while as we weren't familiar with the roads we were travelling on, so I was constantly checking our progress on the route plan. Even when we got there I didn't have time to relax in what was a lovely room, as we were rushing around getting ready.

I nearly always read a little bit about the courses we are about to visit, and I had read that Wincanton had been voted best small racecourse on numerous occasions, when we got there I could see why.

Wincanton has three enclosures; Premier enclosure, Grandstand enclosure and Course enclosure. The two main enclosures are very well laid out; there are a few bars and a really good selection of food ranging from restaurants to mobile units. Everywhere in the enclosures including the toilets are spotlessly clean. Viewing from both the Club stand and the main grandstand is very good, for an extra £3 those holding Member's badges can upgrade to the seated Member's viewing area (limited numbers).

There are toilets for the disabled and viewing areas in both the main enclosures.

The third enclosure is the Course enclosure which isn't in the centre of the course as its name suggests; it has a stand overlooking the course near the second last fence. Food and drink is available in the Course enclosure, though why not take your own and enjoy a family night out in the picnic area which is close to the action. There is children's entertainment at some of their fixtures.

Although we are fans of good music and the sixties one of our favourite decades, the Rolling Clones just weren't for us. There

again it could have been worse, if we had been to their previous meeting we would have been entertained by the Worzels.
Rating: Very Good ★★★★

How to get there:

To get there by road; from the north and west come off the M5 at junction 25 take the A358,A372,A303 into Wincanton then the B3081. From the south and east the A303 and B3081. The course is signposted from Wincanton.
Car parking is free except for the course enclosure which is usually £6.
To get there by rail; Templecombe station which is on the Waterloo to Exeter line is the closest. There is a courtesy bus before and after racing to take you the four miles from the station to the course.
Nearest airport is Bristol (26 miles)
There is accommodation within a few miles of the course but not a great deal, so you may have to search further afield.

Tuesday 23 May 2006

Towcester Racecourse
Easton Neston
Towcester
Northants.
NN12 7HS
Tel: 01327 353414
www.towcester-racecourse.co.uk

Towcester hadn't been the racecourse we had planned to go to
that day, but it was Towcester where we ended up.
We thought it was time to use the rail vouchers GNER had kindly
sent us after our aborted trip to Huntingdon earlier in the year. So
after careful consideration over the courses we still had to visit
we decided Leicester would probably be the best track for us to
travel to by train, and with it scheduled to have an evening
meeting made it even better. We booked one night at the Travel
Inn (Oadby), Leicester south, bought our badges online, and
courtesy of GNER paid for return rail tickets Newcastle to
Leicester.
Justice was done, or at least GNER would have thought so when
Leicester abandoned their meeting. Not to be beaten we checked
the fixture list and Towcester were also holding an evening
meeting that day, and after a few minutes research on the internet
the trip was on.
We were still travelling to Leicester by train; from there we
would get return tickets to Northampton, and from Northampton
station a taxi the 9 miles to Towcester racecourse. This way we
could still stay in our booked accommodation. The only problem
was we wouldn't have time to check in, so we would have to take
our case to the races.
On arrival at Northampton station we headed for the Black Lion,
a pub we could see on the other side of the road opposite the

station. We had a couple of drinks, and from there we phoned a taxi to take us to the races.

On the way to the course I asked the driver if we could book a taxi to take us back to the station after racing. He told us he would be off duty then, but would come back in his wife's car to pick us up for the same price (deal). He dropped us off at the entrance gates, showed us where he would pick us up and even agreed to keep our suitcase for us, that alone was worth the fare.

On the train we had been discussing our betting tactics, one thing I mentioned to Angie was; nearly every time we put our money together to back a horse we backed the winner. So why didn't we try to agree on a horse in each race and have £60 on it. Angie said we should stick to £40, we agreed on £50.

With us having the Racing Post from when we boarded the train at Newcastle, and with a sometimes disputed process of elimination, we had more or less picked our horses by the time we got to Northampton. So we put the system to the test.

Nothing back in the first.

We backed the winner of the second Borehill Joker £50 at evens.

Nothing in the third.

Another winner in the fourth Ask The Umpire £50 at 4/5

Nothing in the fifth.

And even though we had £50 on the last winner Calomeria at 5/2 Angie said she didn't enjoy the system we had used to pick our horses, so we have never tried it again since.

Good as his word our driver was waiting for us when we got to our pick up point. The problem now was we wouldn't get to Northampton in time for the train, but according to the timetable if he took us to Milton Keynes which was only a couple of miles further but in the opposite direction we would catch the same train with time to spare. So he took us to Milton Keynes Central and handed us our case, I handed him some cash, deal done, and we caught our train to Leicester for our overnight stay.

Angie's verdict:

As we got out of the taxi, walked through the entrance gates and up the drive towards the enclosure the whole set up looked rather impressive. When our friends Dorothy and Billy had been there they were staging everything from marquees as the new grandstand hadn't been built. But now it was completed and though it isn't that big it is well designed and fits in well with its surroundings.

As you would expect with it being new everything is spic and span. The viewing is good and a variety of food and drink is available downstairs in the main stand.

Entrance to the course was free, but £20 would get you an upgrade to the first floor of the stand where I presume there would be better facilities and a better view.

Toilet facilities and a private viewing area is available for disabled racegoers

On Bank holidays and Sunday fixtures extra entertainment is provided for children.

We were talking to a couple of locals who told us free admission started when they were still building the new stand and this attracted big crowds. Once the stand was built they started charging admission and attendances dropped dramatically. So the committee decided it would be in their best interest to do away with their admission charge, and sure enough the crowds came back.

I think one or two other courses should take a look at Towcester, and at least try to reduce their entrance fees, surely big crowds would be more beneficial to them in the long run.

Rating: Good ★★★

How to get there:

To get there by road; from the north take the M1 then the A5. From the south, the M1, M40, A43 and A5. From the west, the M40, A422, A43 and A5, and from the east the A45, A43 and A5.

Car parking is free.
To get there by rail; Northampton is the nearest station, this is 9 miles from the course.
Nearest airport is Luton (32 miles).
There are quite a few hotels and guest houses within a 10 mile radius of the course.

Saturday 3 June 2006

The Racecourse
High Yarridge
Hexham
Northumberland
NE46 2JP
Tel: 01434 606881
www.hexham-racecourse.co.uk

Being only twenty miles along the Tyne Valley, Hexham is our
next closest racecourse after Newcastle. We have been there on
many occasions, and to be perfectly honest we had never had
what I would call a really good day. First of all Hexham has
never been a really lucky track for us, though we do usually
manage to pick a winner or two. Secondly we had never been to
Hexham on a good day, weather wise. The racecourse is one of
the highest above sea level in the UK, and being so high you
nearly always get wind or rain or both.
But this was to be our lucky day at Hexham, the weather was spot
on, red hot, no wind and the scene was set for a really good day
out. We were going to have a drink that day so we left the car at
home and went by train from Newcastle to Hexham station; from
here we boarded the shuttle bus to take us the mile and a half
journey uphill to the racecourse.
While standing waiting for the shuttle bus we were talking to this
man from Scotland, he had travelled alone but said he was
meeting friends at the course. He was telling us he always
travelled alone, always by train and though he stuck to the
northern tracks he was a keen racing fan and went whenever he
could. Racing is a fantastic spectator sport and I can only take
my hat off to this man, as he was blind.

179

This was Hexham at its best, we have been to a few courses set in scenic locations, but Hexham set in the rugged landscape of Northumberland is a match for any of them.

The sunshine had brought the crowds out, so we found ourselves a nice little pitch on the grassy slope overlooking the finishing straight. It also happened to be Derby day.

Our betting system for the day was £40 a race alternative picks, I went first.

I thought I was going to get us off to a cracking start when I had £20 e/w on River Alder at 7/2 in the first, only to watch him finish second beaten a neck.

Nothing in the second.

I backed the winner of the third Lord On The Run, £40 at 3/1.

A couple of the course bookmakers were displaying odds for the Derby, and although I didn't bother Angie fancied a bet so she put £20e/w on Sir Percy at 7/1.

In the fourth race Angie was between two, but ended up putting the £40 on Pass The Class at 3/1.

We had been working our way through Angie's water bottle, and I needed to relieve myself before the race started. On the way to the toilet I passed a tote window and decided to have a forecast in the race. I actually fancied Angie's second choice Silver Bow to beat the horse she'd backed. But not wanting to bet against her pick I put a £20 straight forecast on Pass The Class to beat Silver Bow.

Pass The Class won the race with Silver Bow half a length back in second. I didn't say anything to Angie about the forecast until after the race, but she was quite happy going off with both winning tickets. The forecast paid £13.84p, so she came back with a smile on her face and over £400.

All within a couple of hours everything was going right, not only did Sir Percy win the Derby, but I had £40 on the fifth winner Wee William at 5/2.

Even though we gave £40 back to the bookies in the last, we'd just had our best day ever at Hexham races.

We got on the courtesy bus, but didn't go to the station. Instead we got off in town and went on a pub crawl. By the time we did get on a train to Newcastle we'd had a really good drink, and were the subjects of some funny looks as we sang all the back to Newcastle.

Angie's verdict:

If someone gave you a racecourse and asked you to place it somewhere, you would struggle to find anywhere with such a natural setting and as picturesque as Hexham racecourse. The only downside about Hexham is the unpredictable weather. I can only advise you girls by saying if you have long hair put it up as it is nearly sure to be windy, and flat shoes or wedges are a must. The admission prices for Hexham are very reasonable; I would recommend member's badges as you can go indoors if the weather turns bad.
There are two enclosures at Hexham racecourse; the Member's enclosure and the Tattersalls, but with the admission to the Member's enclosure being so reasonable it is well worth the extra couple of pounds as it allows you access to all areas.
Hexham has a couple of bars which are usually very busy and a selection of hot and cold food. I would say the facilities are basic but adequate and kept clean.
Viewing is very good and if the weather isn't too bad the grassy bank where we normally stand when we are there is very popular. There is a special car park for the disabled from where there is also very good viewing. A lift in the main stand gives access to the first floor.
Rating: Average ★★

How to get there:

To get there by road; the easiest way to get to Hexham is on the A69 which runs from Newcastle to Carlisle. Both the A1 and M6 have junctions onto the A69. The course is just south of the town between the B6305 and the B6306.
Parking is free.
To get there by rail; Hexham station is on the Newcastle to Carlisle line and is about a mile and a half from the course. There is a shuttle bus from the station to the track.
Nearest airport is Newcastle (17 miles)
There are a quite few hotels and guest houses in Hexham and the surrounding areas, Newcastle and Carlisle are other options.

Saturday 10 June 2006

Newbury Racecourse plc
Newbury
Berkshire
RG14 7NZ
Tel. 01635 40015
www.newbury-racecourse.co.uk

The nice weather continued, and I don't think there is a better place to be than the UK when the weather is fine. With Hollie and Michael both telling us they were more than happy for us to go away racing whenever we liked and for as long as we wanted, we booked up for what was going to be one of the best holidays I have ever had. We were going away for nine days, and visiting eight tracks on our journey. There was a fair bit of driving to do, including some doubling back on our tracks, but that was all to be part of the fun.

We had started to plan the trip a few weeks in advance, all our hotels were booked, all the route planners printed and we had all our badges except for Leicester's, which was the last course we were going to visit before coming home. We were leaving Friday lunchtime, and because our badges for Leicester still hadn't arrived with Friday morning's post I phoned the course. I was told that the badges had been posted out, but when I explained the situation and that I wouldn't be home for the next week or so, they told me not to worry and we could pick up new badges when we arrived.

So as planned we left Friday lunchtime; six and a half hours and three hundred miles later we arrived at the Travel Inn, Newbury/Thatcham where we had a room booked for two nights. Angie had packed quite a bit of food for our journey, and had put a couple of litres of lemonade in the cooler bag. So the first night we just stayed in our room watching TV, we had plenty of food and plenty cold lemonade, so needless to say we opened the vodka bottle we had also packed for our trip.

The following morning we had breakfast at the hotel and just lazed around until it was time to get ready for the races. We caught a bus from outside the hotel into town and were amazed at the amount of Union Jacks that were on display almost everywhere we looked. It was about a twenty minute walk from the bus stop to the course, during which we took note of an Indian restaurant which was handily situated about half way. The first race was due off at half past six, but we arrived at half past two. We showed our badges at the gates which were already open and made our way to some bench seats which were positioned on the lawn in front of the grandstand. We sat for about ten minutes or so until the big screen came to life with England's opening world cup game against Paraguay. It wasn't a brilliant game but at least England won 1-0.

There was another treat before racing started proper when they held a 1mile 2 furlong race for Arabian horses, which was won by Magie De Faust who got a great reception when it crossed the line.

Long before we left Newcastle we'd had a lengthy discussion on what stakes we would be wagering on our trip. We obviously had to make our kitty last for eight meetings, so it would be no use diving in with big stakes as we could be broke before we'd been to them all. The whole idea of the trip wasn't to win a fortune, though we were hoping to have a few winners on the way. The reason for the trip was to cross another 8 courses off our "courses to do" list.

We decided on £20 each a race, sticking to our e/w policy.

In the first race Angie had £10e/w on the second, Gallego at 6/1

Nothing bck in the second or third races.

We both had £20 on the fourth winner Bustin Justin, Angie took 5/4 and me evens.

I had £10 e/w on the fifth winner Meditation at 6/1

Nothing in the last.

We had taken over £2000 readies on our trip as betting money, so we decided that any returns we would put in the spare purse that Angie had brought with her, which was not to be touched until we got home. We had lost a little bit on the day, but still put nearly £200 in the purse.

After racing we were both feeling a bit tired, a combination of sitting all day in the sunshine mixed with a few glasses of vodka had taken its toll. So we made our way to the Indian restaurant we had passed earlier in the day for an early supper, before getting a taxi back to our hotel.

Angie's verdict:

We'd had a few discussions on which course we were going to leave until last, and as we wanted to finish with one of the bigger courses Newbury was on the shortlist. But with Newbury being an ideal track to start this trip with, we had to knock it off the list as a possible curtain closer.

Just as I had expected, the facilities at Newbury are excellent, everywhere is spotlessly clean and the lawns in front of the stands are really nice, it's hard to believe the site was once used as a prisoner of war camp and a tank testing ground.

There are three enclosures at Newbury; the Member's which has plenty bars and eating places including restaurants, a food hall and snack bars. Viewing from the stand is superb, though we spent most of the afternoon watching from the lawn in front of the stand where we had a seat in the sunshine.

The second enclosure is the Grandstand which also has a number of bars and a wide variety of hot and cold food on offer. The views from the Grandstand enclosure are also very good. The third enclosures is the Picnic enclosure, ideal for a family day out and if you're not keen on preparing a picnic, snacks are available in the Picnic enclosure as well as bar facilities. The Picnic enclosure also has a stand with good views of the course. On weekend and evening meetings the Rocking Horse nursery is open in the Grandstand enclosure (2 hours maximum per child). . There is good viewing for the disabled as well as suitable toilet facilities in all enclosures.

I don't know if it was because the sun was shining or because England had just won their football match, but everyone seemed to be in party mood.

Rating: Very Good ★★★★★

How to get there:

To get there by road; from the north take the A34 then A4, from the south the A34, from the west take the M4 to junction 13 onto the A34 and from the east take the M4 to junction 12 onto the A4. Parking is free except for the picnic area which is £5 a car.

To get there by rail; Newbury racecourse has its own railway station which can be reached by trains from Paddington.

Nearest airport is Southampton (31 miles) Heathrow (37 miles). There are a lot of hotels all within easy reach of Newbury Racecourse.

Sunday 11 June 2006

Bath Racecourse
Lansdown
Bath
BA1 9BU
Tel. 01225 424609
www.bath-racecourse.co.uk

The weather forecasters were predicting the warm spell to continue all week, and even though they don't always get it right, it's nice to hear them talking about summer weather. Living in the north east summer weather isn't a thing Angie or I see a lot of.

We had a bit time on our hands after breakfast, as the journey from Newbury to Bath was only going to take a couple of hours. This was including a 20 mile detour as we both wanted to have a look at Stonehenge as neither of us had been there before. When I say we had a bit of time on our hands, I mean I had a bit of time on my hands, Angie had to pack the suitcases as she insisted all the clothes we had packed for our trip had to be taken out of the cases and hung up.

We got on our way and took the detour to look at the prehistoric building blocks which I know are the subjects of interest to many a scientist and are worshipped by modern day druids, but to me they just looked like what they are, lumps of rock.

We arrived at Bath racecourse a good hour before the first race and after coffees we had a wander around the enclosures, not only to see what was on offer but also to find the first aid post. Angie might carry everything but the kitchen sink in her oversized handbags, but one thing she didn't have was an Elastoplast for the blister she had on her foot from the previous day at Newbury. It was actually quite an experience at the first aid room, I knew racecourses all had them but I'd never been to

187

one and was surprised to see there were 3 other people waiting to see the nurse. It wouldn't surprise me if you had to book an appointment at some of the bigger meetings.

Another sunny day and there were quite a few people getting rather excited in the paddock area as they were getting dressed up as pantomime animals for a charity fund raising race that was about to take place over the final furlong of the course.

So with Angie's foot taped up, and a supply of spare Elastoplasts we were ready for the afternoon's action. But first of all we took our place next to the running rails to watch the charity race. 15 went to post, and I must admit it was quite a laugh watching them charging up the course. I think a couple of them covered the final furlong faster than some of the horses I backed that day.

Nothing in the pantomime race.

Nothing in the first or second races.

We both backed the third and fourth winners £20 each on Lester Leaps In at 5/2 and £20 each on Madhavi at 2/1

Nothing in the fifth, but we both had £20 on the sixth winner Mostarsil at 6/4.

We didn't stop for the last race as we wanted to get on the road for our two hour drive to the Travel Inn, Exeter, where we were staying on Sunday night. Or it would have been a two hour drive if I had listened to my navigator, and hadn't taken a wrong turn as we left the racecourse car park. We ended up somewhere on the outskirts of Bath on a lane that seemed to be getting narrower and narrower the further we went down it. So we turned back and following our instincts and the odd signpost we eventually found ourselves in a traffic jam in Bath city centre.

At least from here we could get our bearings which put us back on the right track. We arrived at our hotel about 45 minutes later than we should have. Again Angie insisted on emptying both suitcases and hanging everything in the wardrobe, so while she did that I went off to find a shop where I bought some nibbles and some cold lemonade (mixer) ready for another night in front of the TV.

Angie was quite happy when she added £360 to our take home kitty.

Angie's verdict:

I was pleased we drove to Stonehenge; I thought it was quite eerie, and even though there is a lot of mystery about the stones I can't understand how people can stand looking at them for hours on end, it's as if they are expecting something to happen. But there again these anoracked enthusiasts probably can't understand why I want to get dressed up to go and watch horse racing.
Bath racecourse is really nice, and another course located in a picturesque setting. There are three enclosures at Bath and I was quite impressed with the whole layout. Everywhere is very clean and tidy.
Although we usually spend most of our racing days in grandstand enclosures, 99 times out of a 100 we buy premier badges as we like to know we can wander almost anywhere we want. But at Bath as we had done the day before at Newbury we spent more time in the Premier enclosure, this was mainly because both days were very busy in the main grandstands.
The Premier enclosure has a couple of bars, a nice restaurant and a bistro and a Champagne lawn. Viewing from the Premier stand which overlooks the winning post is excellent.
The Grandstand enclosure also has bars and a café selling a selection of hot and cold food, there are also a few mobile catering units. Viewing from the Grandstand enclosure is also very good.
There is disabled parking near the turnstiles for blue badge holders, a viewing ramp near the winning post and toilet facilities. Carers of disabled racegoers are admitted free of charge.

The third enclosure is the Course enclosure which has a bar selling both drinks and snacks. With it being such a lovely day I could see quite a few people with picnic baskets sitting near the rails from where they could get the best views of the racing.
The Grandstand enclosure has a play area for kids who can enjoy additional entertainment on family days.
Rating: Good ★★★★

How to get there:

To get there by road; from the north and south take the M5 to junction 15, then the M4 to junction 18 where you take the A46 south. The course is well signposted.
Parking is free.
To get there by rail; the nearest station is Bath Spa which is on the Paddington to South Wales line. A special bus runs from the station to the course on race days.
Nearest airport is Bristol (13 miles)
There are plenty hotels in Bath to choose from.

Monday 12 June 2006

Newton Abbot Races Ltd
Kingsteighton Road
Newton Abbot
Devon
TQ12 3AF
Tel: 01626 353235
www.newtonabbotracing.com

The abandonment of Newton Abbot races on our first intended visit back in April actually worked in our favour, first of all we had the opportunity to switch meetings and go to Kempton that day, and secondly our rescheduled visit to Newton Abbot meant less driving than we would have had to do if the meeting in April had gone ahead.

Because Newton Abbot Racecourse is only fourteen miles from the Travel Inn where we were staying in Exeter we had the luxury of another lazy morning. I had actually got up pretty early and had been out to buy a Racing Post, so we spent most of the morning drinking coffee and browsing through the days racing. Another good idea we had for killing time was not to have breakfast at the hotel, but to stop at the service station that was marked on the route planner on the road between the hotel and the course.

So after drinking probably more coffee than what was good for our health Angie repacked the suitcases for me to load into the car and we set off from the Travel Inn on what was the hottest day yet.

We actually didn't make it to the service station as we spotted a place just off the main road called The Grill On The Hill, so we pulled in there for brunch. We ordered two full English and attempted to eat them indoors, but it was so uncomfortably hot we took our plates outdoors and sat at a table outside facing two of the biggest and tastiest breakfasts we had eaten in a long while. The good thing about a cooked breakfast is it sets you up for the day, or at least I think it does. However when we arrived at the course and for a good hour after Angie was moaning that she'd eaten too much breakfast and felt bloated even though she'd only managed to eat half of hers. I'd finished mine plus an extra sausage that Angie had left and I felt fine.

We'd tried to manage our time the best we could throughout the morning, but even after a stroll around the enclosure there was still quite a wait before racing was due to start. We'd earlier taken a look in the course betting shop where there were a few punters having bets on the televised greyhound racing, so for a bit of fun we went in to join them. We don't go as often now, but we used to go to Brough Park (Newcastle's Greyhound Stadium) at least once every few weeks, where if we weren't betting with the track bookmakers we would bet with the Tote, picking three dogs in a race and crossing them all ways for forecasts which is a fun way to bet and usually gave us a couple of returns during a meeting. So we used these same tactics taking turns to pick three dogs a race and crossing them for £2 forecasts (£12 a race). The stakes weren't big and none of the dividends paid a large amount, but we managed to get 5 out of 6 forecasts right and in the losing race we had first and third.

I would have been better off sticking to the greyhounds, as I never backed a winner at Newton Abbot all afternoon.

Angie did a little bit better and managed three returns;

£10 e/w on Native Commander which finished second in the third race at 9/2.

£20 at 2/1 on Wee Dinns which won the fourth.

Another 9/2 second in the last where she had £10 e/w on Lambrini Bianca.

It wasn't a fortune, but thanks to Angie we had another £100 to put in the purse.

After racing we had another bad start to what should have been a two and a half hour drive to the Travel Inn, Salisbury. We'd encountered a bit of traffic earlier in the day at the roundabouts on the industrial estate as we had driven to the racecourse, but coming out was even worse. As well as the race day traffic making their way home, there were what I presumed to be workers from the industrial units also making their way home, so slowly but surely we got out onto the main road.

The roads to Salisbury weren't too bad and we did pick up some of the lost time, and even though I did pick up three penalty points and a fine for driving through a thirty mile an hour zone at thirty six miles an hour we reached our hotel in just under three hours.

We had hoped to spend an hour or two in Salisbury that evening, but by the time we got there and checked in, Angie had unpacked the cases and we both had baths it was getting pretty late, so we had a couple of drinks in the hotel bar before going to our room.

Angie's verdict:

I imagined Newton Abbot Racecourse to be pretty much in the middle of the countryside, so I was rather surprised to see it right next to an industrial estate. Fortunately the industrial units are set behind the stands, so the view out over the course is still very pleasant.

There are two enclosures at Newton Abbot, the Paddock and the Course enclosures, which means there is no Member's enclosure, so admission prices are very reasonable.

There are a number of places to eat including two restaurants, a self service cafeteria and a few fast food outlets. There are also a few bars, and although it seemed pretty old fashioned to me, everywhere in the enclosure was very clean.

Viewing from the stand is very good, and it was while we were there just before a race started I was asked to leave the stand. Eating in the grandstand is not allowed and there were signs to discourage people from doing so. This is a controversial policy and I don't know if I was shocked or embarrassed when a female member of security approached me and asked me to leave the grandstand while I was eating my ice lolly (Dave of course thought it was very amusing).

There is a viewing ramp for the disabled, and a lift to the upper level of the grandstand.

Rating: Average ★★

How to get there:

To get there by road; from the north take the M5 to junction 31, then take the A38 and A380. From the south the A38 and A380, from the west the A38 and A383, from the east the A381.

Parking is free except on the rails where there is a £3 charge.

To get there by rail; Newton Abbot Railway station which is on the line from Paddington is only three quarters of a mile from the course.

Nearest airport is Exeter (15 miles)

There is plenty of accommodation to be found in the near vicinity.

Tuesday 13 June 2006

Salisbury Racecourse
Netherhampton
Salisbury
Wiltshire
SP2 8PN
Tel: 01722 326 461
www.salisburyracecourse.co.uk

On Tuesday morning I was awake early again, and while Angie
slept I had another read through the previous day's racecard from
Newton Abbot. It's funny how much easier it is the following day
to sort out the form, I was thinking to myself I could have easily
backed three or four winners, but spotting all the vital clues on
the day is a different kettle of fish.

It was another fine morning with clear skies, and all the signs
were there to say we were in for another hot day. Angie woke up
as usual in time with the kettle boiling, so we sat and had a coffee
while discussing our plans for the day. Once again we had to fill
in a lot of time before racing as the Travel Inn in Salisbury is
only six miles from the racecourse, I suggested going into town
for an hour or two but Angie said she was too tired to traipse
round the shops.

Working in the horseracing industry and spending almost every
day travelling from course to course sounds like a glamorous
occupation, but it must be very tiring. It had only been four days
since we'd set off on our trip and it seemed like we'd been
constantly on the go.

Again we skipped breakfast at the hotel and set off in the
sunshine in the direction of the racecourse, looking out for
somewhere to stop on the way. Our port of call was a large
Waitrose store where we bought one or two items including our

papers, before taking a seat in the store's restaurant for breakfast; which looked rather pitiful after the monster portions we'd been served on the previous day.

With little or no chance of Angie moaning on about feeling bloated we left the table and two empty plates and went for a walk in the sunshine. The river Avon is just a stones throw from the supermarket car park, and we soon found a seat on the river bank where we sat for over an hour reading our papers before heading off to the races.

It's common knowledge that the English weather is unpredictable, and on this occasion the unpredictable happened. We had more or less just pulled into the racecourse car park when it started to rain, and the colour of the skies suggested it was going to last a while. It was hard to believe we'd been sitting on the river bank in the glorious sunshine only 15 minutes earlier. We sat for ten minutes waiting for the rain to ease before making a dash for the enclosures, stopping half way to take shelter under a tree while another heavy downpour passed over. Without getting too wet we made it inside where we joined a crowd of people who like us weren't dressed for the weather.

We both had £20 at 15/8 on Sans Reward which won the first. Nothing back in the second or third.

While we had been reading the papers earlier in the day we'd both said we were going to back Frankie Dettori's two rides that afternoon, so we put our money together for his two mounts in races 4 and 5.

In the fourth we had £40 at 2/1 on Island Odyssey, which won. In the fifth we had £20 e/w on Oscar Avenue, which finished third at 6/1.

Nothing in the sixth.

Again we left before the last race as we wanted to get on the road. It was still raining and it had been a damp miserable afternoon, but at least we had another £280 to put in the purse.

It was a hundred and twenty mile drive to our next destination, the Travel Inn, Hereford where we had a room booked for two nights. Once again by the time we had reached our hotel and sorted ourselves out time was getting on, but we were getting bored with hanging around the bars of Travel Inns so we hired a taxi and went into town.

Angie's verdict:

It was a bit of a shock to the system having rain after a few days really nice sunshine, and what made it worse was the dress I was wearing wasn't a good choice for wet conditions. Not only was it raining but the temperature seemed to have dropped considerably, but we were determined not to let the weather spoil our day. There are three enclosures at Salisbury; the Members, Tattersalls and the Course enclosure, all of which have quite good facilities. The Members enclosure has a few bars and a good selection of food ranging from restaurants serving a 3 course carvery lunch to hot and cold snacks which can be purchased at the bars. Viewing from the Members is very good and there is a choice of two stands, one of which has a large seated area.
The Tattersalls enclosure where we spent most of the afternoon also has a number of bars; in the main Tattersalls bar you can also get hot meals and snacks. There are also a few mobile catering units.
We spent most of the afternoon under cover though we did venture out to the parade ring a few times, and watched a couple of races from the grandstand from where the viewing is quite good.
The Course enclosure also has a viewing stand, a well stocked bar where you can also buy food , the Course enclosure also has mobile catering units.
There are disabled viewing areas and toilet facilities in all enclosures.
Rating: Average ★★

Frankie Dettori used to be one of my favourite flat racing jockeys but I went off him a bit that day, even though I had won money backing his two horses. He walked by me on his way to the weighing room after the 5th race so I asked him to autograph my race card, he refused my request. I would have probably had more chance if I'd passed him after the 4th race in which he rode the winner.

How to get there:

To get there by road; from the north take the A345 then A338, from the south the A338 or A354, from the east the M3, A303 and A360, from the west the M4, A346 and A338.
Parking is free.
To get there by rail; Salisbury railway station is 3 miles from the course, from here you can get a bus direct to the racecourse.
Nearest airport is Bournemouth (19 miles)
There is a good range of accommodation to choose from in Salisbury.

Wednesday 14 June 2006

Hereford Racecourse
Roman Road
Hereford
HR4 9QU
Tel. 01432 273560
www.hereford-racecourse.co.uk

I'm usually awake and out of bed by no later than seven o'clock, I think it's because I'm up at five thirty when I'm on early shift, so seven o'clock is a bit of a lie in really. I was quite astonished when I woke up on Wednesday morning to see Angie pottering about; I was even more astonished to see it was quarter to ten. We'd had a few drinks in town the night before and bought a Chinese takeaway which we ate in our room, but it hadn't been that late when we went to bed. I think the combination of four days racing and all the driving was starting to show an effect. The good thing was we were staying in Hereford for two nights which gave us the opportunity to recharge our batteries.
It was back in March when we had originally planned to visit Hereford races, but we cancelled the trip as racing was doubtful due to snow lying on the course. There were no doubts however about racing going ahead this day, there had been a small amount of rain on the Tuesday but nothing like what we'd encountered at Salisbury and the official going was good to firm.
Once again we skipped the hotel breakfast; partly because Angie thought we were having too many cooked breakfasts but mainly because I'd overslept, so we decided to have something to eat when we got to the course. The Travel Inn, Hereford is very close to the racecourse, and the sun shining again made the short walk very pleasant. The other nice thing was we were having a day without driving so we were able to have a drink.

We arrived at the course not long after the gates had opened and after picking up a Racing Post and our racecards at the entrance made our way into the enclosure for an early lunch. After we'd eaten we sat for a while studying the card before going out into the sunshine to enjoy the days racing.

Before racing started there was something that caught my eye, there was a guy standing in a suit and tie, a trilby on his head and round his neck was a pair of binoculars with about a hundred racecourse badges tied to them. When I first started going racing this was quite a common thing to see, but you don't see it so often now. To be perfectly honest I don't know what it is meant to signify, and can only imagine it makes the wearer feel some kind of superiority. Red Indian braves used to get a feather to wear in their head-dress after every battle they fought, and the more feathers they had the more they were respected among their tribe. So I suppose the more badges these guys have tied to their binoculars the higher they feel up the pecking order. I actually saw this decorated warrior later in the day and got a closer look at his feathers which I noticed were nearly all from Hereford.

I had £20 on the first winner Ockley Flyer at 5/2.

We both had £20 at 5/4 on the second winner, Vaughan.

Nothing back in the third or fourth.

We both backed Megaton which won the fifth, Angie at 11/4 and me at 5/2.

I had £10 e/w on the sixth winner Mill Bank at 9/2, and Angie had £10 e/w on Midnight Gold which finished second at 7/2.

Nothing in the last.

Quite an enjoyable afternoon and we had £395 to put in the purse which put us in front of the bookies over the 5 days.

We stayed at the course for nearly an hour after racing sitting on the grass near the running rails enjoying both the sunshine and our drinks. It was very relaxing knowing we didn't have to jump in the car and get on the road as soon as racing finished like we had done at the last three meetings.

As we walked back to the hotel we were discussing the plans for the evening and both thought another night on the town would be a good idea. But a few more drinks in the hotel bar on top of what we'd already had at the races changed our plan. Instead we had a meal in the hotel's restaurant then went back to our room. I put the television on and just lay on the bed watching it while Angie was sorting our clothes out.

We were over halfway through our trip so she decided to put all the clothes we'd already worn into one case which could be left in the back of the car. I thought this was a good idea as it meant less to carry for me. She also put the programmes from the meetings we'd been to along with the now bulging winnings purse in the same case.

We both watched television for a while before falling asleep looking forward to the next day.

Angie's verdict:

I don't think Dave getting up early most mornings has anything to do with his shift work, I think it's because he's getting old and we all know the older you get the less sleep you need.

We had watched the racing from Hereford quite a number of times on television and I always thought it looked like a nice course. When we arrived I wasn't disappointed, the enclosures are well laid out and everywhere is clean and tidy.

There are two enclosures; the Premier enclosure and the Grandstand and Paddock enclosure.

The Premier enclosure has a waitress served restaurant, and also a bar with a good seating area. Viewing is quite good from the stand which leads down to a nice lawn.

The Grandstand enclosure is where we spent most of our day. There are two grandstands in this enclosure, both of which have bars and a selection of food. Viewing from the grandstand was okay, but to be honest I much preferred watching from the running rail.

Disabled facilities include a viewing area and toilet facilities.

Rating: Good ★★★

How to get there:

To get there by road; from the north and south come into Hereford on the A49. From the east and west take the A438 which runs through Hereford close to the course.

Parking is free.

To get there by rail; trains from Paddington go to Hereford station which is only a mile from the course.

Nearest airport is Bristol (48 miles)

There are a few hotels in Hereford itself, and a good choice in the surrounding areas.

Thursday 15 June 2006

Brighton Racecourse
Freshfield Road
Brighton
BN2 9XZ
Tel: 01273 603580
www.brighton-racecourse.co.uk

Five gone, and three to go. I couldn't believe how quickly the days were passing. The drive from Hereford to Brighton was 190 miles, which we were expecting to take about 5 hours, as we were going to make a couple of stops on the way just to break the journey up. The meeting we were going to was an evening meeting which gave us a bit more time to play with. The first race was due off at twenty five to seven, but England's second world cup game against Trinidad and Tobago was also being shown on the big screen at Brighton Racecourse, so we wanted to make sure we were there before kick off at six o'clock.

It was a pretty straight forward journey with no major problems encountered, and our estimated five hours travelling time was only a quarter of an hour out as we arrived at our hotel on Brighton sea front. We had parked the car in a nearby NCP car park, and walked the short distance to our accommodation. I had booked the hotel through a website offering discounted accommodation in hotels throughout the UK and a 40% discount on a sea view hotel on Brighton's promenade seemed to good an offer to miss. Thankfully we were only staying for one night. The whole place looked shabby and dilapidated, and if it hadn't been for the fact our bedroom was clean I think we would have went somewhere else.

It was another red hot day, so luckily Angie had packed all the clothes we had already worn in one case which we left in the back of the car. Meaning we had only one case, a holdall and a suit carrier to take the couple of hundred yards to the hotel.

With the air conditioning in our room not working properly, we spent an hour lying almost naked on top of the bed with the windows open and the ceiling fan on, and even this was only just taking the sting out of the afternoon heat.

We were both glad when it was time to get ready and get out of the room to take the short taxi ride to the racecourse.

We stood among quite a large crowd watching yet another not very entertaining soccer match, half an hour into the game and still 0-0 though England were definitely the better team. Almost time for the first race we walked over to the betting ring to place our bets, we were both backing the same horse Nuit Sombre, but when we got there most of the bookies had no prices showing on their boards. It was more or less at that time when an announcement came over the public address system. They were asking everyone to leave the football and place their bets for the first race as the bookmakers were struggling to form a market.

Nuit Sombre won the first race and we managed to find a bookie who gave us 7/4 for our £40

Nothing in the second, third or fourth.

Angie had £20 on the fifth winner, Sarah's Art at 11/4.

We both had £10 e/w on Cosmic Destiny which finished third in the last race at 5/1.

£15 down on the night, but £225 to add to the kitty.

Two late goals from Crouch and Gerard gave England a 2-0 victory in the football. We didn't see the whole match for obvious reasons, but what I did pick up on while standing amongst those who obviously did, was not everyone was there for the racing. I heard a few people discussing what they were going to do after the football, and horseracing wasn't among their options. They had come in to watch the football on the big screen, and I can only presume got in for free otherwise they'd chosen an expensive way to view the game.

After racing we got into a taxi which was standing just outside the racecourse entrance, and asked the driver to take us into town. It was a Thursday night and not much going on, most of the bars were quiet and we spent most of the night which we finished off in an Indian restaurant in our own company. At least we accomplished one thing by staying out late, we didn't have to spend much time in our hotel.

Angie's verdict:

Before you book into a hotel anywhere I would recommend you read a few reviews about the accommodation, this is one thing we didn't do, and the only nice thing I can say about our hotel was the sea view.

Thankfully Brighton racecourse wasn't in a state of such disrepair, another nicely planned out course and clean and tidy throughout the two enclosures; the Premier and the Grandstand and Paddock.

The Premier enclosure has a restaurant and a couple of bars where you can also order snacks. The Balcony Bar overlooks the winning post. Viewing from the stand which has a covered seating area is very good.

The Grandstand and Paddock enclosure also has a couple of bars; the one on the ground floor is very spacious. There is a selection of food on offer throughout the enclosure, including a few mobile catering units. The grandstand also has a covered seating area; the view from the grandstand was good, though there was no atmosphere there for the first couple of races as nearly everyone was round the side of the stand watching the football.

There is good access for disabled racegoers in both enclosures. There are disabled toilet facilities and lifts to the upper level of the grandstand.

Children's entertainment is provided at fixtures right throughout the summer holidays.

Rating: Good ★★★
I enjoyed the evening at Brighton races, but Brighton itself and especially our hotel was a bit of a let down.

How to get there:

To get there by road; from the north take the M23 to junction 11 then the A23. From the east and west take the A27.
Parking is free.
To get there by rail; trains from Victoria, King's Cross and London Bridge all run to Brighton station which is just over a mile from the course. There is a courtesy bus which leaves from the top of Queen's Road; this is 200 yards from the station.
Nearest airport is Gatwick (22 miles).
Needless to say there are numerous places to stay in Brighton.

Friday 16 June 2006

Chepstow Racecourse
Chepstow
Monmouthshire
NP16 6BE
Tel: 01291 622260
www.chepstow-racecourse.co.uk

I woke up on a rather overcast morning, even though the forecasters said it would be another bright start to the day. The good thing was we were driving up to Chepstow for another evening meeting, so the sun had all day to break through. With Angie still sleeping I sat with a coffee looking out over the sea and watching people as they were going along the promenade in their various ways; dog walkers, joggers, skateboards, pushbikes, roller-skates and even a unicycle. But one very unusual thing I did see were two young men who were either drunk or suffering the effects of stronger substances, but the thing that was unusual about them was one of them was on fire. He had smoke coming from either his shoe or the turn-up in his jeans, I couldn't make out which. I watched them for about 5 minutes as they staggered along the sea front and out of sight; neither of them noticing the trail of smoke that was following them.

We had paid for bed and breakfast at our hotel so we thought we should at least go and see what the food was like; if we didn't fancy it we could always find a café somewhere. Breakfast actually wasn't too bad, and afterwards we had a walk along the sea front before collecting our bags to leave for Chepstow.

The sun was trying to break through as we left the hotel and headed for the multi storey car park. We put our discounted ticket in the machine, paid the tariff then got in the lift to the fifth floor where the car was parked. The doors opened, we stepped out and there was no car. I turned to Angie who already had tears in her eyes and said it's gone. It's strange what goes through your mind when you are confronted with a situation like this. Yes it was a bit inconvenient that we should be so far from home, but getting home wouldn't be a problem. Angie really liked our car so she was upset about losing that, but insurance would cover that, so we could soon get another car. She was also upset about the clothes in the case we had left in the back of the car, but again these could easily be replaced. The thing that bothered me most was the programmes from our first 5 days along with the purse holding our kitty which were also in the car, these weren't so easy to replace. I walked up the ramps to the next level and there was our car standing waiting for us. At least we now know what it feels like to have your car stolen.

We were staying at the Travel Inn, Bristol (Alverston) which is on the opposite side of the Severn Bridge to Chepstow racecourse. So with the car found we set off on our 168 mile journey, Angie was a bit quiet at first but she eventually saw the funny side of what had happened.

We arrived at our hotel (this time the purse and programmes went with us) with plenty time to spare, so we had an hours sleep before getting dressed and setting off on our 10 mile drive to the races.

At least the forecasters had got it right and we arrived at Chepstow to a nice sunny welcome. A good crowd had turned out for what I thought was a poor card, but like I have mentioned once before in these situations you just have to make the most of it.

We put our money together and had £40 on the first winner, Grand Prix at 4/5.

I had £10 e/w on the second winner Full Spate at 4/1 (it actually returned at 7/1) and Angie had £10 e/w on Daville's Lad which finished second also at 4/1.

We didn't have a bet in the third race which was won by the favourite Allegretto at 3/10.

Again we put our money together for the fourth race and again backed the winner, Dove Cottage at 7/4.

Nothing in the last two races.

We had made a slight profit so we came away happy, we had just short of £280 to put in the kitty which meant we were in profit of nearly£180 after seven meetings.

We drove over the bridge and back into England for our last night away from home. We stopped at a shop on our way to the hotel to buy some snacks, a couple of bottles of lemonade and a bottle of vodka as our plans were to stay in our room that night and have a few drinks.

Angie's verdict:

Words couldn't describe how I felt that morning in Brighton when we thought the car had been stolen, and I only hope I never go through the same experience again, and looking back on it I was to blame as much as Dave when we got out of the lift on the wrong floor.

When we arrived at Chepstow racecourse I was really impressed, the whole layout is good and set in a very picturesque location. However I had my doubts about their dress code when a young girl walked past us drinking a glass of wine and wearing a basque along with stockings and a suspender belt. But things became clear when she was later joined by a monk and a Red Indian chief followed by the rest of their friends in various other forms of fancy dress. The nice thing about it was I don't think they were actually celebrating anything and were just out to have a good time.

There are two enclosures at Chepstow; the Premier and the Grandstand and Paddock, both of which are well maintained and very clean or at least they were very clean when we first arrived.

The Premier enclosure, as well as its large restaurant which overlooks the course has a spacious well stocked bar where you can also buy hot and cold food. Viewing is very good from both the stand and the grassy bank overlooking the winning post.
The Grandstand and Paddock enclosure also has a large bar where hot and cold food is also available. There is also a number of mobile catering units. Viewing from the stand is very good, but can I just warn any parents who plan on taking their kids to Chepstow to be vigilant. Kids at racecourses love to climb on the rails to watch the horses go by, but let me warn you that the race support vehicles come very close to the rails as they pass. There is parking, toilet facilities and a designated viewing area for disabled racegoers.
Something I read in the programme might be useful for you to know about, and that is the Severn Crossing Bridge Buster Offer. I don't know if it applies to every meeting, but anyone purchasing two badges could have a full refund of their bridge toll (£4.90p) by presenting their bridge receipt.
The only negative I have was the amount of empty beer cans and plastic glasses that had just been dropped on the ground; there was absolutely no need for it as there were plenty waste bins around.
Rating: Very Good ★★★★★

How to get there:

To get there by road; from the north and south take the M5 to junction 15 then onto the M48. From the east and west also take the M48 via the M4. Come off the M48 at junction 2 then onto theA466.
Parking is free except for the Welsh Grand National meeting.
To get there by rail; Chepstow station is about a mile and a half from the course. Direct trains run to Chepstow from Gloucester

and Cardiff. From London you would go via Newport and from Bristol via Severn Tunnel Junction.

Nearest airport is Bristol (18 miles).

There is a choice of accommodation on both sides of the river Severn.

Saturday 17 June 2006

Leicester Race Co Ltd
Oadby
Leicester
LE2 4AL
Tel: 0116 2716515
www.leicester-racecourse.co.uk

We had celebrated our final night away from home in our room, and it was well after midnight before we had finished the last dregs of vodka and were ready to go to bed. Angie went to get the two extra pillows that were stored on top of the wardrobe and straight away realised the pillow cases hadn't been changed since the room had last been occupied. Not wanting to make a fuss so late at night we put the spare pillows under the two clean ones that were already on the bed.

On the Saturday morning when we were checking out I mentioned the pillows to the young man on reception, I also told him that our double bed had actually been two single beds pushed together, and they had managed to drift apart through the night. He immediately picked up the phone and repeated what I had just told him to who I can only presume was the hotel manager. He listened for a while to whatever the person on the other end of the line was telling him, replaced the receiver then gave us a full refund.

Good start to the last day of our holiday.

So we left Bristol for the final legs of our journey on another hot, sunny morning. Apart from the rain at Salisbury we'd been very lucky with the weather and had enjoyed most of the racing standing outside soaking up the rays. We were on our way home via an evening fixture at Leicester, another course which had abandoned its meeting on our previous attempt to visit.

The drive to Leicester from Bristol is only a couple of hours and we had pretty much all day to get there, so to pass the time we had three long stops at service stations on the way. At the third service station we took the picnic rug out of the car and lay on the grass in the sunshine for a couple of hours.

Because we were going racing in the same clothes we left Bristol in we didn't get suited up, but just dressed casual, and managed to get a wash and clean up at the service station before heading off to the races

When we arrived at the course we went to the racecourse office to pick up our badges. The girl who I had spoken to on the phone before we left for Newbury was actually in the office and said she'd been expecting us. She gave us our badges for the Belvoir Stand and corrected my pronunciation telling me it was pronounced Beaver Stand, she also gave us two complimentary racecards and tokens for a free glass of Pink Champagne. The racecards we were thankful for, the tokens we gave away.

A sunny Saturday night and a good crowd had turned out for what looked like a good card. Even if we'd lost we couldn't have done a lot of damage, but we were hoping to add to the kitty.

We got off to a great start when we both had £10 e/w on the first winner Pippa's Dancer at 4/1.

We only had one more return after that when Angie had £10 e/w on the fourth winner Snowed Under at 9/2.

£30 down on the night and roughly £150 up over the eight meetings wasn't too bad, especially after we'd thought our kitty which at the time was over £1300 had been lost along with our car in Brighton.

So after racing we set off from Leicester to Newcastle for the last 200 miles of our 1400 mile journey. We arrived home to a warm welcome from the dogs, though Cassie by her actions made it clear she was still in a sulky mood with us, Zak was busy sniffing round the cases as he knew there would be a present hidden away somewhere for him. Hollie, Michael and Alex were all in bed asleep and Grant who very rarely slept at home was again staying out somewhere or other.

Hollie had left a welcome home present in the fridge for us; a bottle of vodka and two bottles of lemonade, though we only had one drink before we too went to bed.

It was the following morning before we opened the pile of mail, and among them was a letter from Leicester Racecourse containing two badges for the BEAVER Stand.

It was absolutely amazing how quickly the time had passed by while we'd been away, and to wake up with nowhere to go was a bit deflating, especially when I still had over a week left before I had to go back to work. It was getting harder now to find fixtures that would fit in with my shift pattern, but there were a couple the following week that were strong possibilities.

However I thought it might be better to let the dust settle for a couple of days before suggesting we should have a day at the races.

Angie's Verdict:

I really enjoyed our elongated racing trip, but unlike Dave I wouldn't describe it as a holiday. Holidays to me are lying next to a pool in the sunshine, not packing and unpacking cases every day in between browsing round service stations. In the same breath, to look at us you would have thought we had just come back from a month on the Costa del Sol as our faces and arms had developed deep tans after standing around in the sunshine for so long.

The staff at Leicester racecourse were very friendly, especially the girl in the racecourse office who was really lovely and couldn't have made us feel more welcome. There are two main enclosures at Leicester; the Belvoir Stand and the Grandstand enclosure.

The Belvoir Stand has a couple of well stocked bars and a Champagne and wine bar. There is a good choice of food on offer, including a set menu from the restaurant located in the stand. Viewing from the Belvoir stand is very good.

We spent most of our evening in the Grandstand enclosure, which also has a large, well stocked bar, and a variety of eating places. If you want to go a bit more upmarket there is a restaurant in the Nelson Suite which has panoramic views. We went downmarket, but actually really enjoyed our Chinese noodles which we bought from one of a selection of mobile catering units parked behind the Grandstand.

I like having a look around any trade stands that have set up at the races, and the amazing thing about that evening, and what I thought was a stoke of luck, there was a stand selling nothing but baby merchandise. We had already bought Alex a few of bits and bobs from the service stations we had been to, but we managed to buy him a couple of lovely presents from Leicester racecourse of all places.

There is good viewing from the grandstand where we sat for most of the races; Henry Cecil sat in front of us for one race in which his horse finished down the field. I think he must have smoked three cigarettes in the time between the horses going down and the race finishing.

There are toilet facilities for the disabled in the main Grandstand and a viewing platform overlooking the winning post.

Next to the Grandstand enclosure is the Picnic car park, and kids can enjoy the playground area as well as the extra entertainment provided at weekend and evening fixtures.

Rating: Good ★★★★

I had enjoyed the trip but was also pleased when we arrived home. It was lovely to be greeted by Cassie and Zak, but the thing I was really looking forward to was seeing Alex again the following morning.

How to get there:

To get there by road; from the north and south come off the M1 at junction 21, the course is just off the A6, and can be reached by using the A563 outer ring road. From the east take the A47 and A6, and from the west the M6, M69 and A563.
Parking is free except for the picnic car park which costs between £25 and £32 (4 adults maximum).

To get there by rail; Leicester station which is two and a half miles from the course is on the London, St. Pancras to Sheffield line. A bus runs from the station to the course on racedays.
Nearest airport is East Midlands (18 miles).
Like most cities Leicester has a good choice of hotels, with quite a few close to the racecourse.

Wednesday 21 June 2006

Worcester Racecourse
Pitchcroft
Worcester
WR1 3EJ
Tel. 0870 2202772
www.worcester-racecourse.co.uk

We'd arrived home from Leicester and our eight course trip in the early hours of Sunday morning, and with still over a week before I was due back to work I was pretty determined to fit in another meeting if I got the chance. You might now be thinking it was becoming an obsession, and I suppose it was but in a nice sort of way.

If you can imagine how it is when chocoholics take the lid off a box of chocolates, they simply can't stop eating them until the box is empty. This was my box of chocolates, I'd eaten most of them and couldn't wait to try the rest, and just like a box of chocolates some were better than others.

When I was eighteen and still learning what life was all about, I became really good friends with two ex-sportsmen who were both seasoned gamblers. My best mate at the time Pat, an Irish ex- national hunt jockey whose career ended with a smashed leg in a bad fall at Ayr and Jim (Jinky) an ex-Newcastle United star whose career also ended with a leg injury.

We were standing at the bar one day at Newcastle races and next to us were three men who were celebrating their big day, Newcastle had just completed their tour of all the GB racecourses. I thought this was great and although I would have loved to have been in their shoes, I didn't think I would ever be in the situation where I could follow in their footsteps. At the time I was paid weekly on a Thursday, and like most eighteen year olds I was skint by Monday morning and borrowing money from my parents until payday came around again. So there was no way I could have possibly been able to afford to visit all the tracks. But circumstances change, and my opportunity came, and nobody was going to take my chocolates away.

Angie wasn't keen on having another night away from home so soon after our recent trip, especially when I had been planning with Darren (who we'd been to York with) a weekend in Dublin in early July. So I suggested a day trip to Worcester and Angie gave it the thumbs up.

It meant an early start as it is a four and a half hour drive from our house to Worcester, and we wanted to be clear of Newcastle before the rush hour traffic hit the road. We set off at seven o'clock and drove to Tibshelf services on the M1 where we stopped for breakfast and a fuel top up before continuing our drive to Worcester Racecourse.

After another trouble free drive, we arrived at the course well before the first race. The course itself is close to the city, and the river Severn runs right alongside which I believe causes flooding problems at times, but that certainly wasn't going to be the case on the hot sunny day we were there.

We agreed on £40 a race, alternative picks and to start making our way home after the sixth of the seven races on the card, Angie went first.

A good start when Angie had £20 e/w on the first winner Classic Crocco at 4/1.

I had £40 on the second winner September Moon at 3/1.

In the third race Angie had £20 e/w on Mabel Riley which finished second at 5/1.

Nothing back in our last three races.

With the start we'd had it looked like we were in for a cracking day and I was even considering staying for all seven races, but our luck fizzled out. Even so, after our expenses; including fuel, food and admission we had finished up more or less level, and that is still a satisfactory days racing in my book.

Angie's verdict:

By now I was getting quite used to the travelling, and the truth be known, I was really enjoying it, especially with the weather being so fine. We both liked the look of Worcester as we approached the racecourse, and more or less at the same time said "We should have booked a room for the night."
Worcester Racecourse has three enclosures; the Club, the Grandstand and the Course enclosure. The Club or Member's enclosure, apart from its viewing restaurant on the second floor of the grandstand has a spacious bar on the first floor which also has a self service restaurant. Viewing from the Club enclosure is very good.
The Grandstand enclosure is where we spent most of our day enjoying both the racing and the sunshine. Like the Member's enclosure there is a spacious bar on the ground floor of the Grandstand enclosure which also serves snacks as well as drinks. There are also quite a few mobile catering units parked on the concourse. We watched a couple of races standing at the rails which was okay, but not as good a view as at some courses, viewing from the stands however is fine. Taking advantage of their closeness to the river, there are mooring facilities behind the Grandstand for riverboat hospitality.
There are toilets for disabled racegoers and a viewing area overlooking the course and parade ring. There is also a lift to the upper level of the stand.
The course enclosure also has a bar and a variety of snacks and fast foods. There is no stand in this enclosure. There is however a picnic car park and a kiddie's playground, and at weekend fixtures children can also enjoy the extra entertainment on offer. Although the people were pretty friendly, for some reason everybody seemed to be dashing about in a mad hurry even though it was such a hot day. I didn't get that warm welcoming feeling that I'd felt when visiting some courses, but that didn't

spoil a really enjoyable afternoon at Worcester races. One thing is for sure, the next time we go we are stopping overnight.
Rating: Average ★★★

How to get there:

To get there by road; from the north and south take the M5, coming off at junction 6, then the A449 to Worcester city centre. From the east take the A442, and from the west the A44.
Once in Worcester it is well signposted to the racecourse.
Parking is free.
To get there by rail; Worcester's Foregate Street station is less than half a mile from the course.
Trains from Paddington, Birmingham, Bristol and Cardiff all run direct to Worcester.
Nearest airport is Birmingham (27 miles).
There is a fair amount of accommodation to be found quite close to Worcester racecourse.

Sunday 2 July 2006

The Curragh Racecourse
County Kildare
Ireland
Tel: +353 (0) 45 441205
www.curragh.ie

Darren and I work at the same place but we are on different shifts
so we get very few days when we are off together, especially
weekends. So we were lucky that Irish Derby weekend fell on
one of the rare occasions we were able to go racing together. We
were flying out to Dublin on the Friday night and returning to
Newcastle early Monday morning. I was working on the
Thursday night when Darren rang me to make final arrangements
for the following day; he also told me he'd been given a tip for
Toldo which was running in the Northumberland Plate on the
Saturday. I did a little bit research on the horse that night and
decided it would have little to no chance on the expected good to
firm ground that was predicted for Newcastle.
Darren and Jane arrived at our house early Friday evening; from
there we went to Newcastle airport by taxi. None of us had been
to Ireland before so we were all really looking forward to our trip,
though Jane seemed a bit nervous about the flight. I mentioned
my findings on Toldo to Darren who said he too had been
looking through its form and agreed it would be well left alone.
Our flight was scheduled for 22:00 so we had time to have a
couple of drinks in the airport lounge getting our weekend off to
a good start and helping to calm Jane's nerves.
The flight was on time and we arrived in Dublin at 22:50 and
took a bus from outside the terminal building to Dublin city
centre. From here we got into a taxi and asked the driver to take
us to our hotel, The Best Western Ashling Hotel in Parkgate
Street. The big mistake we made was making it obvious to the
driver it was our first visit to Dublin, and for our mistake he

221

ripped us off. Even though it was late when we checked in, the hotel bar was still open, so we took our bags to our rooms and came back downstairs where we sat until well after midnight, drinking in the company of a great couple from Belfast who were in Dublin on a business trip.

Surprisingly after the late night we all made it to the breakfast table and it wasn't long before we were out and about. A short trip from just outside our hotel on the Luas (Dublin's light railway system) took us back into the city centre. Our main objective of the day was to find a bar that was showing live coverage of England's quarter final World Cup game against Portugal. The bar we chose was The Turks Head in the Temple Bar district, an area renowned for its drinking establishments. There was plenty of time to kill before the match kicked off, so Angie and Jane went off shopping while Darren and I found a seat in the sunshine and read the racing papers.

Confident of backing a few winners we made our way to The Track Bookmakers, which we had spotted earlier on and which is close to The Turks Head bar. Having a few bets before we were due to meet Angie and Jane, we managed to take a few Euros off the bookie, so we picked two horses each and placed an e/w Yankee on races that were being run later in the afternoon, the bet included Greenwich Meantime which was well fancied and was running in the Northumberland Plate.

The girls arrived at our agreed meeting point quite happy with their purchases but complaining about the heat, they told us the tar on the road through Temple Bar was actually melting. After we'd listened to the shopping stories we made our way to The Turks Head to get good seats for the match. Good seats we got and a good drink we had, but the match turned out to be a big disappointment, and England's exit from the World Cup was inevitable early in the second half when David Beckham went off injured and Wayne Rooney was sent off for violent conduct. However they did manage a 0-0 draw but went out on a penalty shootout.

England going out of the World Cup wasn't the only disappointment we were going to have that afternoon. I had been popping over to The Track Bookmakers to follow the progress of our Yankee; we had two winners, a nowhere and a third. The third was Greenwich Meantime 9/2 joint favourite beaten a neck and a short head, Toldo the horse Darren had been given the tip for won the Northumberland Plate at 33/1. So with the World Cup over as far as we were concerned for another 4 years and kicking ourselves for missing a 33/1 winner we left The Turks Head and made our way to The Track Bookmakers to pick up our money (€130) only to find the shop was shut, which just about rounded the afternoon off.

They all said they needed something to eat, so they went into The Hard Rock Cafe, while I not feeling hungry said I would just go for a wander and found myself in Paddy Power's bookmakers a short distance away. There was coverage of a couple of greyhound meetings, so with no better way to pass the time while waiting for the diners I had a few bets. My first bet was €20 on a loser followed by €50 on a 5/2 winner, my third and final bet was €100 on another 5/2 winner, so I made my way back to The Hard Rock Cafe €355 better off.

We spent the rest of the evening in Temple Bar before making our way back to our hotel and bed ready for our big day at The Curragh

Sunday morning arrived and again we all made it to the breakfast table where Darren told us he'd received a text message saying his friends Alan and Carl who were brothers along with their partners Faye and Pauline had managed to book a night at our hotel, and were catching a morning flight from Newcastle which would get them to the hotel in good time to go racing.

We were going to the races by train, and luckily Heuston station is just a two minute walk from The Ashling hotel as the new arrivals to our party arrived with less than an hour to spare before the train was due to depart. When they came out of the airport and got into a taxi, the driver took them to a different Best

Western which is located on the other side of town. There was also a panic as they needed to get ready for the races and their rooms weren't ready. So the girls went to Darren's room and the boys went to ours, and half an hour later we were all set to go. Finally we were on our way, and boarded an already crowded train with virtually minutes to spare. The train stopped at The Curragh station which is no more than a platform on either side of the track, and only used on certain race days. The platforms are really low compared to the height of the carriages, so the guard had to help quite a few people down from the train by placing a wooden box on the ground to act as a step. It took under ten minutes to walk from the train to the enclosures as we joined the droves of people that were heading for the entrances.

Being Derby day we knew it was going to be busy, but it seemed like everyone was arriving at the same time. Darren and I already had badges for the Premier stand as we'd bought them online, Alan and Carl tried to purchase similar badges but as expected they were sold out. But at least they gained admission and to keep the party together we didn't make use of our Premier status.

As far as betting was concerned, I suggested €40 each a race, and it was at this point I told Angie about the money I had won at Paddy Power's the day before, and that I had more money than I had left Newcastle with. €40 each a race it was.

Nothing back in the first, I had €40 on the second winner Dandy Man at 11/8.

We had both said we thought Kieren Fallon might have a good day and both fancied him to win the third on Bonus, so we put our money together and had €40 e/w at 6/1 only to watch him be collared on the line and beaten a head into second.

Fallon won the next two races on Holy Roman Emperor and Dylan Thomas on which he won The Derby, neither of us backed either horse.

Angie backed the sixth winner, and even ignored our normal e/w policy when she had €40 on Telemachus at 11/2.

Nothing back in the last two races.

We were slightly down on the day and considered ourselves a bit unlucky, but you can't win all the time, at least we came out better than Darren and Jane who never backed a winner all afternoon. Alan and Carl also finished down on the day. We made our way back to the railway platforms which were crowded on both sides of the track, and it wasn't long before the train arrived to take us back to Dublin. We went to bed early that night as we were getting up at 04:30am to catch a 06:00am flight back to Newcastle. There was something about our first taste of Irish racing that was both different and very exciting, and our trip to The Curragh was going to open a brand new chapter in our lives.

Angie's verdict:

As soon as we had checked our bags in and were sitting in the airport lounge the fun started. Jane was coming out with some really funny stories and seemed to be having a great time even though she was convinced we were all going to end up in the Irish Sea that night.

A day in Dublin wasn't a lot of time to see much, but at least I noted a few landmarks that would come in handy for future trips, including one or two nice hotels that were a lot more central than the one we were staying in.

The eight of us spent most of the afternoon standing by the rails near the finishing line where the viewing was pretty good. I did manage to watch one race from the grandstand however when Jane and I went to the bar upstairs, Jane for wine and me for lemonade, as the water bottle was also having its first trip to Ireland. Funny enough the race we watched was my 11/2 winner Telemachus, the viewing from here was excellent, I don't know who was the more excited when my horse won me or Jane.

When I eventually got to the front of the queue to pick up my winnings, the bookie took my slip and handed me €150 then started to deal with his next punter. I stayed glued to the spot and said "that's wrong" but he just ignored me and carried on paying the rest of his queue. It was his colleague who told him there was a problem, he then looked at me and without even asking what the problem was he took another €110 from his bag and paid me the rest of my winnings. He had obviously known what he was doing, so a warning to you ladies, make sure you know exactly how much money you are expecting to collect when you hand in your winning tickets at any race meeting.

There is a good variety of bars and restaurants throughout the enclosure and a number of fast food outlets. There is a picnic area and a children's playground, though I must warn you Derby day is the one meeting when under 15's don't get into The Curragh free of charge. There is a special viewing stand close to the parade ring for the disabled and all areas of the course are wheelchair accessible.

Rating: Very Good ★★★★★

How to get there:

We have an Irish AA road atlas which shows the location of the racecourses, using the atlas and a printed route planner we have found the roads in Ireland are very easy to navigate.

When we first started visiting the Irish tracks I found the racecourse guides I was using not very informative on road directions. For this reason I have included where possible more detailed directions (which I believe to be accurate) to the Irish courses.

To get there by road; take the N7, the main Dublin-Cork/Limerick road, continue onto M7 coming off at junction 12, at roundabout take the second exit onto the Curragh

There is plenty free parking.

Bus Eireann run a race day bus, which leaves from Busaras, Dublin city centre bus station.

To get there by rail; although the Curragh has its own stop it is only used on certain race days; Kildare is the next nearest from where there is a race day shuttle bus.

Trains from Dublin (Heuston), Waterford, Cork and Galway all stop at Kildare.

Nearest main airport is Dublin (25 miles).

There are quite a few hotels in Kildare including a couple close to the course.

Tuesday 4 July 2006

Thirsk Racecourse Limited
Station Road
Thirsk
North Yorkshire
Y07 1QL
Tel: 01845 522276
www.thirskracecourse.net

We spent Tuesday morning carrying out domestic chores, Angie on general housework while I was cutting the grass after having the dogs out for a walk. We'd gone to bed early the previous night as we'd been up since 04:30 to catch our flight home from Dublin and were totally worn out by the evening. Early to bed early to rise meant all our jobs were done by lunchtime, so the four of us (dogs included) set our stalls out for an afternoon basking in the sun. We'd been in the garden about an hour just chatting and reading the papers when Angie mentioned there was very little on television that night." Why don't we go to Thirsk" was my reply, and within half an hour the garden chairs were folded away and we were getting ready for another evenings racing.

We'd only been to Thirsk once before when we went one evening with Hollie, which was pretty remarkable and especially for me as I'd been to most of the other Yorkshire tracks umpteen times. Before general betting duty (tax to us) was abolished in the betting shops my mates and I used to go racing quite regularly if local meetings were on. This was because there was no tax to pay with the course bookmakers, and even though the Yorkshire tracks aren't exactly local we usually managed to get a couple of free badges which made it a cheap day out. Why Thirsk got the miss I don't know.

Betting tax was abolished in 2001 and before that betting shops would take 10% of your winnings for the government. You did however have an option of paying the tax out of your stake which meant you paid even if you lost. Changes in the betting taxes and the introduction of internet betting to me have totally changed the atmosphere at the races. Not so much in the stands where everyone is lifted by the excitement of the race, but more in the betting ring where at one time you could feel the tension as punters were hungrily pacing the rows of bookies looking for the best odds for their chosen horse. You still get the odd gamble taking place during racing, but I think a lot of the big players have placed their bets long before racing has even started, and probably just stay at home watching the racing in comfort.

Our previous visit to Thirsk had left no happy memories, it was a nice evening when we first arrived but that soon changed. A sudden drop in temperature brought on by heavy rain along with backing six consecutive losers made the night a miserable experience if not a total disaster.

This trip turned out to be the total opposite on both counts.

We still hadn't decided what our best system of betting was as we seemed to be doing alright no matter which one we chose on the day. The one thing that did make a big difference was keeping to the same stakes. At Thirsk we went for £40 a race alternative picks. Angie went first.

A great start to the night when Angie had £40 on the first winner Aahgowangowan at 11/4.

Nothing in the second or third.

A winner for me in the fourth when I had £40 on Rosbay at 7/4.

Another winner for Angie in the fifth, Minister Of State, £40 at 6/4.

And I finished the night by backing the winner of the last race, Whispering Death, £40 at 5/2.

Angie's verdict:

Compared to our previous visit to Thirsk races this trip was a real treat. As I have mentioned before, things look totally different when the sun is out, and Thirsk racecourse was no exception. Most of the crowd were outside, ladies in their seasonal dresses and gentlemen in their short sleeved shirts making the most of what was turning out to be quite a good summer. The course itself looked really lush in the radiant sunshine.

Thirsk is one of what I would describe as a quaint and almost old fashioned racecourse, everywhere is clean and tidy and everyone very friendly. A restaurant and bar facilities can be found in the club enclosure from where you get the best views over the course and finishing line. However we spent most of the evening taking in the sun's rays sitting on the steps in the grandstand of the tattersalls where the viewing is also very good. The tattersalls enclosure also offers bar facilities and a variety of fast food.

There is a third enclosure, the family enclosure which also has a bar serving drinks and snacks. There is a viewing stand in the family enclosure but it is quite a way from the finishing line. The nice thing about this enclosure is it is ideal for a picnic and with admission only being £3.50p and children under sixteen admitted free when accompanied by an adult it can be a not too expensive family day out.

Thirsk is a very friendly racecourse well worth a visit, especially on a sunny day.

Rating: Average ★★★

How to get there:

To get there by road; take the A1/A1M coming off on the A61.
The race course is just off the A61 west of Thirsk itself.
There is plenty free parking.
To get there by rail; Thirsk railway station is less than a mile
from the course, the station can be reached using the Kings Cross
line, though you will need to change trains en route.
Nearest airport is Teesside (19 miles).
There are a number of hotels and guest houses very close to
Thirsk racecourse.

Thursday July 20 2006

Epsom Downs Racecourse
Epsom Downs
Surrey
KT18 5LQ
Tel: 01372 726311
www.epsomderby.co.uk

Epsom, home of the English Derby, and probably the most famous horse race in the world was on the shortlist of courses we were considering leaving until last. But there were three things that contributed towards Epsom being scratched off the list. Being off work was the most obvious reason; secondly it was an evening meeting which gave us plenty of time to get there. Thirdly and most significantly it was one of the four Epsom live meetings, where they have live music after racing. Quite a few courses now have live entertainment after racing in the summer months, but you will find in a lot of cases the acts that are playing are either has-beens or simply unheard of. There are a few courses however that go for the bigger names, and with UB40 playing after racing at Epsom we couldn't resist the temptation to go.

UB40 isn't everyone's idea of entertainment but we enjoy their music, as does Angie's sister Karen and her husband Ken who couldn't believe it when we told them the band were playing live after racing and at no extra cost. They had just recently paid £37 each a ticket to watch UB40 at Newcastle Arena where no drinks are allowed in the concert hall. We had paid nothing extra for the entertainment, and people were drinking in the stands while swinging their hips to the Reggae rhythm.

We had a room booked for one night in The Travel Inn, Epsom Central, and as it a five and a half hour drive from Newcastle to

Epsom we set off mid morning leaving Hollie and Michael to their now well accustomed duties.

Arriving at our hotel at about half past three in the afternoon and with the first race not being until six fifteen we had ample time to get ourselves ready for our night out.

Suited up and still almost an hour and a half before racing started we decided to walk the two and a half miles from the hotel to the racecourse. This seemed like a good idea as it was such a lovely evening, what we didn't realise was how lovely an evening it was and by the time we reached the course we were both feeling a bit hot under the collar.

Once inside the stand we were able to sit down and cool down aided by a nice refreshing drink. We'd looked at the papers earlier on in the day when we'd stopped for lunch on our way from Newcastle, so we had a good idea which horses we fancied.

We had a few quid in the kitty so I suggested £40 each a race but Angie wasn't happy with my suggestion and said we should stick to £40 and £20. My argument was we had been betting €40 each in Ireland to which she replied "that was different". What she meant by that I'll never know, so £40 and £20 it was.

Nothing back in the first race.

We both backed Envision which won the second, £40 at 2/1 and £20 at 7/4.

We went on to back the same horses in the last four races.

We had £60 on Pagan Crest which finished last in the third at 2/1.

We then hit a lucky streak and had £60 on the last three winners; Croon at 3/1, Scrummage at 2/1 and Carloman at 5/2.

I made sure I got to the front of the bookie's payout queue after the last race, as Angie went into the stand to get a prime position close to the stage where the after racing entertainment was going to perform. After collecting our money and a couple of bottles of lemonade from the bar I joined Angie in the stands.

Once the show was over we just walked back to the hotel, this time it was a more pleasant experience, not only because it had cooled down but we were nearly £450 up.

Two meetings in a row we'd backed four out of six winners, and although we'd won nearly £200 more at Epsom having separate bets than we had done at Thirsk where we'd had alternative picks, it didn't help to prove which system was the best. That was because we'd backed the same horse in five of the six races at Epsom.

Angie's verdict:

After the huge crowds we'd encountered at The Curragh for the Irish Derby, I'm pleased we hadn't planned our trip to Epsom to watch the English equivalent. There was still a good crowd however, and this became more apparent at the end of the evening when everyone started to make their way outside to watch UB40 on stage.

I don't think there is much I can really say that you wouldn't have already guessed about the facilities at Epsom. There are plenty of places to eat and drink though I did think it was a bit overpriced. Everywhere throughout the enclosures is very clean and the staff are quite friendly.

We had started the evening having a drink in the Queens stand which is very nice and offers a great view of the course and the finishing line. From here we moved to the Grandstand enclosure which is also very good and like the Queen's stand has a good view of the finish. It was while standing at the rails in this enclosure I realised just how much of a slope the course has, but with the track being renowned for the speed at which horses can cover the ground it obviously doesn't hinder their performance in any way.

There is also the Lonsdale enclosure which is opposite the Queens stand overlooking the winning post. This enclosure has free admission for meetings in April, September and October. There are fast food outlets located in the Lonsdale enclosure.

Finally there is the Hill, a large grassy area in the centre of the course which has free admission for pedestrians and cars can park for a fee (from £10-£15). This area is ideal for picnicking.

The main stands have ramps and toilets for the disabled as well as lifts to upper floors. Children under 16 are admitted free if accompanied by an adult although this doesn't apply to the Queens stand. Children are also charged admission on Derby Day or if there is a live band playing after racing.

Rating: Very Good ★★★★★

The concert after racing was great. I got great pleasure out of phoning my sister Karen and her husband Ken while their favourite UB40 song "Kingston Town" was playing. They actually put the phone down on me.

How to get there:

To get there by road; from all directions make your way onto the M25, come off at junction 8. The course is well signposted from here.

Parking is free at most meetings; it is advisable to book your parking space if you are planning to go to the Derby.

To get there by rail; there are 3 stations in Epsom;

Trains to Epsom station leave from Waterloo, Charing Cross and Victoria. From Epsom station you can take a bus or a taxi to the course.

Epsom Downs station can be reached from Victoria.

A better option could be Tottenham Corner station which is on the line from either London Bridge or Charing Cross and is only a short walk from the course.

Nearest airport is Gatwick (12 miles)

There is a good selection of accommodation all within easy reach of Epsom racecourse.

Friday 11 August 2006

Haydock Park Racecourse
Newton-le-Willows
Merseyside
WA12 0HQ
Tel: 01942 725963
www.haydock-park.co.uk

Hollie and Michael had just been told they had been accepted by a housing association and were promised they would be given the keys to their newly built house within the next week. This was great news for Hollie, Michael and Alex, and was good news for us as well as far as having the house to ourselves again was concerned, but it also meant we were losing our resident dog sitters.

To make the most of the last weekend before our house guests moved to their new residence, we set off on a two day trip to visit Haydock and Ascot. Neither of us had been to Ascot before but we had both been to Haydock. Haydock is one of Angie's favourite courses and in fact had been her favourite until Cheltenham took over the top spot. I also think Haydock is a very good course except each time I've been there the stands have been packed like sardines, and the queues at the bars were just mad.

So this time we bought two badges for the Premier Suite which has a balcony overlooking the winning post and is limited to 400 people, so at least we would have some space to ourselves. We also booked a room for the night at The Holiday Inn which is right next to the course at Newton-le-Willows, which meant we could leave the car and just walk to the races.

We waved goodbye to Hollie and drove west to join the M6 which we followed all the way to Haydock, we did meet some heavy traffic when we reached the Manchester/Liverpool area but that didn't cause us any major delays.

Arriving at The Holiday Inn late afternoon we went to our room and Angie started to unpack the case, but something was missing. It was as bad as going camping without a tin opener; we'd left our bottle of vodka sitting on the kitchen bench at home. So we jumped back in the car and made the short drive to the village where we had a twenty minute wait for the off licence to open before the situation was rectified.

The walk from the hotel to the course was really pleasant on what was yet another glorious summer evening. We'd tried on a few occasions to book a room at the Holiday Inn when we'd been to Haydock, but this was the first time we'd managed to get one. It makes a big difference when you can just walk to the races and not have to join the queues of raceday traffic.

We arrived at the course a good hour before racing started and found ourselves seats at a table. Even though there were ten bar staff serving I still found myself having to queue at the bar, but at least I knew it would still be nothing like the chaos that would be going on at the bars in the County stand a floor below us.

We were betting £40 and £20 a race but because we were upstairs and at the time I was having a lot of trouble with my knee, I had no intention of running up and down the stairs to the betting ring. So I placed 6 X £40 wins in the betting shop on the ground floor on the horses I'd marked earlier on in the Racing Post. Angie was betting with the tote.

Angie had £10 e/w on the first winner Linden Lime which paid £7.60p a win and £2.10p a place.

Nothing in the second.

We both had the third winner Wid; £40 at 11/10 and £20 on the tote paying £2.10p a win.

Only one more return on the night when my selection Endless Summer won the fifth race at 100/30.

Another very enjoyable evening at Haydock Park, and a very small profit on the night. A short walk back to the hotel followed by a nightcap in the hotel bar, and we were ready for a nights sleep.

Angie's verdict:

This was a trip I was really excited about, not only for my first visit to Ascot but also for going back to Haydock as I am a big fan of racing at Haydock Park. I wasn't so sure about having badges for the Premier Suite, as on previous visits we had been in the County Stand where we had enjoyed a good atmosphere and always had a good laugh. I think the Scouse and Geordie sense of humour is very similar.

The Premier Suite, set in the Centenary Stand is very nice, and we couldn't have asked for a better view than the one we had from the balcony. But the atmosphere wasn't the same and my personal preference would be for the County Stand where there are numerous bars and eating places offering a good range of food, though as Dave says you might need to be prepared to join a queue.

There is also the Tattersalls enclosure which also has bars and eating places, there is a seated viewing area in this stand.

Last but not least is the Newton enclosure which is situated furthest from the winning post. This enclosure has a raised viewing gallery and a children's playground close by. Children under 16 get in free when accompanied by an adult.

Even though it is always busy the toilets are kept nice and clean, even the gents which I went into by mistake receiving some rather amusing comments from those relieving themselves at the urinals.

Disabled racing fans are very well catered for at Haydock Park.

Rating: Very Good ★★★★

How to get there:

To get there by road; Haydock is only about a mile off junction 23 of the M6.The main car park can be easily accessed from the A580 (East Lancashire Road) which links Manchester and Liverpool.
Car parking is free.
To get there by rail; Warrington and Wigan stations which are on the London to Glasgow line are both about an 8 mile taxi ride from the course.
Newton-le-Willows station which is on the Manchester/Piccadilly to Liverpool/Lime Street line is the closest being 2.5 miles from the course.
Nearest airport is Liverpool John Lennon (14 miles).
There is a very good choice of accommodation in the area, including quite a few close to the racecourse.

Saturday 12 August 2006

Ascot Racecourse
Berkshire
SL5 7JX
Tel: 01344 876876
www.ascot.co.uk

When you tell people you have been to Ascot, whether they are racing fans or not they automatically think you have been to The Royal Meeting. Although Royal Ascot is probably the biggest event in the social calendar, Ascot racecourse has a lot more to offer, staging high quality racing, both flat and national hunt right throughout the year.

The meeting we were going to was The Dubai Duty Free Shergar Cup; two teams of jockeys, one from Great Britain and Ireland and the other team representing the rest of the world.

They compete against each other on a points system, each race having 10 runners with 5 jockeys from each team taking the mounts. 40 points a race are awarded; 15, 10, 7, 5 and 3 for the first 5 horses past the post and the team with the most points at the end of the day lift the trophy.

We had quite a long day in front of us starting with a three and a half hour drive from Haydock to Ascot, this we broke up by stopping for breakfast and a refuel at Warwick service station on the M40.

We left the Holiday Inn at Haydock at 09:00am and arrived at Ascot an hour and a half before the first race. As we made our way from the entrance gates towards the stands we passed a staged area where Charlotte Church, who was performing live after racing was setting up her equipment, and judging on what I heard I was glad we were driving straight to Newcastle after the last race.

We had time for a good look around before sitting down for a coffee and a read through the Racing Post and our racecards. Angie did disappear for twenty minutes however, when she joined the queue of people who were lined up to meet the jockeys. She came back with our programme signed by all the members of each team (nice keepsake to add to our ever increasing programme collection).

Before racing started there was a 6 furlong duel between the two team managers; Jason Weaver for GB. And Ireland riding Pic Up Sticks against Michael Roberts for the rest of the world riding Who's Winning. The result looked cut and dry when a fit looking Muis Roberts set off at a blistering pace, leaving Jason Weaver who was carrying a bit of personal overweight in his wake. The reaction of the crowd was electric as Jason started to pull back the deficit and went away inside the final furlong to win 5 bonus points for GB. and Ireland setting the tempo for a great days racing.

GB. And Ireland; Jamie Spencer- Ire.(captain), Seb Sanders- GB., Mick Kinane- Ire., Hayley Turner- GB., Ryan Moore- GB. and Robert Winston- Ire.

Rest of the World; Frankie Dettori- Italy (captain), Glen Boss-Australia, Doug White-South Africa, Emma-Jane Wilson-Canada, Gerald Mosse-France and Yuichi Fukanaga-Japan.

We were just going to use the same stakes as we had the night before £40 and £20 and because of the cold breeze that had rustled up, we decided just to stay inside and bet with the Tote. Another good start when I had £40 on the first winner Dark Missile which paid £5 a win.

Angie kept the ball rolling with £20 on the second winner Eddie Jock which paid £4.70p a win.

We had nothing back in the third race, but things started to really pick up when we both backed the fourth and fifth winners; Dorothy's Friend paying £3 a win and Young Mick which paid £2.50p.

Nothing to collect from the last but we'd had a good day showing over £250 profit. GB. and Ireland walked away with The Shergar Cup 158 points to 87.

We drove away on our five and a half hour homeward journey leaving the rest of the Ascot crowd to watch Charlotte Church strut her stuff.

Angie's verdict:

As we said farewell to Haydock and drove south down the motorway there had been a notable change in the weather, the skies had clouded over and the temperature which had dropped a few degrees felt even colder in the strong breeze.

I had read about the newly built £24,000,000 stand at Ascot, and even though the reviews I had read were good, they didn't justify the magnificence of the design and the whole layout of the new Ascot.

When we first went in and were on the escalators heading for the fourth floor I thought it resembled an airport terminal building (but in a nice way).Security is understandably tight, Ascot and Aintree are the only two courses where my bag has been searched at the entrance. Ascot also have security staff on the escalators, ensuring people don't wander off where they shouldn't be.

With such a lot to look at it wasn't long before we were walking around seeing what was on offer. The grandstand is over 350 metres long and has six levels. Most racecourses have their stands positioned horizontally with the premier enclosure being nearest to the finishing line. Ascot's stands being built vertically give more people a chance to see the horses cross the line.

The top two levels are private boxes I believe; we were in the premier on the fourth floor, where there is a good selection of bars, restaurants, delis and coffee shops, we also had an excellent view over the course. The lower concourse level also offers a good variety of bars and eating places, and naturally everywhere was spotlessly clean.

The parade ring behind the stand is also quite spectacular with enough space for thousands to enjoy the view.

Disabled racegoers have access to all enclosures where there are designated viewing areas. Children are very welcome at Ascot where they have a free to join colts and fillies club who arrange activities for the under 16's, a supervised crèche is available for younger children.

The whole design of the refurbished Ascot is amazing and it is a course I would definitely put on your "to do" list.

What made the racing so different that day was; even if I knew my chosen horse was beat, I was still cheering the mounts of the home team. There again I was only betting £20, those betting in 1000's or even 100's probably wouldn't have been so exuberant.

Rating: Excellent ★★★★★

How to get there:

To get there by road; Ascot is on the A329 and easy accessible from the M3 and M4 motorways. From the north M1, M25 to junction 13. From the south and east M3 to junction 6 and from the west the M4 to junction 6. Once off the motorways the course is well signposted.

Free parking is available in car park 6 for most meetings; there is a £6 charge in the other car parks except for the Royal meeting where parking is from £14-£18 per car.

To get there by rail; Ascot railway station is less than half a mile from the course. There are frequent services from both Reading and Waterloo.

Nearest airport is Heathrow (15 miles)

There are a number of hotels within a 5 mile radius of the course.

Bellewstown Racecourse
Bellewstown
County Meath
Tel: 353 41 984 2111
www.bellewstownraces.ie

Hollie had told us that Michael had agreed with her and we should just carry on booking our racing trips as if they were still living with us, and that it would be no inconvenience for them to stay at our house while we were away. So taking Hollie's advice we carried on booking them.

On our previous trip to Ireland, the late flight that we'd used from Newcastle to Dublin and the early return flight had been ideal for Darren and Jane as they had to fit the flights to suit their baby sitting arrangements. With Angie and I travelling alone this time we could be more flexible, and although we'd booked to come home on the same early morning flight, we flew out at the much more sociable time of 08:00. By 09:15 we'd collected our case from the baggage claim at Dublin airport and were standing in the queue at the taxi rank for a cab to take us into the city.

On the way to our hotel the taxi driver asked us if we had been to Dublin before and having learned from our previous mistake we told him we had been there many times. Our destination was The Jurys Inn, Christchurch which is just off Temple Bar and a hotel we'd taken note of on our previous trip. When pulling up, the driver asked us for a fare that was only half as much as the fare we'd been ripped off with on our first visit and for a journey more than twice the distance.

We checked in but were told our room wouldn't be ready for at least an hour, so we left our case with reception and set off into town to find somewhere to have breakfast. I'd managed to find a very good detailed map of Dublin in the hotel reception area, and with its help we found the location of Dublin's central bus station (Busaras).This we needed to know, as it was from here that Bus Eirran were running a special bus to Bellewstown races later that afternoon. After finding out the bus departure time from the information desk we made our way back to the hotel via The Track Bookmakers in Temple Bar. This was to collect the €130 from the yankee Darren and I had put on the day before the Irish Derby, and were unable to collect as the betting shop had closed early.

It worked out to be a good idea finding the location of the bus station, as we knew exactly how long it was going to take us to walk from the hotel. We joined about two dozen others as we boarded the bus and set off right on schedule for the 32 mile, one hour trip to Bellewstown racecourse.

Apart from watching the racing from Bellewstown on At The Races on Sky TV, the only thing I knew about the course was; Bellewstown was the course where Barney Curley allegedly pulled off one of the biggest betting coups in Irish racing with a horse called Yellow Sam.

Most of Ireland's courses are set in picturesque settings, and Bellewstown is no exception. Sited on the hill of Crockafotha it gives great views of the mountains of Mourne and the Irish Sea. We were betting the same stakes as we had on our previous visit to Ireland €40 each a race.

Although they were both short prices we put our money together and backed the first two winners; Impetious at 4/6 and Davenport Democrat at 4/6.

At least it was a winning start; even if they are a short price you still get a thrill out of picking a winner. Unfortunately I didn't pick another winner all night.

Angie managed to salvage the situation a little by backing the last two winners; €40 on Whataboutya at 2/1 and €40 on Athlumney Lad at 5/2.

We got back to Dublin just before ten o'clock and because we were up early the next morning we went back to the hotel stopping at Charlie's 2 a Chinese takeaway for our supper which we ate back in our room. We were standing at the door when our taxi pulled up at 05:00 the next morning.Ryanair who we were flying with were operating two flights a day from Dublin to Newcastle at the time; the early flight that we were flying on and an evening flight. This meant if we didn't take the early flight we would be hanging around all day for the later one. But Angie wasn't happy with the early morning calls and told me I had to sort something better for our next trip.

Angie's verdict:

As the bus pulled into the parking area at Bellewstown we stayed in our seats letting others get off before us, quite a few of them wishing us good luck as they made their way past us down the aisle. It seemed like most of them knew each other, obviously through racing and nearly all of them knew the driver (Andy) who was a regular driver on the raceday specials put on by Bus Eireann. On the way to the entrance we were approached by women selling programmes, but as nobody else was buying them we too declined.

Bellewstown racecourse is small but set in a lovely location and one thing I really liked about it was, unlike the Curragh where we stayed in our own little group, here we felt part of it and were getting a real taste of what Irish racing was all about. As the night went on we had been bumping into people who had been on our bus, they all acknowledged us and some even stopped for a chat. Viewing was okay, but with being so many people in such a small area we just had to find the best spot we could.

The enclosure at Bellewstown may not be very big but is quite well planned out, there is a self service cafe, a snack bar and a few bars; including the one we made base camp which was in a marquee where there was live music playing in between races, and which also gave us shelter from the rain.

There are designated parking and toilet facilities for the disabled, and there are fairground rides for children, though most of the kids seemed more interested in the racing (must be in the blood). There were a couple of trade stands, one of which was selling racing pictures and prints. I wasn't sure whether I wanted a racing picture on the wall but one picture caught my eye, Dave asked me if I wanted the picture but I still wasn't sure so told him I'd think about it. On the way out I called into the toilet and while I was there Dave had bought the picture.

At the exit gates were the same women who were selling programmes on the way in. This time they had stalls made up from pram chassis and wooden boards from which they were selling fruit and chocolate (Toblerones) a custom we would find to be common at Irish racecourses.

Rating: Good ★★★

How to get there:

To get there by car; From the M1, Dublin to Belfast motorway come off at junction signed Drogheda south,Julianstown and Laytown. Take the turning after Gormanstown service station and the racecourse is about two miles further on.

Parking is free.

Bus Eireann run a special bus from Dublin central bus station (Busaras).

To get there by rail; Gormanstown station is the closest being four and a half miles away, Gormanstown has a line from Drogheda.

Drogheda station is on the line from Dublin Connolly to Belfast Central, from Drogheda you can get a taxi the seven miles to the course.

Nearest airport is Dublin (25 miles).

There are hotels in Meath that aren't too far from the course and are worth a try, but the Bellewstown festivals are very popular so you may have to try a bit further afield.

Sunday 1 October 2006

Longchamp Racecourse
Route de Tribunes
Bois de Boulogne
Paris 75116
Tel: 33 1 44 30 75 00
www.longchamp.com

The trip to Longchamp for the Prix de l'Arc de Triomphe had
been planned a couple of months earlier while sitting in our local
social club one Sunday night with our friends Mark and Michelle.
Michelle was looking for something special to do for Mark's
birthday, and it wasn't long before Longchamp got everyone's
vote. We arranged the trip through a local newspaper which had
been advertising a weekend trip to Paris, highlighted by a day at
Longchamp for the big race. The trip was paid for by Angie and
Michelle who are best friends and who had just had 5 numbers on
the lottery together. They had won around £1500 and were over
the moon, I was gutted as it had been a triple roll over jackpot
and one more number would have been £13,000,000.
The races and Paris itself were very enjoyable, the coach journey
or should I say nightmare coach journey was nothing short of a
horror show.
Mark and Michelle live on the same street as us, and it was from
here we went by taxi to Newcastle Central railway station from
where the coach was leaving at 06:00 on the Friday morning.
What we weren't aware of and should have realised when the
coach had empty seats was we weren't going straight to Dover.
The coach had to pick up the rest of the passengers, so we first
went to Middlesbrough followed by York and then Leeds where
the rest of the vacant seats were filled. It was also at Leeds where
the courier joined the coach. Finally we were on our way and
hadn't been on the road ten minutes when she started. There was

an historic building that was hardly visible from the road, but we had to sit and listen to the history of the families that had lived there for what seemed like the last 10,000 years. The coach made three stops on the way to Dover which Angie and I were very grateful for, as it gave us a break from our continuous history lesson. Newcastle to Dover is 350 miles and a 6 hour drive, but because of our pick ups and stops we didn't arrive at the ferry port until after four o'clock in the afternoon and had missed the ferry we were booked on to. Luckily one of our two drivers managed to get us on the next ferry but we still had nearly an hour to wait before boarding the ship for our 90 minute crossing. It was dark by the time we reached Calais so we didn't have to listen to her babbling on as we headed north to the Quality hotel in a district on the outskirts of Paris. It was five minutes before twelve when we reached our destination, it was also five minutes before our drivers maximum driving time ran out, as they had set off from Ayr in the early hours to drive to Newcastle. Before we got off the coach our courier told us the plans for the following day; a guided tour of Paris or if anyone wanted to do their own thing they could be dropped off in the city "we went for option 2".

We skipped breakfast as we were in need of a lie in after the long day we'd just put in on the Friday, and only just made it downstairs in time to get onto the bus for our lift into the city centre; and again she started. This time about the restaurants she'd eaten in on her visits to France and how to recognise which restaurants served horsemeat. "Who wants to know? I don't", the only time I want to look at a horse is in the parade ring or on the racecourse, not on a dinner plate covered in some fancy French garnish.

The majority of us got off the coach at the Arc de Triomphe while a few diehards stayed on the coach to suffer the guided tour. We were getting picked up at the drop off point at 22:00 so we had the whole day to ourselves. Mark and Michelle went off on their own to ride around on the Metro system, while we had a stroll down the Champs-Élysées where we had lunch before going on a river cruise along the river Seine. We met up with them again in Planet Hollywood where we drank cocktails before sampling a few of the Parisian bars on the way back to our pick up point. When we reached the hotel the courier told everyone the coach would be leaving at 10:00 the next morning for the races. She was told it was far too early, but she was adamant and said people were free to make their own way if they wished. We actually considered doing that, but because the coach was already paid for we thought we might as well get on it.

We arrived at the course over an hour before the gates opened, and again we were given options; after racing we could either go to the Latin Quarter where there were a choice of restaurants and bars, or if we wanted we could go to Montmartre to see the Sacré Cœur which just happened to be her favourite sight in Paris. Almost everyone on the bus said they would prefer to go to the Latin Quarter, so she reluctantly agreed that was where we would go.

Even though there was still an hour before the gates were due to open the crowd was massive. The strange thing about it though was nearly everyone in the crowd was Japanese, it was more like we were queuing to go and watch the Japan Cup. One of the leading contenders for the Arc was Japanese horse Deep Impact and they had turned out in thousands to support the horse from their homeland.

The jockeys were mounted for the first race when we finally agreed on our betting strategy; €40 a race, alternate picks, me to go first.

Angie had only agreed to let me go first because I said I was backing Sergeant Cecil (one of her favourite horses) in the first race. Sergeant Cecil obliged winning by 3/4length and paying €2.20 on the Pari-Mutuel which is the equivalent to our tote, and is the only means of betting on French racecourses as there are no bookies. We watched the first race with Mark and Michelle before agreeing a meeting place and splitting up to do our own thing.

We had two more winners that afternoon; Mandesha which paid €2.20 and Holy Roman Emperor paying €2.80 a win.

Betting for the big race was crazy; all the Pari-Mutuel windows at the front of the stands were packed with Japanese. We had been warned earlier on in the day by an American guy who had been racing the previous day where again thousands of Japanese had turned out and he told us to put our bets on early, which we did at a window behind the stands. Because of their obsession there was €1,587,263 placed on the Japanese horse Deep Impact sending him off the 1/2 favourite.

Rail Link trained by Andre Fabre won the Arc, the horse we backed Hurricane Run could only manage fourth, one place behind Japanese invader Deep Impact. Not only did they have the disappointment of watching their horse finish third, two weeks later Deep Impact retired after being disqualified from the race after failing a blood test.

When we got back to the coach the courier was standing with the two drivers asking how everyone had done at the races. We were only about €30 down, but listening to the comments of everyone as they boarded we'd had a better day than most. Once we were all on board the bus set away with conversations mainly in the small groups of people that were travelling together. It was when someone noticed we were passing the Moulin Rouge for the second time the mood on the bus changed. The Moulin Rouge is in the Montmartre district; we had been kidnapped!

As she was in Paris the courier was not going to be deprived of seeing her favourite sight, but what she didn't realise was; the coach was 95% full of racegoers most of which had just done their money in and were in no mood to listen to her twittering on about the Basilica of the Sacré Cœr. Fearing a mutiny on board she wisely redirected the bus.

When we arrived at the Latin Quarter we were told we had an hour and a half before the bus would be heading back to the hotel

as the drivers would be having a long drive home the next day.
As you can imagine she got some grief as people both made their way off the bus and as they got back on after their 90 minute night out.

When we got back to the hotel there were quite a few of us went into the hotel bar where we had quite a good night. We all had something in common now and without realising it the stupid woman had united us all.

The following morning when we got on the coach for our journey home, one of the drivers read out a note that had been slipped under his door through the night. It was from the courier stating she wouldn't be travelling home on the coach due to the aggressive behaviour of some of the passengers the previous evening.

Although the journey home was a long one, it was a quiet one.

Angie's verdict:

I think Dave has said just about enough about the coach, so all I can add is; unless you live in the southern counties or are very fond of long bus rides, this is not the ideal way to travel to the Arc.

I was looking forward to my visit to Paris as the only time I'd set foot on French soil in the past was on a booze run to Calais.

We had a nice day on the Saturday notably the walk down the tree lined Champs-Élysées and the river cruise, though the shops in this area of Paris were very expensive to shop in.

Longchamp Racecourse is quite impressive; I particularly liked the marble stairs of the stand leading down to an asphalt path in front of the running rails, the viewing isn't brilliant from here but this is compensated for by a giant screen in the centre of the course.

There is a panoramic restaurant for which you will need to book in advance as well as a tea room and a brasserie. There are a few other outlets selling chips, pancakes, drinks and sandwiches made with French sticks which seemed to be the most popular snack of the day and must have been selling in their hundreds.

At the back of the grandstand there is a nice seating area shaded by trees, with hedges and lawns nicely cut, in fact the whole enclosure is clean and nicely laid out.

The souvenir shop from where Dave bought me a jacket was swamped by Japanese who were just buying anything and everything, luckily I'm bigger than most of the Japanese women, so at least I managed to get my jacket.

Kids between 6-10 years can join in the fun organised by the Space Children, who have supervised activities. There is also Space Ponies, but I don't know if these are just for experienced riders.

One of the biggest surprises was the admission price; it was only €8 to get in, and apparently prices are double on Arc day.

A very good trip but if I went again I would insist on flying.

Rating: Very Good, Trés Bon. ★★★★★

How to get there:

The French aren't as passionate about horse racing as we are, and most meetings are poorly attended. The Prix de l'Arc de Triomphe is the only meeting where Longchamp can boast a full house. On a typical Arc weekend a third of the crowd will have travelled from the UK. and most of them on organised trips. There are quite a few tour operators offering travel and accommodation with varied prices. If you shop around you will find a package that suits your budget.

If you are travelling independently, I would recommend you use public transport from Paris, however if you do want to take the car (good luck) you can find the course quite easily from the Paris ring road though it will be very busy if travelling on Arc day.

Parking is €2.

In my opinion public transport is your best option, taxis being the easiest.

If you want to be a bit more adventurous you can take the Metro to either Porte Maillot (on line 1), or Porte d'Auteuil (line 10) from where there is free shuttles.

The nearest airport is Orly (12 miles) Charles de Gaulle airport (20 miles) both have transport links to the city centre.

Paris has a wide range of accommodation available to suit everyone's taste.

Thursday 19 October 2006

Punchestown Racecourse
Naas
County Kildare
Tel: 045 897 704
www.punchestown.com

Having already pencilled in the dates for the last four UK tracks
in our diaries meant I could get to work researching the Irish
tracks. Racing doesn't take place every day in Ireland, and with
some of the tracks only having a few meetings a year it wasn't
going to be an easy task fitting them in with my shift work. After
our first two trips to Ireland Angie had asked me to find better
flight times for our return journey than the early morning flights
we had previously used. I actually agreed with her on this; it
wasn't because I minded getting up early, it was more to the fact
we couldn't let our hair down the night before for fear of missing
our flight.
With the winter months fast approaching my concentration was
mainly on the 2007 fixtures, but I did find a couple of meetings
we could quite easily fit in before the end of 2006, the first of
which was Punchestown.
After carefully working out the times of the flights to and from
Dublin, the times of the first and last races combined with the
journey time from Dublin to Punchestown, I reckoned we could
comfortably do it on a day trip. The day trip to Punchestown is a
day trip we will never forget.
Again we flew on the 08:00 flight from Newcastle, and as we had
no baggage we were soon through passport control in Dublin
airport and standing outside the terminal building. With plenty of
time on our hands we boarded the 747 Airport / City Centre bus
getting off at the Central bus station where we checked the
departure time of the race day special going to Punchestown.

Our next port of call was The White Horse Inn on George's Quay overlooking the river Liffey.This is where we'd had a substantial breakfast on our previous visit and decided to go back for a second helping. Breakfast over and still three hours to kill we went for a walk along Grafton Street towards St. Stephen's green. Angie had mentioned she needed a new pair of comfortable shoes for walking the dogs, so this was as good a time as any to find a pair. Amazingly it only took four shops before she found a pair she liked.

I also found the whereabouts of St. Stephen's Luas (light railway) station, as I knew we would need to know its location for a future racing trip.

The time soon passed and we made our way back to the bus station where Angie put her shoes in a luggage locker so she didn't have to carry them around with her all day.

Punchestown is only 22 miles from Dublin and the journey only took 50 minutes. The last race was quarter to six, so even if the bus left half an hour after the last race, we would still be back in Dublin with nearly an hour to get to the airport as we had to check in no later than 20:00, "perfect planning"

We kept to €40 each a race as we had on our previous trips to Ireland.

After nothing back in the first two races and the third race being a very tricky 25 runner handicap hurdle, I was thinking it was going to be a losing day.

Neither of us were sure what we were going to back as we made our separate ways around the betting ring. When we met back up we had both had €20 e/w on the same horse, Clearwaterdreamer ridden by Ruby Walsh and both had taken 13/2.

We turned out to be good judges and my thoughts of a losing day soon cleared when Ruby drove Clearwaterdreamer to the front close home to win by a length.

We put our money together in the fourth race and took the 4/6 on offer for War Of Attrition who had earlier that year won the Cheltenham Gold Cup. It was when War Of Attrition jumped the last clear of the field I realised just how passionate the Irish are about their racing. As he passed the stands to win his race by 11 lengths absolutely everyone young and old applauded a true champion racehorse.

I made it 3 in a row when I had €20 e/w on Matlock Ranger which won the next at 11/2.

We drew a blank in the sixth, but backed the first and second in the last, I had €40 on the winner Stadbrook at 3/1, and Angie €20 e/w on the second, Windy Harbour at 7/2.

€300 up we made our way back to the bus which was already half full, and by ten past six we were only waiting for two people. Andy was all but ready to drive off thinking they had found alternative transport, when somebody said they were definitely travelling back on the bus. It was almost 15 minutes later when they turned up and we joined the queue of traffic making their way home from the course. It was a long slow crawl and Angie was already checking her watch. I tried to reassure her by saying it would be fine once we got onto the motorway, but deep down I was also having doubts whether we were going to make it in time. What I hadn't calculated for in my "perfect planning" was the rush hour. We arrived at Busaras just before twenty to eight, and sods law there were no taxis standing by. Looking back, what we should have done was got off at Heuston station which we passed at twenty five past seven and where the taxi rank was full of cabs. We could have given Andy the key for the luggage locker, and the shoes could have been left at the bus station office for us to collect on our next visit.

Angie rushed in to collect her footwear while I managed to flag down a cab. It was now twenty to eight so I told the driver there would be a €20 tip if he could get us to the airport before eight o'clock. He seemed quite pleased with his efforts and qualified for his bonus as we pulled up at the departure terminal at two minutes to eight. But by the time we reached the check in desk it was two minutes past eight and we were told we had missed the check in deadline. I told the girl on the desk we had no luggage to check in and were only two minutes late, she said it was out of her hands and directed us to Ryanair's customer service desk. We were told there was a strict check in policy and there was no way we could be put on the flight. We were then told we would have to wait until the next day where there were available seats on the early morning flight to Newcastle.

Not wanting to spend the night in Dublin airport we asked if there were any other flights that would get us back to the UK that night, and after checking the schedules she offered us either Leeds/Bradford or Edinburgh. Because the Leeds/Bradford flight was due to depart at 21:10 we opted for that at a cost of €150, which was more than we had paid for our original return flights. Not thinking things could get any worse we made our way to the departure gate. We were then hit with a double whammy; as we passed the Newcastle gate the passengers were still sitting and didn't even look like they were ready to board, and then an announcement to say the flight would be delayed an hour.

So just after 22:10 we took off, arriving in Leeds/Bradford forty minutes later. From the airport we got a taxi to Leeds railway station followed by a train to York and another to Newcastle. Finally we jumped into a taxi to take us home where we arrived at 03:30 having spent all our winnings in the proceeds.

Angie's verdict:

The day had started off really well, a good hearty breakfast followed by a few hours shopping time which had been more pleasurable by the fact Dave wasn't continuously moaning as we made our way up Grafton Street. It was only when we reached the top I realised he had willingly tagged along only because he wanted to know where St. Stephens Green station was on the Luas line.

It had been sunny in the morning but by the time we reached Punchestown racecourse it had clouded over. Luckily we only got a few spots of rain and it was still very warm for October.

There are a number of bars and eating places throughout the grandstand, with everywhere including the toilets very clean. The view from the grandstand is very good; unfortunately there were no races on the Banks course the day we were there as I can imagine they are pretty spectacular to watch.

Disabled people can also enjoy all the facilities at Punchestown. There is reserved parking close to the entrance as well as reserved areas overlooking the racecourse and parade ring. There are lifts to all levels of the grandstand.

I particularly liked the bar we were in on the first floor which has a balcony overlooking the parade ring. The furnishing is also quite unique; we were sitting on stools pulled up to a table that had been constructed from an old turnstile.

It's a shame our day was spoiled by our elongated journey home, but I would definitely recommend a visit to Punchestown Racecourse, and just for the records; "I've still got the shoes."
Rating: Very Good ★★★★

How to get there:

To get there by road; Punchestown is only 3 miles from Naas on the Naas-Ballymore Eustace road. Take the N7 followed by the R410; Punchestown racecourse is well signposted from Naas. Parking is free.

Busaras run a special bus during the national hunt festival at the end of April.

Bus Eirann and other private coach firms have buses for other fixtures.

To get there by rail; Newbridge is the nearest railway station, from here you will need to take a taxi ride the 9 miles to the course.

Trains from Dublin (Heuston) to Kildare and Inter City trains from Dublin (Heuston) to Waterford stop at Newbridge.

Nearest airport is Dublin (30 miles) Ireland has 5 international airports and 7 regional airports along with a number of airstrips.

The airports we are recommending are those that have regular scheduled flights from the UK.
There is a choice of hotels within easy reach of Punchestown racecourse.

Monday 30 October 2006

Plumpton Racecourse
Plumpton
East Sussex
BN7 3AL
Tel: 01273 890383
www.plumptonracecourse.co.uk

By the time we got in the car and set off for our trip to Plumpton, a trip that right up to the last minute was nearly cancelled, we were just glad to be getting away to take our minds off the terrible week we had just been through.

Originally we had planned to go away with our friends Billy and Dorothy who had already been to all the existing UK courses. We were going on a two day trip and were hoping to go racing to both Great Leighs and Plumpton, but with Great Leighs going through a number of setbacks it meant the course wouldn't be open in time for our planned trip. Because of this Billy and Dorothy pulled out, but told us they would definitely come with us once the Essex track was up and running.

Hollie was still quite happy with dog sitting as long as we let her know in advance of our planned trips, and she knew this trip had been planned in for quite a while so she had agreed for herself, Michael and Alex to stay at our house.

The problem was Alex; he had developed high temperatures and was almost permanently crying, and even in such a young face you could see he was in painful discomfort. We took him to hospital where they took blood samples and kept him in for a couple of nights while monitoring his condition. After the second night they were happy to send him home and advised Hollie to give him Calpol to keep his temperature down.

The morning after his release Hollie rang us to say in her opinion Alex's condition had worsened and the Calpol was just making him sick, so she asked us if we could take them back to the hospital. I hadn't even finished putting my clothes on when the phone rang again. On answering it Angie burst into tears; the hospital had just rang Hollie to tell her an ambulance was on its way to pick Alex up as his blood tests had revealed he had meningitis. There are two medical conditions that send the fear of God into families; one is cancer and the other is meningitis, and knowing the horrific complications meningitis can bring on with young children, it seemed like our world was falling apart.

We arrived at the hospital and the ward Alex had been taken to where we saw Michael standing in the corridor where he'd been asked to wait. Hollie was in a room with Alex who was on the bed surrounded by a team of medical staff. The door to the room was open and although we couldn't see everything that was happening, I can still to this day remember Alex's screams. The next few critical sleepless days we spent travelling back and forward to the hospital, mainly to sit with Hollie and Michael as Alex lay with various tubes releasing saline, morphine, feed fluids and medication through his bloodstream in order to flush out the poisons.

After the fourth day the tubes were starting to be removed and the doctors were confident they'd won the battle, but said they would keep him in a couple more days under observation.

On the 28th of October Alex was released from hospital having been given the all clear. Before we left the doctor sat down to have a few words with Hollie and Michael, he told them that Alex had been very lucky as the meningitis and especially the meningococcal septicaemia which his young body had been fighting against carried with it a big percentage of fatalities. They were also told that even though the meningitis was clear his immune system would be weak and would take a long time to build back up. His last piece of advise was for Alex to have a hearing test as deafness is a common side effect (his test was fine).

A couple of days before his release we were sitting talking in his hospital room, the subject of racing came up and Hollie asked if we were still going away at the weekend. Alex who was in his hospital cot playing with a soft toy was definitely on the mend, so we told her we would still go racing but only if we could find alternative arrangements for the dogs, as she and Michael along with Alex needed some rest. Grant was the obvious choice, but soon after Hollie and Michael had moved in with us we were seeing less and less of him and he was now living with his girlfriend Kelly. Kennels were out of the question, and we only knew one more possibility or the trip would be postponed.

A few of the lads at work when going on holiday leave their dogs with Anne who is married to John. John is a work colleague and has been a friend of mine for over twenty years. We rang Anne and told her our predicament and without hesitation she told us there would be no problem, as long as we picked them up again before Tuesday lunchtime when she was expecting another canine lodger to turn up with his suitcase; so the trip to Plumpton was on.

We had a room booked for the Sunday night at the Travel Inn, Boreham, Chelmsford which was originally booked because it is close to Great Leighs, and even though Great Leighs was now a fixture for the future we didn't cancel the hotel booking as we wanted to wake up in the southern counties on Monday morning to give us a shorter drive to Plumpton

On the Sunday lunchtime we drove away, and after dropping Cassie and Zak off with Anne we set off for the Travel Inn Chelmsford where we had a really good nights sleep. The following morning we stopped about halfway through our two hour drive to Plumpton for breakfast and to phone Hollie who told us Alex was getting stronger by the minute.

There were seven races but we decided to only stay for six as we were driving straight home after racing.

We were betting £40 a race alternative picks and me to go first.
So with me having races 1, 3 and 5, I lost £40, £40 and £40.

Angie fared a lot better in races 2, 4 and 6.
In the second race she had £20 e/w at 9/2 on Poncha Train which
finished third. In the fourth she had £40 on the winner Hill Forts
Henry at 9/4, and in the sixth she had £20 e/w on rank outsider
Master T which won at 16/1.
No thanks to me we set off on our journey north nearly £350 in
profit, and after collecting the dogs we went home where we had
another really good nights sleep.

Angie's verdict:

Family has always come first to me, and seeing Alex in his pain
was one of the most frightening experiences I have ever
encountered. Hollie is not only a lovely daughter but an excellent
mum and reacting on her instincts at an early stage of Alex's
condition probably prevented a much more serious outcome.
The trip to Plumpton was a welcome break from our anxiety as it
enabled us to wind down.
My best memory of Plumpton was my 16/1 winner Master T,
when I told Dave what I'd backed he just shrugged his shoulders
saying it was my choice. When they jumped the second last I
though Master T was going to be in a battle for second place.
When they jumped the last and made their way to the post I was
probably the loudest person in the stands as Master T crossed the
line a length in front. It was quite funny, as the bookie that I had
put my bet on with had recognised me earlier in the afternoon and
turned round to the lad standing next to him and said the
Geordies are here. When I collected my winnings he actually
congratulated me and told me I was the only one on his book who
had backed the winner.

There are three enclosures at Plumpton; the members, the tattersalls and the silver ring, the entrance fee to all three include a race card.

The member's enclosure has a restaurant with a view over the course. There is a bar which serves hot and cold snacks as well as a variety of drinks. The stand has both seating and standing areas, both giving good views of the action.

Bars and eating places can be found in the tattersalls where there is good viewing from a stand which also has a seating area. There are toilets for the disabled as well as access ramps in both the member's and tattersalls enclosures.

The silver ring is in the centre of the course and is ideal for a family picnic. There is no stand in the silver ring but there is a bar.

Rating: Average ★★★

How to get there:

To get there by road; From the north, make your way to the M25, from here take the M23 south followed by the A23 towards Brighton come off onto the B2116 from here you will pick up signs to the racecourse. From the south take the A23 followed by the A273 and B2112. From the east the A27 and A275 and from the west the A272 and A275

Parking is free.

To get there by rail; Plumpton station is less than a quarter of a mile from the course and is on the London Victoria to Hastings line which runs an hourly service.

A train to Brighton is another option; from here there is a free bus shuttle on race days.

Nearest airport is Gatwick (17 miles).

There are a number of hotels in the area; Brighton is also a good alternative

Friday 3 November 2006

Down Royal Racecourse
Maze
Lisburn
County Antrim
BT27 5RW
Tel: 48 28 926 21256
www.downroyal.com

With family affairs settled once more and everyone pretty much
back to their normal routine another racing trip wasn't going to
cause any problems. Once again we were going racing in Ireland
on a day trip this time to Down Royal. Learning from the
situation we found ourselves in when coming home from
Punchestown when we missed our check in deadline, I checked
the timetables over a few times before booking our flights.
This was another first for us as we were flying to Belfast which
has daily flights from Newcastle through Easyjet to Belfast
International Airport, and a scheduled 07:15 flight estimated to
land in Belfast at 08:10. We took the car and left it in the short
stay car park at Newcastle Airport, which not only made things a
lot simpler but the extortionate parking fees still worked out
cheaper than taxis to and from the airport.
Hollie and Alex were coming to our house at lunch time as well
as Daisy (Angie's mam) who was going to sit with Alex while
Hollie walked the dogs.
 It was just after 08:15 by the time we got off the plane and
walked through the terminal building of Belfast International
Airport. Belfast has two airports the other being Belfast City
(George Best) both having transport links into the city.
From just outside the terminal building we boarded the Airport
Express 300, a service bus that departs every 10 minutes for the
30-40 minute journey to Belfast Europa bus station in the city

centre. The Europa bus station is quite unique as it is also a train station and it was from the Europa train station we would start the next leg of our journey, a train to Lisburn.

But first things first, we had been up since 05:30 and were feeling the need for nourishment so we went into the bus station diner and ordered two breakfasts (the full works). Although we weren't staying overnight on this occasion we knew we would be stopping in Belfast sooner or later, so after breakfast we went out onto Great Victoria street to see if there were any hotels nearby. We didn't have to look far as there are a few hotels that are very close to the bus/railway station, and one in particular, Jurys Inn which we made a mental note of. We didn't have a great deal of time to look around but enough to get an idea of what was in the area and a few landmarks from which to set our bearings.

After making the 25 minute train journey to Lisburn we shared a taxi with a guy who was also going to the races. We were in November now, the weather was unbelievably warm and there was an abundance of wasps annoying people in the stands. We were sure the bookies would be accepting both Euros and Sterling but we took both just in case. Angie said Christmas wasn't far away so we should only bet €40 a race alternate picks. For a quiet life I agreed though I didn't know what Christmas had to do with it as I had no intention of changing any Euros into Sterling, not even for Santa coming.

Angie got us off to another flying start when she backed the first winner Deputy Consort at 5/2.

After losing my €40 in the second race (beaten a neck), Angie recouped my losses in the third having her €40 on Grangeclare Lark which won at 11/10.

We just watched the fourth race in which the very impressive Iktitaf won at 1/7.

We drew blanks in the fifth and sixth, and I saved face a little when I took 6/4 for Powerberry which won the last.

So at 16:15 and €80 up we started our journey home. Our flight wasn't until 20:55 so we had loads of time to get to the airport.

What we weren't expecting was; the taxi to arrive straight away, the train to arrive straight away and the bus driver to think he was Stirling Moss. We arrived at the airport at 17:40 which meant a three hour wait for our flight. We looked on the departure board to see if our flight was even on it when we noticed another Easyjet flight to Newcastle that was due to take off at 18:20. Taking a chance we went to the Easyjet desk and asked if there was any chance we could get the 18:20 flight. While the girl was making a phone call to see if we could get on the flight we stood and listened while an Irish couple were pleading without success to another Easyjet customer service rep. to let them onto a flight for which they had missed their check in deadline (memories of Punchestown). Our girl told us to go to the check in desk, then without any delay straight to the boarding gate as they were letting us fly on the 18:20 to Newcastle. The amazing thing is the check in deadline for the 18:20 had passed a good 5 minutes before we were told to check in.

Angie's verdict:

As well as going racing it is sometimes nice to spend a bit of time in the places we are visiting, and with it being our first trip to Belfast I would have much rather stayed overnight. There are only two racecourses in Northern Ireland, Down Royal and Downpatrick so our next trip to the North would have to include an overnight stay.

It was a really warm day for the time of year, so we bought two coffees and sat outside the hospitality suite on a bench seat to drink them. Inside the suite was a roomful of people sitting at tables listening to some chap giving his tips for the afternoons racing, and although the windows of the suite were open we couldn't quite hear what he was saying. One thing I did hear him say was he strongly fancied Ruby Walsh to win the first race, so taking his word I backed Deputy Consort ridden by Ruby Walsh which won giving us a good start to the day.

While walking around before racing started we were talking to a young man at a trade stand who was selling prints and Christmas cards of famous horses that he'd sketched. He was from England but told us he now lived in Ireland and spent most of his time going around racecourses selling his work. We talked quite a while about the courses we had each been to before we said farewell and left with two packs of Christmas cards.

The facilities at Down Royal are very modern and everywhere including the toilet facilities is clean and well maintained. There is a self service restaurant, a cafe and several fast food outlets. There are also a number of bars offering a full range of drinks throughout the enclosure.

Because we'd watched the first race from the stands we thought that must be our lucky spot so we watched all the races from there, and even though there were a few wasps buzzing around we had a great view enhanced by a big screen in the centre of the course.   Rating: Good ★★★

How to get there:

To get there by road; Down Royal is best reached by the A1 Belfast to Dublin road.

From Belfast, turn right across the A1 carriageway following the brown heritage signs before Hillsborough roundabout onto Harry's Rd.

From Dublin, take the first turn left off the A1 after the Hillsborough roundabout onto Harry's Rd.

Follow Harry's Rd. and go straight over the crossroads onto Achnatrisk Rd, at next crossroads turn right onto Kesh Rd. which will take you to the course (2 miles).

Parking is free.

To get there by rail; Lisburn station is 4 miles away, from here you can get a taxi.

Lisburn is on the Belfast to Portadown line and regular trains run from both Belfast central and Europa Buscentre stations.

Nearest airport is George Best Belfast City (16 miles) Belfast International (20 miles)

There is a good variety of accommodation in the area.

Thursday 9 November 2006

Ludlow Racecourse
Bromfield
Ludlow
Shropshire
SY8 2BT
Tel: 01584 856 221
www.ludlow-racecourse.co.uk

Angie's mam Daisy who also likes a day at the races, and who always shows an interest when we are planning a racing trip was sitting having a coffee with us one afternoon in our house. We got onto the subject of racing and Angie told her we were thinking of going on one more trip before the end of the year, so naturally she asked us where. When we told her Ludlow she first asked us where Ludlow was and then said "You can't have many more to do now."

We then told her we were going on a two day trip and were also going to Cheltenham on the second day. This stirred up a much bigger reaction, and my mother in law's eyes lit up. She immediately said "book us a room as well," us meaning Daisy and her partner Joe (who also likes the odd bet). When we said do you not think you should ask Joe first, she just said "Oh he'll be alright".

Taking Daisy's word for it and hoping that Joe would be alright I booked two rooms at both the Travel Inn Hereford which is only 25 miles from Ludlow racecourse and the Travel Inn Cheltenham Central. Angie and I had stopped at both hotels before and knew they were okay.

We left our house at 05:45 on the Thursday morning as we'd arranged to pick them up at 06:00, and even though they only live two minutes away from our house we left early as we knew they would be standing at the door waiting for us. Joe was alright, but

271

he jokingly said as he was getting in the car that he was sick of people organising his life for him.

Hollie, Michael and Alex were coming to our house mid morning and were staying the two nights we were away to look after Cassie and Zak.

So off we went on our last trip of the year, starting with a 260 mile drive to Ludlow racecourse. We headed west on the A69 and were almost at Carlisle where we were joining the M6 south when dawn started to break. Once again the sun was rising in an almost cloudless sky and it felt more like a spring morning even though it was the second week of November. The amazing thing was that most trees still had their leaves which were predominantly green and only a few were starting to turn into their autumnal colours.

After stopping for breakfast on the M6 we only made one more stop for fuel before arriving at Ludlow racecourse.

Angie had already bought a few Christmas presents but still had as many to buy, and even though our racing kitty was quite healthy I was still surprised when she suggested £40 and £20 over the two days racing. I had been going to suggest £20 and £20, so without questioning her suggestion I agreed.

In the first race I had £20 e/w at 20/1 on Heathyards Joy which finished a well beaten third. Joe backed the winner Pilca which returned 8/11 but I don't know how much for.

Joe backed the second winner Its a Classic at 4/1, again I don't know how much for.

Angie and I both backed the next winner Ericas Charm, I had £40 at 5/2 and Angie got 3/1 for her £20. Joe told me he'd lost everything he'd won in the first two races on Charlton Kings which finished second. Only he knows how much he lost, but I know it wouldn't have been coppers as he's not frightened to have a go.

Although Daisy loves a day at the races she only bets £2 a race and particularly likes to back grey horses.

The rest of us left the fourth race alone as the favourite was trading at 2/5 but Daisy still had her £2 bet with the tote. She backed the favourite My Turn Now which won by a distance and paid £1.40p a win and an 80p profit for Daisy.

No more returns until the seventh and final race where Angie and I put our money together and had £60 at 7/4 on the winner Lady Roania which beat Joes horse Risk Challenge into second.

So with 58 of the 59 courses completed and over a hundred pound in profit we set off for our night in Hereford, Daisy hadn't lost much and only Joe knows how he finished up. The following day at Cheltenham Angie and I had a cracking day winning just short of £400. Daisy didn't lose much and only Joe knows how Joe finished up, but I was starting to wonder if he really did wish people wouldn't organise his life for him.

Angie's verdict:

I usually see my mam 5 or 6 times a week but I was still pleased when she said she was coming away with us as it had been a long time since we had actually been on a trip anywhere together. We had been a little bit worried in case the bad weather suddenly appeared and spoiled the trip, but as it turned out our worries had been needless. The first day at Ludlow was sunny and the second day although it was overcast the temperature was still well above average for November.

Ludlow racecourse is pretty neat and compact and has 3 enclosures. The member's enclosure where there is very good viewing from the stand or the rooftop viewing above the stand. There are two restaurants in the member's enclosure and even though all but one of Ludlow's fixtures are held midweek I would still recommend if you wish to use the restaurants you book in advance.

In the second enclosure the grandstand or paddock there is a self service cafe as well as a bar. Viewing from the stand is very good though there isn't much cover. There is a viewing ramp for the disabled and disabled toilet facilities on the ground floor.

The third enclosure is the course enclosure from where the best viewing is on the rails, there is also a bar and snack facilities available. We found Ludlow to be a very friendly racecourse to visit.

Rating: Average ★★★

How to get there:

To get there by road; Ludlow racecourse is just off the A49 a couple of miles north west of Ludlow. From the north take the A49 from Shrewsbury and from the south the A49 from Hereford. From the east the A44 from Worcester then the A49 and from the west the A4113.

The course is signposted from both the A49 and the A4113. Parking is free.

To get there by rail; trains from both London Paddington and Euston will take you to Newport. Ludlow station is on the Newport to Crewe line and is 2 miles from the course.

There is a free bus from the station which leaves a quarter past the hour before the first race is due off and returns after the last race.

Nearest airport is Birmingham (43 miles).

Although there isn't a vast amount of accommodation in the immediate vicinity there are still quite a few hotels and guesthouses within a 20 mile radius.

So we ended our 2006 travelling in the same way we ended 2005 with another exciting and successful day at Cheltenham. We'd had some great trips throughout the year, highlighted by our eight course adventure in June and our introduction to racing in Ireland There was still a lot of speculation about Great Leighs; in fact it was becoming a pain in the butt. A lot of people including myself were starting to doubt whether it was ever going to open. We wanted to leave Sandown as our last course to visit, but a decision had to be made so we thought up a plan. Great Leighs had been given a full fixture list for 2007, so we chose a meeting in April that preceded a meeting at Sandown. The plan was; if Great Leighs still hadn't opened by then we would go to Sandown anyway. We'd been pretty successful with our betting in 2006, which I think the weather played a big part in as the long spell of dry weather we'd had gave us consistent ground conditions making the form book a lot easier to follow. I also liked the systems we were using;

Meetings where we were having alternative picks were invariably meetings where one or two horses were jumping out of the paper and where we were quite confident of picking at least one winner on the day.

Other not so easy cards we were backing two horses a race, or one if we both fancied the same horse. Backing two horses in a race obviously reduces your winnings, but it gives you more of a chance of collecting something. Even if you aren't convinced this is a good idea it is certainly worthwhile backing a couple of horses in handicap races where the odds are usually a bit more generous.

Stick to a level stake, though I must admit I have broken this rule on occasions.

Finally, if a horse is 7/2 or greater back it each way.

You are never going to win a fortune, but you will find you will get at least one return at most meetings, we have had some very successful days using this simple system.

Saturday 6 January 2007

Cork Racecourse (Mallow) Ltd
Mallow
County Cork
Tel: 353 22 50210/50207
www.corkracecourse.ie

Looking forward to 2007, one way or another we were going to complete the UK courses and we were hoping to have a good run at the Irish tracks.

I think most people know that the name steeplechase comes from a race between two gentlemen who for a wager of a cask of wine raced four and a half mile across countryside from one church steeple to another. What most people don't know is the famous race that put the name steeplechase into the dictionary was from the steeple of St. Johns, Buttervant to that of St. Mary's, Doneraile which are only a few miles from Mallow, County Cork.

Christmas 2006 hadn't been much fun as I had to work right through the festive season including Christmas Eve, Christmas Day, Boxing Day and New Years Eve. So with a 17 day break starting at the beginning of January 2007 I was ready to start my celebrating while most people were recovering from theirs.

We'd received a booklet through the post which included special offers on hotel rates and among them was the Jury's Inn Christchurch in Dublin which was offering two nights for the price of one. So after studying the fixture list for some time we booked three nights for the price of two at the Jury's Inn which would allow us to go racing at both Cork and Naas. I know you're thinking it would have been easier flying to Cork, but scheduled flights weren't daily from Newcastle to Cork and seemed mainly to fly in the summer months.

Hollie was more than happy to look after the dogs while we had a weekend away and at 09:00 Friday morning our Ryanair flight

276

touched down in Dublin. We weren't racing until the Saturday and had all day to kill so we just took the airport bus into town, had breakfast then made our way to the hotel. We weren't expecting our room to be ready, but the girl on reception told us they weren't that busy after the Christmas rush and our room was in fact available.

After a couple of hours just chilling out in our room we decided to go for a walk. We had no intention of going for a drink as we had to be up reasonably early the next morning to catch a train to the races. It wasn't cold outside but it was wet with the occasional heavy shower of rain. We had only been walking 5 minutes and were halfway through Temple Bar when one of the heavy showers started so we took shelter in the Oliver St. John Gogarty pub. Because we were there we thought we might as well have a drink, so I ordered a couple of vodka and lemonades. The pub wasn't packed but there was a few in enjoying the live music being played by an Irish show band. I was at the bar ordering our second drinks when this guy spotted the Newcastle United crest on my polo shirt. He introduced himself as Justin and told us he'd been to Newcastle just recently with his pals and thought it was a great city for a night out. We'd been talking for a minute or two when this other fellow came over and asked Justin if everything was alright."Fine" he said, and introduced us to his brother Paul who towered over my meagre 6ft. I can't remember who bought the first round but we ended up drinking in their company. It was while Paul was at the toilet that Justin told us Paul was a hero in Dublin and compared his status to that of Alan Shearer's in Newcastle. Paul (Bealin) had won an All Ireland medal playing Gaelic football with Dublin.

After a few hours and quite a few drinks later the brothers said they were going to another pub and asked us to join them. We told them we weren't dressed for a night out, so after hand shakes, hugs and exchange of E mail addresses we parted company; them to the nightlife of Dublin and us to our hotel room via Charlie's Chinese takeaway.

We didn't get up as early as we had intended the next morning so we skipped breakfast at the hotel. Once we were ready we took a taxi to Heuston railway station where we bought sandwiches, pastries and drinks for our two and a quarter hour train journey to Mallow. Another taxi from the station to the racecourse got us there well before the first race.

We still had quite a few Euros in the pot, but because we were racing over two days and the card didn't look that hard we decided on €40 a race, alternative picks and Angie to pick first. We managed to find two winners on the day; Angie backed the first winner Significant at 100/30 and I backed the fourth winner Wins Now at 5/4.

So, slightly down on the day we jumped into a taxi from outside the course and got dropped off at a pub close to the railway station where we had a couple of drinks before catching our train back to Dublin.

We arrived back at our hotel just after nine o'clock and went into the hotel bar for a nightcap before going to bed for a good nights sleep, and the prospects of a good day at Naas the following day.

Angie's verdict:

I know Dave gets a lot of quality time off work, but when Christmas and New Year falls into his shift pattern it really is "Crap", especially Christmas when families are supposed to be together, and because Dave was on night shift meant I spent most of the time on my own. I think Hollie was feeling a bit sorry for me and when Dave's rest days came along she was more than happy to look after the dogs and let us get away for a few days. Although we'd only been there a couple of times we were becoming quite familiar with Dublin city centre, and we liked it so much we often said if we ever came into money we would buy a second home there.

I think travelling by train is the most relaxing form of transport, and the journey from Dublin to Mallow not only gave us time to relax but gave us plenty time to read the Racing Post. This wasn't a luxury Dave was used to as nine times out of ten when we go racing he is driving.

Cork racecourse (Mallow) is in the county of Cork but is actually 22 miles from the city of Cork. When the taxi pulled up at the course I was quite impressed with what I saw, and even more impressed when we got inside.

Being so soon after Christmas and New Year I wasn't expecting many people to be there, but a good crowd had turned out, and the nice thing was it was a real friendly atmosphere and we found ourselves chatting with quite a few people.

There is no shortage of places for you to recharge your batteries between races with bars and eating places in both the old and new stands.

Viewing from both stands is very good, as is the viewing from the rails where there is a designated area for the disabled.

A great start to the New Year.   Rating: Good ★★★★

How to get there:

To get there by road; from Cork or Limerick take the N20, go under the railway bridge at the roundabout in Mallow town, from Dublin or Waterford take the N72 the N73 and take the town park bypass to reach the roundabout. From the roundabout take the Killarney road and it is about a mile to the course which is on the left hand side.

There is free parking.

To get there by rail; Mallow station is just a short journey from the course. Trains from Dublin, Cork, Killarney and Tralee all stop at Mallow.

There are taxis and a free shuttle bus to and from the racecourse. Nearest airport is Cork (27 miles).

Cork is the natural choice for accommodation as there is a huge selection of hotels to choose from.

Sunday 7 January 2007

Naas Racecourse
Tipper Road
Naas
County Kildare
Tel: 353 45 897 391
www.naasracecourse.com

We'd really enjoyed the previous day and our decision to have a good night's sleep paid its dividends, though Angie's idea of a good nights sleep is about two hours longer than mine. So by the time Angie's eyes first got a glimpse of Sunday I had been for a Racing Post, drank two cups of coffee and had a good idea of what horses I was backing that afternoon. The weather was still pretty mild but damp and miserable with rain forecast for the whole day but at least the racing was going ahead.

Once again we'd missed breakfast in the hotel, and after joining Angie for another coffee we got ourselves ready and made our way to the bus station (Busaras). We had considered getting a taxi to the bus station but it wasn't raining at the time so we just walked.

As we made our way through Temple Bar Angie started to reminisce about the weekend we'd been away with Darren and Jane, and said how the soaking wet road we were now walking on had been melting with the heat when we'd been there back in July. It was all a memory now and seemed like a lifetime ago, but as we walked by the Hard Rock Cafe and Paddy Power's bookmakers I too had vivid recollections of our first weekend in Ireland.

We were travelling to Naas on the race day coach put on by Bus Eireann, and with the first race being at one o'clock we thought we had better go to the bus station to find out the time of departure before allowing our hungry stomachs the satisfaction of food. As it happened we had 45 minutes before the coach was leaving, so we went into the Isaac Butt cafe bar opposite the bus station where we had late breakfasts.

Cork races on the previous day had been quite busy, but that was a Saturday meeting which nearly always have the best attendances. Sunday meetings were also becoming quite popular and we were expecting to see a big queue when we went back to the bus station. We were rather surprised to see there was only a dozen people waiting and when the bus pulled into the stand we were still the last ones in the queue.

When the bus pulled out of the bus station it started to rain, and it rained for the whole of the half hour journey from Dublin to Naas. It was soon to become apparent that the forecasters had got it right on this occasion and the rain was in for the day.

There hadn't been many folk on our bus but there was a pretty big crowd at the course, most of whom were indoors sheltering from the rain. Luckily the weather didn't totally spoil our whole day and we managed to find three winners.

We just stuck to the €40 alternative picks that we had been betting the day before.

I had €40 on the first winner Black Harry at 6/4.

Angie had €20 e/w with the tote on the fourth winner Chelsea Harbour, which paid 7.10 a win and 3.20 a place.

Unlike the UK where the tote only pays the first four places in handicaps of 16 or more runners, in Ireland the tote pays 4 places in all races having fields of 16 or more.

I finished off the day backing the last winner Rinroe €40 at 7/4.

It was dark when we got back to Dublin but the rain had stopped and it was pretty mild and quite a nice night to have a wander around. We had been to the bars in the Temple Bar district so thought we would try somewhere else for a change. Temple Bar is very lively; it has many pubs and restaurants and is very popular especially with the younger generation. Nearly every time we have flown to Dublin there has been one or two hen or bachelor parties on the plane, and you can bet your life their destination is Temple Bar. Because of its popularity and just like the popular pub crawling routes in most towns and cities you pay top dollar for your drinks.

A couple of minutes' walk from the bus station, and we found ourselves on Talbot Street where we tried a couple of bars. One of the bars we tried and where we stayed for a few drinks is part of the Celtic Lodge Hotel and had a live band playing. The bar was as lively as most of the bars in Temple Bar; the good thing was the prices weren't Temple Bar prices. With the Celtic Lodge Hotel being so close to the bus station we agreed to give it a try on a future overnight stay in Dublin..

Another handy thing we had found out while we were booking the trip was Aer Lingus also flew from Newcastle to Dublin, and although we flew out with Ryanair we flew back with Aer Lingus who had an early afternoon flight to Newcastle.

Angie's verdict:

One of the main factors that gives the Emerald Isle its greenness is the amount of rain it gets, and although we have been lucky enough to have enjoyed some glorious sunny days while in Ireland the rain is never far away, so go prepared

Because of the weather we spent most of the day inside, but so did everyone else which made things a little bit crowded. The bars were very busy and it was an impossible task finding an available seat. There was a good selection of hot and cold food on offer, but again the serving areas were very busy.

I think the catering staff at Naas struggled to keep pace with the numbers of people that day, and empty glasses and food wrappers were left cluttering the tables and anywhere else people could find to put them down, which made the place look rather messy. Even the viewing was spoiled by the thick drizzle and the kick back making it very difficult to pick out your jockey's colours.

Rating: Average ★★★   I would like to go back on a nicer day.

How to get there:

To get there by road; Naas is just less than 20 miles south of Dublin off the N7. From the N7 take the junction signed for Naas and the racecourse is on the left just before you reach the town. Parking is free.

Bus Eireann run a special bus from Dublin bus station (Busaras). To get there by rail; a train service runs from Dublin, Heuston to Sallins from where you can get a bus the 3 miles into Naas. Taxis are also available.

Nearest airport is Dublin (25 miles)

There are a few hotels in Naas, Dublin is another option.

Thursday 15 February 2007

Thurles Racecourse
Thurles
County Tipperary
Tel: 353 504 23272
www.thurlesraces.ie

I will never forget his words, "Not in this province."

We'd booked flights to and from Dublin, and a room for one night in the Best Western, Park Gate St. Our plan was to go racing at Thurles on Thursday 18th Jan. 2007. On the Wednesday there was torrential rain across Great Britain and Ireland, so I thought it would be wise to phone the course to make sure racing would be going ahead. Why shouldn't it be was the reply I got and when I mentioned the widespread rain he simply said "Not in this province." Brilliant, see you tomorrow was my reply. We were up early the following morning and drank coffee as we watched the weather forecast on Sky news. Not only was it raining everywhere but there were gale force winds across the Irish Sea. Angie isn't a bad traveller but she is very nervous when flying through turbulence, so I asked her what she wanted to do and flying to Ireland certainly wasn't what she had in mind. So we aborted our trip and went back to bed. We got back up just as our intended flight would have been landing in Dublin, and after brewing another caffeine fix, I put the teletext on only to find out Thurles races had been abandoned.

Four weeks later we tried again, the weather was still unsettled but nowhere near as bad as it had been in January. It was raining when our plane took off from Newcastle, and although it was overcast when we landed in Dublin it was dry, so we were hopeful it would stay that way. On the way to the Best Western I mentioned to our taxi driver there seemed to be a lot of taxis on the road. He told us that since new legislation had came out there were more taxis in Dublin than what there was in New York (because a taxi driver told us this I researched it when we got home and found it to be true).

Although our room wasn't ready at the Best Western, we checked in and left our case in their luggage lock up and walked across to Heuston Station to catch our train to Thurles. We had travelled about a quarter of our eighty minute journey when the rain started, and it rained, and it rained and it rained. When we reached Thurles station we boarded the courtesy bus to take us to the course. I don't know whether the bus was leaking or it had been carrying wet passengers before us but the seats were absolutely soaking wet: at least it got us to the races and it was free.

We thought we would try a different approach to our betting; we staked €40 a race each and picked two horses in every race, alternatively having first choice of horses. Before this when we had been betting separately we had often picked the same horse, this new approach meant we were guaranteed to have two horses in every race, and even though it would greatly reduce our profit margin it would guarantee us more chance of winning.

Angie had first choice in the opening race.

We backed the second and third in the first race; I had the second By The Brook €20 e/w at 7/1, and Angie the third Joys Island €20 e/w at 5/1.

Second and third again in the next race where I had the second Ballycullen Boy €20 e/w at 7/2, and Angie €20 e/w on the third Tawnies at 6/1.

Nothing in the third, but better luck in the next when Angie staked €20 e/w with the tote on the winner Jog On, paying 8.60 a win and 1.40 a place.

I had €40 on the fifth winner Templers Hall at 6/4, and Angie €20 e/w on the second Grangehill Dancer at 9/2.

Another winner for me and another second for Angie in the sixth; Sea Diva and Bryansford Belle both for €20 e/w and both at 7/2.

It was one of those days when everything was going right and it continued into the last race when again I had the winner Sophocles €40 at 5/2 (returned 5/1) and Angie again had the second Shuil Dara €20 e/w at 9/2.

So despite the rain and the heavy going we'd had a cracking day, and I know luck played its part but I would like to think most of it was down to good judgement.

By the time we were ready to make our way back to Dublin the rain had stopped, so we thought it was very amusing watching these two old guys putting their waterproofs on to keep them dry when they got on the minibus.

We finished the night off drinking in a couple of bars close to our hotel in Dublin. The following day we flew back to Newcastle on an afternoon flight.

Angie's verdict:

If you are a person who goes racing to be wined and dined, with waitresses serving you a 3 course meal followed by afternoon tea, then your trip to Thurles is going to be a bit of a culture shock. The facilities at Thurles are basic, but if you are like us (what Dave calls proper people) you will be able to adapt to what's on offer and you will find the facilities are adequate, though I would recommend trying not to go on a rainy day.

Once inside you have access to all areas of the enclosure including the two grandstands which give you very good viewing over the course, which in my mind is the most important facility as the whole idea of being there is to watch horse racing.

There is a self service restaurant, a tea room and a few bars, including the one we were in at the back of the grandstand and where the rain decided to join us through a leaking roof.

There is designated parking and a viewing ramp near the grandstand for the disabled.

We met some really nice people at Thurles, and it is another course I would like to go back to on a drier day.
Rating: Average ★★

How to get there:

To get there by road; Thurles racecourse is 5 mile off the main Cork-Dublin road. Come off the M8 at junction 5 onto the N75 continue forward onto the N62 and R498.
There is ample free parking.
To get there by rail; Thurles station is on the line from Cork to Dublin (Heuston)
There is a free mini bus service to the course which is about 1 mile away.
Nearest airport is Shannon (50 miles)
There is quite a good selection of hotels and bed & breakfast accommodation in and around Thurles.

Wednesday 28 February 2007

Downpatrick Racecourse
71 Lismore Road
Bishopcourt
Downpatrick
Tel: 48 446 12054
www.downpatrickracecourse.co.uk

The short walk we took along Great Victoria Street on our previous trip to Belfast helped make the planning for our trip to Downpatrick a piece of cake. We flew on the same morning flight with Easyjet from Newcastle to Belfast International airport, and boarded the 300 Airport Express to the Europa Bus Centre which is only a couple of hundred yards from the Jurys Inn where we had booked a room for one night.
We arrived at the Europa Buscentre before 09:00 so headed straight to the cafe inside the bus station building for our Goldliner breakfast before walking the short distance to the hotel. Angie wanted to have a look around the city centre, so with an hour and a half to kill before our bus was due to leave for Downpatrick, we put our case in the hotel's baggage lock up and went for a walk around. I don't know what women find so intriguing about city centre shops, because to me all towns and cities have the same things on offer. Nearly every corner will be a coffee house and every third shop in between will be selling mobile phones, and the people who keep these enterprises in business are there to be counted.
The next time you walk through a town centre just count how many people you pass who are either carrying a cup of coffee or talking into their mobile phone and give yourself a point for each one, give yourself a bonus point for spotting someone doing both.

Nearly one hundred points later, and Angie not managing to spend any of our money we made our way back to the Europa Buscentre for our bus to Downpatrick and our day at the races. The bus journey from Belfast to Downpatrick racecourse took just under an hour. We knew it wasn't far to the racecourse and considered walking, but not knowing exactly how far it was we thought a taxi would be a safer option. This proved to be a wise choice as we'd only just gone through the turnstiles when it started to rain. We took shelter in the snack bar and ordered two coffees, and while drinking them we started chatting to one of the racecourse groundsmen. When the weather came into the conversation he told us there was a well known local saying; "If you can see the mountains of Mourne rain is on its way, and if you can't see them it's already raining." Thankfully the rain didn't last long and we were all set for a good days racing. Because of the success we'd had at Thurles we stayed with the same system of backing two horses in every race to a €40 stake. (The bookies were accepting both Sterling and Euro, but we stuck with Euro).

I had the first winner Good Company €40 at evens, and Angie backed the third Running Wild €20 e/w at 7/2.

The second race caused us a bit of a dilemma as it looked like it was going to be a very closely contested race between two horses, and this reflected in the betting as they were both trading around even money.

We decided not to have two win bets but went for a €40 straight forecast which we managed to get the wrong way round.

A better result in the third race where Angie had €20 e/w on the winner Mono at 7/2, and I had €20 e/w on the second Jakeups Fold at 9/2.

Another winner in the fourth, and another winner for Angie; €20 e/w on News Item at 9/2.

Nothing back in the fifth or sixth races, but Angie having €40 on the last winner Chestnut Charlie at 3/1 put us slightly up on the day.

After racing and now knowing how far it was, we walked back to the bus station, and didn't have to wait long before our bus arrived to take us back to Belfast.

Once we got back to the Jurys Inn we collected our case, checked in and freshened up before calling into a few pubs on our way to the Indian restaurant we'd taken note of earlier in the day.

Angie's verdict:

I enjoyed my look around Belfast, but could have done with a few hours more but without moaning Dave in tow.

I thought the bus ride to Downpatrick was also quite nice as I like to see new places, even if it is only passing through them. When we got out of the taxi at the racecourse entrance and the rain started, it looked like we were in for another soaking. But as Dave mentioned it didn't last long, and once it had passed we were able to enjoy the rest of the afternoon outside.

The facilities at Downpatrick are quite basic but adequate; there are three bars and a fast food restaurant offering a range of hot and cold foods (including traditional Irish stew) as well as tea and coffee.

A viewing platform for wheelchairs is available at the grandstand.

Viewing from the grandstand is spectacular; I had read that the course has undulations but never expected them to be so extreme. It really is like a roller coaster with a steep uphill climb to the finish.

A course well worth a visit.   Rating: Average ★★★

How to get there:

To get there by road; From Belfast take the A2 to Bangor then follow the signs to Downpatrick. From Dublin and the south follow the NI to Newry then the A1 to Lisburn and again follow the signs to Downpatrick.

Car parking is free.
To get there by rail; Downpatrick station is now a railway museum, so the nearest stations are Belfast and Lisburn which are both just over 20 miles away. Taxi services are available from both.
By bus; The 215 Goldline Express leaves every hour from Belfast Europa bus station and terminates at Downpatrick bus station which is less than a mile from the course.
Nearest airport is George Best Belfast City (28 miles) Belfast international (36 miles).
There is a selection of hotels and bed and breakfast accommodation in Downpatrick.

Wednesday 21 March 2007

Auteuil Hippodrome
Route des Lacs
75016 Paris
France
Tel: 33 (0)1 40714747
www.france-galop.com

I won't even repeat what Angie told me to go and do with myself
when I suggested a racing day trip to France; I think her trip to
Longchamp had left scarring memories.
Easyjet had started scheduled flights from Newcastle to the
Czech Republic, so I was on their website checking out the
flights as I'd always fancied going to Pardubice to watch the
Velka Pardubicka, A six thousand nine hundred metre
steeplechase cross country held once a year and very popular
with British racegoers.
While browsing the site I also found out they had scheduled daily
flights to and from Paris, Charles de Gaulle airport. After a bit
more time studying the French transport network and the French
racing calendar, I worked out we could quite easily travel to
Auteuil races and back home in the same day.
So after printing off the times for planes, trains, first and last
races I put my case forward, and after carefully going over my
figures Angie agreed I should go ahead and book the flights.
A couple of days before we were due to fly we were in our local
bookmakers and asked how to get the Racing Post supplement for
the French racing. They kindly told us they would order an extra
copy and tell the newsagent we would pick it up from the
newsagent's shop.
Because we were travelling back the same night Hollie said she
would come round mid morning to walk and feed the dogs, so
early Wednesday morning we drove to the airport via the

newsagent where we picked up our paper. The 1 hour 35 minute flight got us to Charles de Gaulle airport mid morning and a short walk from the terminal building brought us to the airport railway station.

The queue at the railway ticket office was massive, and we actually stood in the queue longer than what the 35 minute train journey took to get us into the centre of Paris. After the train we used the Metro system to take us to Porte d'Auteuil (the Parisian underground railway isn't too hard to navigate). From the Metro we walked through a subway which brought us out facing the racecourse. As we approached the entrance gates we picked up a free race card from a full rack fixed to a notice board, though unlike our racing programmes these were just printouts on a broadsheet of recycled paper (but at least they were free).

The first thing that catches your eye when looking over the course from the grandstand is the "Rivieres de Tribunes" a spectacular water jump which compared to ours is more like a swimming pool. Water jumps although good for spectators have become a controversial topic here in the UK. A lot of our top trainers have a concern that the unconventional fence is unnecessary and if misjudged by horse or rider can cause serious back injuries to the horse. There are no water jumps at any of Ireland's national hunt courses, and only 16 of the 41 British national hunt courses have such an obstacle. I think it is just a matter of time before they are phased out altogether.

There are two water jumps at Auteuil and the rest of the fences on Auteuil's chase course are varied and real challenging. The hurdle course is also quite interesting as the hurdles stretch the whole width of the track, so a horse running out at a hurdle is totally out of the question.

We'd both studied French at school, but obviously hadn't studied hard enough as the free race card meant nothing to us, so Angie tucked it away into her handbag and brought out our Racing Post supplement.

Before racing started we'd decided to "Screw the loaf" (not do anything stupid) and only stake €20 e/w in every race. Philip Carberry had come over from Ireland and had 3 rides at the meeting so we said we would back each of them, and take two races each from the rest of the card.

Carberry was beaten a neck in the first on Passion Des Bordes paying 4.40 a place.

Nothing in the second.

Carberry was beaten a short head in the third on Pyla paying 3.20 a place.

Nothing in the fourth or fifth.

Philip Carberry's horse O De Montot was going well and challenging in the sixth race when it was brought down at the second last.

I saved the day backing the winner of the last Orgeres paying 6.50 a win and 2.80 a place.

Although the journey home meant travelling through the centre of Paris during rush hour we didn't have any delays. We were actually back in Dudley having a drink in our local social club at 20:40, which meant we'd travelled to Paris, had an afternoons racing and travelled home in 5 hours less time than it took us just to get to Paris when we went to Longchamp.

Angie's verdict:

I can't remember telling Dave to go and do anything with himself, and if I did it wouldn't have been as vulgar as he is making it out to be. Since Punchestown I have been a bit dubious about his planned day trips, but this one turned out fine.

The train journey from Charles de Gaulle airport was quite intriguing; we passed through some really nice areas on the outskirts of Paris, but as we got closer to our destination things deteriorated. Derelict buildings, slum areas, the biggest gypsy site I have ever seen and everywhere and everything covered in graffiti. I know all cities have similar problems, but to anyone travelling this way into Paris for the first time, it would surely kill off any fantasies they might have about Paris being Europe's most romantic city.

Auteuil racecourse however is a different kettle of fish; I can honestly say it is one of the best kept courses I have seen. The groundsmen had the course and parade ring looking absolutely lush on the day, and looking out from the grandstand with the Eiffel tower in the background was quite spectacular.

What really impresses me about the Parisian tracks is how cheap the entrance fees are, Auteuil entrance fees are €3 on weekdays, €4 on Sundays and bank holidays and only €8 for the Grand Steeplechase du Paris which is their biggest meeting of the year. Facilities inside the grandstand include; lifts and escalators to all floors, a panoramic view restaurant, a brasserie, bars and spotlessly clean toilets.

Rating: Very Good ★★★★

How to get there:

Auteuil is literally a stone throw from Longchamp, and if you do have the desire to drive there, from the Paris ring road come off at the exit for Porte de Passy or Porte d'Auteuil.

Parking costs €1 on weekdays and €2 on Sundays and bank holidays.

Taxis from the city centre would be the easiest choice.

The Paris Metro is a good option, Porte d' Auteuil Hippodrome is on line 10, and the course is right outside the station.

Nearest airport is Orly (12 miles) Charles de Gaulle (20 miles) both have transport links to the city centre.

Paris has a wide range of accommodation available to suit everyone's taste.

Leopardstown Racecourse
Foxrock
Dublin 18
Tel: 353 1 289 3607/8
www.leopardstown.com

Easter weekend to me has always meant the start of the warm
weather.

When I was young my parents owned a holiday caravan which
they had sited close to the cliff top overlooking the Solway Firth
at Auchenlarie Holiday Farm, a caravan site near Gatehouse of
Fleet, South West Scotland. Easter weekend was always the
weekend when we had our first holiday of the year, and as my
sister Elaine and I had a lot of friends at Auchenlarie we always
looked forward to Easter. Elaine actually met her husband Tam at
Auchenlarie a few decades ago.

Even now I still look forward to Easter, but more for the warmer
weather than anything else. This Easter weekend however was
going to be special as we had a trip planned to visit both
Leopardstown and Fairyhouse, two of Ireland's better known
racecourses.

Hollie and Michael didn't have anything planned for the holiday
weekend, so once again agreed to stay at our house dog sitting
while we were away.

We had a room booked for Saturday and Sunday night at the
Celtic Lodge on Talbot Street, a hotel we'd found while on
walkabout the evening after we'd been to Naas races and which is
only a short walk from Busaras (the central bus station)

The eight o'clock flight from Newcastle gets you in Dublin just
before nine, which is ideal except for arriving at your hotel too
early invariably means your room won't be ready. We arrived at

the Celtic Lodge before ten o'clock and as our room wasn't going to be available until early afternoon, once again and what was now becoming part of our itinerary we put our bags in the hotel baggage lock up. We made our way to St. Stephens Green from where we were travelling on the Luas (light railway system) to Leopardstown for the first of our two days racing.

We still had a bit of time before it was time to catch our train so we went for a look around St. Stephen's Green shopping mall, which Angie took great delight in as it has quite a number of shops. Once she'd had her shopping fix we went into the cafe on the second floor of the mall for a late breakfast.

We sat at a table at a window overlooking the park and the Luas station where a young boy was sitting on the platform near a ticket machine. I watched him get to his feet as an elderly couple approached the machine, he started pointing out something to them on the ticket machine, then after a few seconds held out his hand in which the elderly man put something. The train came and the train went, leaving the platform empty except for the young lad sitting next to the ticket machine. Once again when a couple approached the machine he went through the same procedure, and at the end held out his hand.

When it was time for us to make our way for the train, and being intrigued by what he was up to, we deliberately went to the machine the young lad was sitting next to. At first he didn't move, but as soon as he heard our accents he got to his feet. He asked us where we were going, pointed out the route on the map, pressed a few buttons then asked us to put our money in the machine. He handed us our tickets, then asked if we could spare him €1 as he didn't have enough money to get home and held out his hand. He couldn't have been more than twelve years old, but not a bad little scam as trains leave the station every 5-7 minutes. So after crossing his palm with silver, we got our train from St. Stephens Green to Sandyford, from where we walked the twenty minutes or so to Leopardstown Racecourse.

While we were booking our flights and accommodation for our trip we were looking at buying our badges online, and although we didn't buy badges for Fairyhouse we did for Leopardstown. The badges we bought gave us a seat on the first floor of the grandstand from where we had great views over the course. One thing that did surprise me was the number of empty seats there was, and after talking to one of the security staff we found out why. He told us it was Easter weekend and a lot of people would be at their holiday homes.

Because we were having two days racing we agreed on €40 a race alternative picks, and because we were on the first floor away from the betting ring decided to back on the tote, I went first.

We got off to a fantastic start to the weekend as we backed the first three winners.

All My Loving 4.90 a win, Arch Swing 1.90 a win and Warriors Key 3.70 a win.

We had one more winner on the day when I backed the last winner, Seasoned which paid 4.10 a win.

On the way out we came to an office where they were selling badges at discount prices for Fairyhouse the following day. The reason we hadn't pre-booked our badges for Fairyhouse was because we hadn't decided on what day we were going. We fancied Monday for the Irish Grand National but were a bit worried about catching our flight home on the Monday evening, so we decided to go for the offer and bought badges for the Sunday.

We took the free shuttle bus back to the train station, and went back to Dublin and our hotel where we checked in before enjoying a couple of hours of live music in the hotel bar.

Angie's verdict:

The only problem I have with low cost airlines is the baggage allowance. If you are going away for a couple of days in mid summer or mid winter you can quite easily make a decision on what outfits to pack, going away at Easter isn't quite as easy. Easter usually means the start of the warmer weather but it can be very unpredictable, so a very careful choice of clothes had to be made both to stay within the baggage allowance while at the same time being prepared for all weather conditions.

The few days before we travelled however had been quite mild and the forecast was for the mild weather to continue over the holiday weekend which made packing a little bit easier, though it wouldn't have been the first time the forecasters had got it wrong. At least they got it right for Easter Saturday and it was a warm sunny morning when we arrived in Dublin, where we spent an enjoyable few hours before going to Leopardstown

Being a sunny day it was a pleasant walk from Sandyford train station to the racecourse, though I wouldn't call it a short walk so if you have any doubts I would advise you to wait for the free shuttle bus.

When we arrived there was a nice couple setting up a stall near the entrance, they were selling racing pictures and prints and I couldn't resist giving them a sale before we went into the racecourse.

The whole layout at Leopardstown is really nice, and you feel welcomed by a very friendly atmosphere. I have read that Leopardstown was modelled on Sandown Park in the late 60's, and like Sandown it is one of the top dual purpose courses in Europe.

There is disabled access around the enclosure, and also a crèche for children between 2 and 10 years old. I personally think if you take your kids to a race meeting you should encourage them to watch the racing with you, as they are the racegoers of the future.

There are plenty bars and eating places within the enclosure, and everywhere including the toilets are very clean.

Viewing from the grandstand is good, and the first floor seating where we were has excellent views over the course.

In a survey carried out on racehorse owners in 2006 asking which was their favourite Irish racecourse, Leopardstown came out top with 20% of the votes.

Rating: Very Good ★★★★★

How to get there:

To get there by road; on race days there are two entrances, one is on Leopardstown road and the second is off the M50 at junction 15 at Carrickmines.

From Dublin take the N11 southbound signed Wexford; turn right at the traffic lights at Whites Cross junction onto the R113 (Leopardstown Rd.). The racecourse is less than a mile along this road on the left.

From the north, south and west; plan your route to join the M50 coming off at junction 15, from here follow the signs to the course.

Parking is free.

There are raceday buses operating from Busaras (Dublin's central bus station).

To get there by train; Blackrock is the nearest station, from here a 3 mile taxi ride will take you to the course. Trains run regularly to Blackrock from Dublin, Connolly.

Another option is the Luas (Dublin's light railway system). The green line runs from St. Stephen's Green, Dublin to Sandyford. From here there is a courtesy bus.

Nearest airport is Dublin (23 miles)

You will have no problem finding accommodation in Dublin; there are quite a few hotels close to the course.

Sunday 8 April 2007

Fairyhouse Racecourse
Ratoath
County Meath
Tel: 353 1 825 6167
www.fairyhouseracecourse.ie

It would have been nice to have gone to Fairyhouse on Easter
Monday for the Irish Grand National, but worrying about whether
we were going to get back to Dublin in time to catch our flight
home would have put the dampeners on it. The Irish Grand
National was obviously top of the bill at Fairyhouse that weekend
but Easter Sunday also promised to be a good days racing, so
after breakfast I ventured out to buy a Racing Post.
Being Easter Sunday and still quite early it took me a while to
find a newsagent that was open, but perseverance paid off and
eventually I got my paper and made my way back to the hotel.
The streets were pretty quiet, but as I reached O'Connell Street
there was quite a bit of activity going on as they were making
preparations for the annual Easter 1916 Commemoration Rally.
When I got back to the room Angie was lying on the bed reading
Tony McCoy's autobiography, so I brewed up and sat down with
the Racing Post to go through the day's runners.
We were travelling to the races with Bus Eireann, and with the
bus station only being a few minutes walk from the hotel we were
in no hurry to get ready. When it was time to go Angie put the
book she'd been reading in her bag which was already pretty full
with her normal racing accessories. When I told her the trip to
Fairyhouse wouldn't take that long so she wouldn't have much
time for reading, she said "I'm not going to read it, Tony McCoy
is riding at Fairyhouse today and I'm going to ask him to sign it."

When we got to the bus station there was already a long queue waiting for the raceday coach, and ten minutes after joining the queue there was as many behind us as what there was in front. The bus pulled in and was soon filled up leaving us about half a dozen places from the front of the queue, but an inspector said not to worry as another bus for Fairyhouse was on its way and would soon be pulling into the bus station. Luckily we were near the front of the queue as again the bus filled up still leaving about twenty desperate looking people who were hoping to spend the afternoon at the races. This time the inspector wasn't as reassuring as he told the remainder he wasn't promising but they were doing their best to try and get another coach. Whether they found another coach or not I don't know, but if we'd arrived at the bus station ten minutes later we too would have been left behind.

Half an hour after leaving Dublin the coach parked up at Fairyhouse racecourse. There were hundreds of people making their way from the coach and car parks towards the course and there were quite big queues at the turnstiles. Luckily we'd bought our badges the previous day at Leopardstown so we joined the smallest of the queues at the pre-paid turnstile and it wasn't long before we were inside and ready for the afternoon's action. Sticking to €40 a race alternative picks, I went first again and had €40 e/w on the first winner, Royal County Star and 7/2. Nothing in the second, but a quick recovery in the third with €40 on Aitmatov which won at 9/4.

We were talking to these fellows who had travelled from Cardiff for the weekend when Angie said she wouldn't be long as she was going to the parade ring to have a look at the horse she was backing in the fourth race.

She was away ages, and when she got back I asked her what she'd been doing. Not saying anything she took her book out of her bag and opened it to reveal Tony McCoy's signature. Apparently she stopped him and asked him to sign the book when he was on his way to the parade ring.

Whether she really fancied it or whether it was because Tony McCoy had signed her book she backed King Johns Castle which Tony McCoy was riding in the fourth race. They seemed to be going okay early in the race, but lost touch with the leaders and pulled up before jumping the third last.

Nothing back in the fifth or sixth races.

€20 e/w at 4/1 on Mick The Man which finished second in the last race meant we hadn't lost too much on the day.

Back to Dublin and a night on the town. The following day our flight wasn't until the evening so we spent the day at Dublin Zoo which is in the North West of the city and close to where Phoenix Park Racecourse was sited until it closed in 1990.

Angie's verdict:

Fairyhouse may not be the house of fairies as its Gaelic name Tigh na Siog suggests, but it certainly does house some kind of magic. I can't remember any other race meeting where so many people were laughing and smiling and really having a good time, it was almost like a party atmosphere and I shudder to think what Grand National Day would be like.

The grandstand at Fairyhouse is big and has a number of bars (which were all very busy) and plenty eating places offering a good variety of food. With there being such a big crowd it was inevitable the enclosure would be strewn with litter by the end of the afternoon, and even the toilet facilities were looking a bit worse for wear.

Disabled racegoers are well catered for at Fairyhouse; all areas of the stands are accessible by lifts and there are a number of viewing areas as well as parking and toilet facilities.

There is a supervised crèche for children up to nine years old and without trying to sound to repetitive, if you take your kids to the races let them share the enjoyment with you. Being a mother and now a grandmother myself I know its nice for someone to take the kids off your hands for a couple of hours, but believe me kids really enjoy horseracing especially if you let them pick a horse and you put a small bet on for them.

Viewing from the stands is very good, but as the afternoon went on we had to be careful as we manoeuvred through the crowd up the steps to where we wanted to stand to watch the action as there were quite a few broken bottles and glasses lying around.

All in all we had a wonderful day at Fairyhouse, though I think they should employ a few more staff on litter picking duties.

Rating: Very Good ★★★★★

.

How to get there:

To get there by road; from Dublin take the N3 towards Navan, after approx. 6 miles turn right onto the R155 signposted Ratoath/Fairyhouse, the course is two miles on the right hand side.

From the north take the N1, N2, and R155 signposted Ratoath. Go straight over crossroads at Ratoath and the course is on your left.

From the south and west, make your way onto the M50 northbound, exit onto N3 towards Navan, after approx. 6 miles turn right onto the R155 signposted Ratoath/ Fairyhouse, the course is 2 miles on the right hand side.

There is plenty free parking.

Bus Eireann run raceday buses from Dublin's central bus station (Busaras).

To get there by rail; the nearest railway station is Dublin Heuston which is 14 miles from the course. There is a taxi rank at the station.

Nearest airport is Dublin (18 miles)

There are a number of hotels in Meath and Dublin is a good second option.

Friday 27 April 2007

Sandown Park Racecourse
Portsmouth Road
Esher
Surrey
KT10 9AJ
Tel: 01372 463072
www.sandown.co.uk

Because we'd intended to make Sandown the last UK racecourse
to visit, waiting for the opening of
Great Leighs had meant us missing several opportunities to go
racing at the Esher track.
At the beginning of 2007 we had made arrangements with our
friends Billy and Dorothy to go to Great
Leighs which was scheduled to have an evening meeting on
Thursday 26th April, followed by an afternoon fixture the
following day at Sandown. Construction of the Great Leighs
course was already eight months behind its intended completion
date and problem after problem kept delaying the grand
opening. So what we decided was; if Great Leighs still hadn't
opened its doors to the public by the date we were due to travel
we would still all go to Sandown on the 27th April.
Although there had been some progress made with the new
course, it was becoming more and more obvious it wasn't going
to be ready in time , so we started making plans for our
rescheduled trip. Long before we knew which racecourse would
be the 59th and last of the UK's courses we would visit, I
thought I would contact whichever course it was and try to get our
names in the race card for the day we would be there. So I rang
Sandown and explained the situation. The lady I spoke to was
very nice, and said she would see what she could do and asked me
to send an e mail giving details, dates and contact numbers. A

couple of days later Angie received a phone call from a girl who was in public relations at Sandown who thought it was amazing that we'd been to all the courses in such a short space of time. She was talking about us having our photographs taken by the press, a radio interview and even a live interview on the day during the television programme being broadcast by Racing UK. She then asked Angie if we subscribed to Racing UK and when Angie told her no, the girl said it wouldn't matter and she would start the ball rolling. It obviously did matter as we never heard any more from her and our 15 minutes of fame never happened, we did however get our names mentioned in the race card.

We could have comfortably driven down to Sandown on the morning of the races, but we thought it would be nice to drive down south the day before and have a night out. Derek and Norma who are friends of Billy and Dorothy live in Essex and were always asking them to go down for a visit, so this was as good an opportunity as they were going to get. We booked rooms at the Travel Inn, Thurrock west, and Billy arranged with Derek to meet up with them on the Thursday night.

With Hollie left as kennel girl we set off on our journey south. As you can probably imagine the main topic of conversation on the way was racecourses, and between us we probably went round them all again. We were all looking forward to our night out, and soon after checking in to our hotel we had freshened up and were having a thirst quencher in the hotel bar before getting a taxi to our rendezvous, the Treacle Mine, a pub in Grays, Essex. Angie and I hit it off straight away with Derek and Norma, and an hour later when we set off for the Stifford Clays Social Club it felt like we'd been friends for years.

Whether it was the good company the night before, the Chinese takeaway we'd taken back to the hotel, the prospects of a good days racing, a good night's sleep or a combination of all we woke up with clear heads. This I thought was a miracle as we'd put away nearly twice as much alcohol as we would have on a normal night. By the time we'd eaten breakfast and sorted ourselves out it was well into the morning, so we set off on our hours drive to Sandown and arrived not long after they'd opened the gates.

I had been told to go to the main reception where there would be complimentary racecards waiting. I was half expecting complimentary badges, that didn't happen but at least we were given the racecards, though if my name had been Fred I would have also been given a badge. BetFred were sponsoring the days racing, and anyone with proof of the name Fred somewhere in their name were being admitted free of charge.

Our betting strategy for the day was £40 and £20, and what made the day a bit more special was it was a mixed meeting of both flat and national hunt.

We couldn't have had a worse good start than we had; we both fancied Arcalis to win the first race but it was trading at 8/13. We decided to put our money together and have £60 win with the tote as the tote screens had it around even money. Arcalis dead heated for first paying 80p a win, so we had £60 on the first winner and lost £12.

Nothing back in the second race, but Angie had £10 e/w on the third winner Desert Dew at 10/1 by mistake. She had been to the parade ring with Dorothy, and when she went to put her bet on she gave the bookie the wrong racecard number. She realised her mistake when she walked away, but instead of going back to change the bet she decided to go with destiny; this time destiny paid off.

Nothing back in the fourth, fifth or sixth races.

We put our money together and had £60 on the favourite, Spume in the last at 6/4 trying to get back some of our losses, but it wasn't to be as Spume finished well down the field.

So we finished off at Sandown our last UK course losing a few quid, but we'd still had a great day. Billy and Dorothy had also lost on the day, but one thing I did pick up on was the number of decent priced horses Billy had backed to win only to see them finish second or third. We explained to him our theory of backing horses each way if they were 7/2 or more, and since that day he has been using the system and having quite a bit of success.

We only had a three mile drive from the course to our accommodation at the Travel Inn, Cobham. After dropping our cases off in our rooms we sat in the sunshine at a table outside the hotel bar for a couple of drinks before getting a taxi. We asked the driver to take us somewhere with a few good pubs close together. I don't know exactly where he dropped us but give him his dues there were a few bars in the vicinity, and I can honestly say they were the most expensive bars I have ever drank in. The funny thing was they were getting more and more expensive as we went along. So before the bank went bust we got another taxi back to Esher, which was a tenner well spent as not only were the price of the drinks more down to earth, the people we met were more our type of people. At the end of the night we got another taxi to take us back to our hotel where the driver told us on arrival that the fare was £15 and tried to justify the price by saying Sandown races had been on. I know I keep going on about taxi drivers, but this one was totally taking the Mickey. I gave him £10 and told him that included his tip; he took the tenner, thanked us and wished us goodnight.

On the way home the following day, we stopped off for an afternoon at Ripon races where we did no better than break even.

Angie's verdict:

Visiting Sandown our last UK course ended a wonderful experience. I know we can go to all the courses again and quite a few of them we have already been back to, but it is a lot more exciting visiting somewhere for the first time as you don't know what to expect. The good thing was we still had quite a few to visit for the first time in Ireland.

The phone call I received from Sandown added a bit more excitement to the build up to our visit, but we soon came to realise they weren't going to contact us again, and it certainly didn't spoil our day.

We couldn't have picked a better racecourse to finish off with, and certainly couldn't have had better travelling companions. The two main enclosures at Sandown are the Premier and the Grandstand; in the Premier enclosure as well as its restaurants there are bars that sell food and a good selection of drinks. The bars in this enclosure stay open for two hours after racing has finished. Viewing is very good from the Premier stand.

The Grandstand enclosure's bars also sell food, but we thought the food court had a better selection; it also has a quite large seating area. If you just want a quick snack while on the move there is a number of mobile catering units. Everywhere is very clean and well maintained. This enclosure also has good viewing of both the course and the parade ring.

It was after Dorothy and I left the parade ring I put my money on the wrong horse, how I managed to do it I don't know but the main reason I didn't go back to try to change the bet was because Barry Hills the trainer of Desert Dew came down from the stands and was standing just a few yards from us watching the race, which I thought might have brought me luck. Thankfully I didn't change it as Desert Dew was the only horse that won us any money all afternoon.

There is parking for the disabled as well as access ramps to all areas, toilets and viewing platforms.

The third enclosure is the Park enclosure which has a family picnic area and a large playground, a crèche is available for children under 5 years of age.

Rating: Very Good ★★★★★

How to get there:

To get there by road; Plan your route to join the M25, come off at junction 10 and take the A224, the course is well signposted.
There is plenty free parking.
To get there by rail; Esher railway station is only a half a mile from the course. Trains to Esher leave from London, Waterloo.
Nearest airport is Heathrow (8 miles)
Sandown is another course with plenty of accommodation in its surrounding areas.

Sunday 3 June 2007

Radotinská 69
Praha 5
Velká Chuchle
159 00
Czech Republic
Tel: 420 242 447 031
ww.velka-chuchle.cz

I had watched the Velká Pardubicka steeplechase a couple of times on television, and when Easyjet started a scheduled flight to Prague the first thing I checked was the date of the big race and how it fell in with my shift pattern at work. Unfortunately it didn't fit in with my shifts, so a trip to one of the world's most challenging horse races had to be put on hold for a future date. What I did find interesting was the Czech Republic has 15 racecourses which is more than any other eastern European country, and one of them Velká Chuchle holds regular Sunday meetings throughout the summer. The other thing I found interesting about the track is its location as it is situated in one of the outer districts of Prague.

Angie really enjoys visiting new places, so it didn't take much to persuade her to have a few days in the Czech capital with of course a day at the races included.

The flights from Newcastle to Prague had become very popular, not only attracting the parties of cultural visitors, but the parties of stags who were out to sample the cheap booze and lap dancing clubs for which the city had become renowned.

We flew mid morning on the Saturday and arrived late afternoon local time; we were staying 3 nights at the Hotel Da Vinci just a short walk from Wenceslas Square in Prague's city centre. A twenty minute taxi ride from the airport took us to the hotel entrance, like all city taxi drivers the drivers in Prague will rip you off if they can so it is a good idea to negotiate a price before you get in the car. It was a nice sunny afternoon when we arrived, but by the time we had sorted ourselves out and were ready to hit the big city it was dark, but still very warm. We called into a few bars as we made our way towards the city centre and couldn't believe how cheap the drink was compared to back home. We ended up in Rocky O'Reilly's, an Irish sports bar where we stayed for a couple of hours before calling into the nearby steakhouse for supper before returning to our hotel.

After a good night's sleep and a very nice buffet breakfast it was time to set off on our expedition, a trip to the races. We didn't dress for the occasion as we didn't even know for certain if we were going to get there as most people we'd tried to communicate with couldn't understand English, never mind our Geordie accents, I had however done some research and knew we had to catch a Metro train on line B (yellow line) to Smíchouské nádraží from where we could catch a bus to the course. Luckily as we were trying to work out how to use the ticket machine at the Metro station (which wasn't far from our hotel), a young man who spoke good English helped us out, and as he was also on our train he told us where to get off.The bus station is right outside the Metro station, and after about half an hour our bus pulled in, number 172, which dropped us off right outside the main enclosure of the racecourse.

Once inside we had a look around and a bite to eat before getting down to the nitty gritty. We were both betting 400 Koruna (about £12) each race and it took a couple of races to fathom out how it all worked, and with the help of one girl who was working at the window of their equivalent of the Pari-mutuel and who could speak a little English we got by.

You can obviously back your horse to win which we did, but you have a number of options for place betting as you can back your horse to finish in the first 2, 3, 4 or 5 with the odds decreasing the more number of places you opt for. The other thing is the odds are displayed on a screen which is changing all the time, just like our own tote screens. The difference over there is once you place your bet the price is secured. I personally couldn't make head nor tail of the race card, but Angie seemed to have got the gist of what it was all about and managed to back 3 of the 8 winners on the day; Mantilla in the first, Ediggio in the third and Cool Glen in the seventh. I didn't go away empty handed however as I backed Shaman which won the sixth.

After racing we stayed in the racecourse bar for a couple more drinks before making our way back to the city centre, more or less finishing level on the day. Angie wasn't too keen on touring the city pubs, so we had another night in Rocky O'Reilly's sports bar. The Monday was a free day, and I knew Angie wanted to get stuck into the shops, but we had been told if we were in Prague we would have to visit Charles Bridge as it was full of street artists and a real treat for tourists. We did go to the shops and we did go to Charles Bridge, but neither of us was very impressed, what did catch our eye just before the bridge was a museum of medieval torture, so we spent an hour in there.
Monday night saw us once again in the Irish sports bar, and Tuesday saw us on our flight home.
Angie enjoyed the races but didn't like Prague so with her hating our time in the Czech capital so much and Easyjet no longer flying from Newcastle to Prague, I doubt we will ever get to see the Velká Pardubicka live.

Angie's verdict:

I was really looking forward to visiting Prague when we first booked the trip, but as it was getting closer to the time to go I was getting more and more negative thoughts in my mind. We are friendly with a lot of people in our village who know we travel around the racecourses, and we are often asked where we are going on our next trip. When I was telling people we were going to Prague, there was quite a few of them told me to be careful as they nearly all knew somebody who'd had a bad experience over there, mainly the victims of crime.

On top of this, about a week before we went we watched a documentary on the escalating problems the Czech government was having trying to keep the streets of its capital city in order. Drugs and corruption were bringing a lot of wealth to the gangs in Prague, and violence and street crimes were an every day occurrence. A taxi driver who was interviewed on the programme said it was that bad that he and a lot of his colleagues carried a gun in their cabs. So with all these things on my mind I just couldn't relax, in fact the only two places I felt comfortable were at the Irish bar and the racecourse.

Once we were inside the racecourse enclosure it didn't even feel like we were in Prague, though the language barrier did cause us one or two minor problems.

There is a restaurant with a nice seating area giving a panoramic view on the upper level of the grandstand as well as a nice bar. The lower level also has a nice seating area that spills out onto a patio overlooking the finishing straight.

There is also a small cafe on the lower level where fast food is cooked to order, and luckily there were pictures of the food on offer on posters so we could point to what we wanted.

The grandstand has plenty seats and is covered, from here you can see right round the course, binoculars are handy here but make sure you know your colours as you won't understand the commentary.

There wasn't a very big crowd there on the day and most people seemed to have gathered in the area close to the parade ring where there were a few mobile catering units.

Rating: Good ★★★

I'd really enjoyed the day at the races and was quite looking forward to shopping on the Monday. The shops in Wenceslas Square include the likes of Marks and Spencer and C&A, and with the food and drink costing so little in Prague I thought I was going to have a field day. Unfortunately the merchandise in the English shops still had English prices and I ended up buying very little.

How to get there:

To get there by road; it is probably easier using public transport, but if you are driving take the main road south from Prague towards Strakonice. About 6 miles from the city centre you will come to Dostihova Street, turn right for Velká Chuchle and after 400 yards turn left just before you get to the crossroads, keep going past the grandstand where you will come to the car park.

There is parking for 400 cars.
To get there by rail; There are trains that run from Prague's main railway station (Hlavní nádraží) to Velká Chuchle station which is a 5 minute walk from the course.
Alternatively you can get a tram (yellow line) or a train to Smíchovské nádraží; from here you get the 172 bus which drops you at the entrance to the course.
Nearest airport is Prague (16 miles).
There is a really good selection of hotels in Prague.

Sunday 8 July 2007

Limerick Racecourse
Greenmount Park
Patrickswell
County Limerick
Tel: 061 320 000
www.limerickraces.ie

We'd now been to ten courses in Ireland, and apart from our night
in Belfast all of our overnight stays had been in Dublin. We'd had
some great nights in the capital, but we were looking forward to
branching out and taking a look at what else Ireland had to offer
and a two night stay in Limerick was a good start.
Limerick is served by Shannon airport which is only 16 miles
from the city; unfortunately there are no direct flights from
Newcastle. So our easiest option was a flight to Dublin from
where we could either hire a car or travel by rail for the 123 mile
cross country trip to Limerick. After taking everything into
consideration we decided on going by train, and once again
leaving the dogs in Hollie's capable hands we flew out on the
Saturday morning to Dublin. A taxi from the airport got us to
Heuston station in good time to catch the 10:00 Intercity to
Limerick Junction from where we boarded our connecting train to
Limerick.
When we arrived at Limerick station the sun was shining and
there wasn't a cloud in the sky, so we were pretty eager to get rid
of our suitcase and get out to enjoy the afternoon. As it happens
we could have walked to our hotel in 10 minutes, but as we didn't
know Limerick we took a taxi from outside the station to our
accommodation, the Old Quarter Lodge on Denmark St. which
also took nearly 10 minutes (ripped off again).
Not long after checking in we were on walkabout, we were in a
city centre it was a Saturday and the amazing thing was Angie
wasn't interested in shopping. This was because I'd suggested we

316

find the location of Limerick's greyhound stadium as we could spend the evening at the dogs which Angie thought was a great idea. The stadium didn't take that long to find, so we walked back into town stopping off at a pub for a cool drink. While we were there the racing was on the TV and the horses were going down to the start for the Eclipse at Sandown. Angie asked me if I was having a bet but I said no as I fancied the Derby winner Authorized to also win the Eclipse but it was too short a price. However Angie did want a bet, so she sent me out to have €20 e/w on Notnowcato, luckily the bookie's shop was just 50 yards from the bar and I managed to get the bet on before all the horses were in their stalls. By the time I got back the race was running and when I looked at the TV screen it looked like the bet was beat. All the horses were running on the far rail except for Notnowcato which jockey Ryan Moore had brought across to race alone up the stands rail. After the race the TV pundits had nothing but praise for the ingenuity of Ryan Moore as he had found the better ground for Notnowcato and won the race by a length and a half, beating Authorized and George Washington into second and third. Whether Notnowcato would have won if the whole field had raced together we'll never know, but Angie wasn't bothered as she had backed the best horse on the day at 7/1.

Her winnings gave us a nice start towards our night at the dogs where we spent the evening standing in the sunshine. We backed 3 winners out of 10 more or less breaking even on what was a great night, which we finished off in a Chinese restaurant.

Sunday morning I was first awake as usual, so I went for a walk to find out how far it was to the bus station from where we were getting the race day special coach later that day and also of course to buy a Racing Post. We hadn't noticed it but the bus station is right next to the railway station and I was surprised at how quickly I'd walked there after the taxi had taken so long taking us to our hotel on the previous day.

By the time I got back to our room Angie was up and ready, so we went for breakfast.

When we arrived at the train/ bus station the whole area was packed with people wearing green and white (Limerick's standard colours). They were there to catch a train to Thurles where Limerick were playing Waterford in the Munster senior hurling championship final. Just outside the station was a mobile unit doing a good trade selling various items in the Limerick colours, we actually bought a green and white braided wristband which Angie fastened to the handle of her handbag hoping it would bring us good luck for the day.

It didn't take long for the coach to make the 7 mile journey to the racecourse, and when we arrived the sun was shining, but one or two black clouds were threatening the afternoon with some rain. Still with plenty money in our Euro kitty we went for a €40 stake each.

The lucky charm served us well in the first race as we both had our €40 on the winner Cloone Rocket at 7/4. Nothing in the second.

We didn't bother with a bet in the third race as there were only six runners and the favourite Quinmaster was 2/5. As it happened the second favourite Field Commander turned the favourite over. Angie had €20 e/w on the fourth winner Hegrid at 13/2. Nothing in the fifth.

First and second in the sixth where I had my €40 on the winner Phelans Fancy at 3/1, and Angie had €20 e/w on the second Arc En Ciel at 5/1. Nothing in the last but we were still showing a profit on the day.

There had been a couple of rain showers during the afternoon, but by the time we'd got back to Limerick it was falling heavily and it looked like it was in for the night. Limerick had been beaten by Waterford in the hurling final, but the green and white supporters who were finishing their day with a few drinks were still in pretty high spirit, and we had a good night in their company before once again going for a taste of Oriental cuisine.

We decided to spend Monday morning in Limerick and to travel back to Dublin in the afternoon to catch our evening flight home.

Angie's verdict:

I couldn't have agreed with Dave more when he said it was time to see more of Ireland, and to be perfectly honest we couldn't have chosen a better place to start than Limerick. We both really enjoyed our stay and even though a Limerick judge had nicknamed his domain "Stab City" we were made to feel welcome by everyone we met in what we found to be a very friendly community. On top of that the prices of things in Limerick were a lot less expensive than what we'd been used to paying on our stays in Dublin.

Limerick racecourse is one of my favourite Irish courses; the Hugh McMahon stand is outstanding, it is spotlessly clean and has all the facilities inside to make your day at the races a memorable one.

As well as the corporate boxes and panoramic restaurant which are located on the top two floors of the stand, the lower two floors have bars and a good range of food to choose from.

There is easy access into the stand via a ramp near the betting ring, and there are toilets for the disabled on each floor.

We watched the racing from a few different spots as we were dodging the rain showers, but no matter where we stood we had a good view. I would recommend a day at Limerick races.

Rating: Very Good ★★★★

How to get there:

To get there by road; the course is on the Annacotty to Adare by-pass.

From Dublin and Galway, drive through Limerick and follow signs for the N20 (Cork, Tralee and Killarney). On the outskirts of Patrickswell turn left at the first roundabout, straight over the second roundabout and the course is half a mile on the left.

From Cork follow the signs for the N20 towards Limerick. After Croom follow signs for Limerick and turn left onto the new road, at the end of the road turn right towards Crecora go straight over the roundabout and the course is half a mile on the left.

Parking is free.

To get there by rail; Limerick station which is 7 miles from the course can be reached via various routes.

Buses run from the station to the course on race days.

Nearest airport is Shannon (24 miles).

There are plenty of hotels to choose from in Limerick.

Tuesday 7 August 2007

Roscommon Racecourse
Racecourse Road
Roscommon
County Roscommon
Tel: 353 903 26231
www.roscommonraces.ie

It was coming up to my seventeen days off from work again, and the nice thing was it was the beginning of August. The way my shift pattern works means I get a minimum of five seventeen day breaks a year, and these long breaks were the ideal time to knock a few courses off our "to do" list. Hollie was aware of this and when it was coming up to my seventeen off she would ask us what days she would be required to look after the dogs. The Irish fixture list for the first week of my break had five consecutive evening race meetings at tracks we hadn't yet been to. The five meetings were scattered all over Ireland but it was too good an opportunity to miss, and with Hollie happy to fall in with any plans we might have I set to work planning the trip.

With the help of Andy, a learned ex Royal Navy work mate of mine, we planned the routes and found the accommodation for what was going to be a zigzag trip around Ireland. Because they were all evening meetings it made things a bit easier, but careful choice of accommodation was essential. We needed to find Hotels or Guest Houses as close as possible to the courses, as I didn't want to take the car we were going to hire to the races as I fully intended having a drink.

When planning a route in the UK you simply enter the post codes of your starting and finishing points into the AA route planner and it will give you directions to the doorstep of your chosen destination. With Ireland not having a postal code system you can't be so exact, so detailed street maps and an Irish road atlas were also essentials for our trip.

So with everything we needed for the trip filed together and the dogs in safe hands we flew to Dublin on our usual 08:00 Ryanair flight on the Tuesday morning. When we arrived at Dublin airport we made our way to Hertz car rental and picked up our hire car a Toyota Yaris and set off on our mission.

The first of the five meetings was at Roscommon where we had a room booked at the Gardens Guest House, situated at the Walk, Roscommon which is just over a mile from the course. En route we made one stop for breakfast at Enfield which wasn't the brightest of moves; the breakfast was fine but we'd pulled off a toll road to get to Enfield and had to pay to get back onto it to continue our journey.

We reached our accommodation early afternoon and after a couple of hours relaxation we set off walking to the racecourse on what was a hot sunny summer evening. I can remember as we were walking up the road passing a nice bungalow with a large garden. Sitting at the front door of the bungalow was a huge German Shepherd who was watching our every move, looking like he was ready to pounce if we decided to invade his territory. It brought to mind a sign I'd once seen that was posted in a farmer's field occupied by a bull, it read; MAYBE YOU CAN CROSS THIS FIELD IN 12 SECONDS, THE BULL CAN DO IT IN 10.

We arrived at the course in good time and joined a good crowd who had turned out to enjoy the sport in the glorious sunshine. Even though our Euro kitty was doing very well we were going to five meetings so we reduced our stakes to €20 each a race. We enjoyed our evening but it wasn't a brilliant night as far as betting was concerned as we only had two returns between us on the night.

I had €10 e/w on the second winner Newparks Doughter at 5/1 and Angie had €20 on the last winner Paco Jack at 9/4.

We'd had a couple of drinks at the races and fully intended going into town for a couple more, but it had been a long day and by the time we'd walked back down the road we thought an early night was a better idea.

Angie's verdict:

Maybe it was just a psychological thing because we were starting our 5 night trip by flying, but this one felt more like we were going away for a holiday. That was until the Wednesday morning when we brought the luggage downstairs. We'd put our two cases next to the front door while waiting for our taxi to arrive, and I was putting one or two last minute items in our hand luggage when Dave handed me a road atlas and a thick folder containing route plans and street maps. We'd never hired a car in Ireland before, and most of our time in Ireland had been amongst the hustle and bustle of Dublin, so as you can imagine when he handed me this pile of papers I thought I was in for a nightmare of a trip.

This didn't turn out to be the case, as once we got away from the airport and the boundaries of Dublin not only were the roads a lot quieter they were easy to navigate making the journey quite enjoyable. The street map of Roscommon was also very useful as it helped us find our accommodation without any fuss.

Roscommon is another racecourse set in a lovely location, and the sun shining made it all the better. One of the nice things I have found about the Irish courses is the people we have spoken to have always been warm and friendly, and Roscommon was no exception as we met some really nice people that evening.

The enclosure isn't very big but is nicely laid out; there are three bars and hot and cold food is available from the self service restaurant and snack bar.

We don't usually stay in the same place when watching the racing, but we watched all the races from the stand that night from where the viewing is very good. There is a designated viewing area and toilet facilities for disabled racegoers.
Rating: Average ★★★

How to get there:

To get there by road; from Dublin take the N4 then follow signs onto the N6, come off at junction 12 onto the N61. From Cork the N6, M8, N62 and N61. From Galway the N6, N17 and N63. Once in Roscommon take the N60 towards Castlebar and the course is about a mile on the left hand side.
Parking is free.
To get there by rail; trains from Dublin Heuston go to Roscommon station from where you can get a taxi to take you to the course which is less than 2 miles.
Nearest airport is Galway (46 miles).
There is a nice selection of accommodation in Roscommon to choose from.

Wednesday 8 August 2007

Sligo Racecourse
Cleveragh
Sligo
County Sligo
Tel: 353 71 62484
www.countysligoraces.com

Wednesday morning we joined a couple of nice gentlemen from Dublin at the breakfast table. It so happened that not only had they been to the races at Roscommon the evening before, but like us they were driving to Sligo after breakfast where they were having a game of golf before going to the races in the evening. We left Roscommon shortly after breakfast to drive the 53 miles to the Sligo City Hotel, our next port of call. Once again the weather had been kind to us as we pulled up in the hotel car park in glorious sunshine. Not wanting to miss any of the fine weather, Angie quickly unpacked our cases and we went for a stroll around town. We stopped for a coffee at a cafe which had a terraced seating area where we sat watching the world go by. We'd been there about twenty minutes and were nearly finished our second coffee when the sky darkened and down came the rain. We made our way back to the hotel via a couple of shops which Angie couldn't resist going into for a look around, then spent the rest of the afternoon in our room until it was time to go racing.

We had a pretty good idea where the racecourse was as we'd seen road signs that morning when we drove into Sligo, and although the sun was back out and we had plenty of time to get there we thought it was a bit too far to walk so we went by taxi. The driver took a different route to the road we'd come in on and it actually wasn't as far as what we'd thought.

We arrived at the course over an hour before the first race so Angie suggested we should go for something to eat. Even though we'd had nothing to eat since breakfast I wasn't hungry, but Angie said she needed something so said she would go and buy a sandwich. While she was away I wandered over to the mobile Tote betting shop and because I was there I thought I might as well have a bet. The runners were down at the start for a race that was being televised from Pontefract. After quickly looking through the field in my Racing Post I went to put €40 on Divine Spirit which had won its previous two races only to be told it was a non runner. The horses were starting to go behind the stalls so after another quick glance at my paper I put my €40 on The History Man. Angie by this time had bought herself a sandwich and a drink and came over to see what I was doing, I told her I'd had a bet in the race that was just about to start, but she was more interested in her sandwich and told me she'd be on the grass down by the running rail. It was a photo finish which The History Man was involved in, and although it was only a couple of minutes before my horse was confirmed as the winner it was over half an hour before the Irish Tote could confirm the win dividend. The History Man paid 13.90 a win giving me a return of €556 which more than covered our €20 each stakes at Sligo that night. Nothing back in the first two races.

I had €20 at 100/30 on Incline which won the third race.

We both backed Tai Lass which won the fourth and both took 5/2.

Nothing in the fifth, but we both backed the last 2 winners; Spaxdotcom at 4/6 and The Chip Chopman at 9/4.

After racing and now knowing how far it was we walked back into town over €650 in profit. We called into one or two bars, and in one we got into a conversation with this lady who lived in Sligo who was out for a couple of drinks with her father. I can't remember how it came into the conversation but she asked us our surname, when we told her it was Conroy she said the Conroys came from the west of Ireland. I looked this up when we got home and according to the web site I found, the Conroys come from Galway.

Angie's verdict:

Unlike the previous morning and with a new found confidence in my navigational skills I was quite looking forward to our drive from Roscommon to Sligo. The journey itself took just over an hour, but with the sun shining and passing through some really scenic countryside it gave me a big lift to the start of my day. The few rain showers we'd had in the afternoon had passed over and the sun was out again by the time we went racing, even the grass was dry enough to sit on. We bumped into one of the gentleman we'd met at breakfast near the parade ring and he told us they had been soaked to the skin while playing golf in the afternoon.

I have often mentioned racecourses in scenic locations, and Sligo has to be up amongst the best of them. What made it even better was the sun had moved to the west and was shining on the cliff faces in the background as we looked over the course making it a pretty spectacular view.

The facilities at Sligo racecourse are basic but suffice; there is a spacious bar and a self service restaurant/snack bar selling hot and cold foods. The people are very friendly and everywhere is nice and clean.

Viewing from the stand is good, but we enjoyed watching from the grassy slope overlooking the finishing straight. It was while we were standing on the grass that three young boys stopped close to us and were discussing the horses running in the third race. One of them, who looked the oldest and was no more than twelve years old had just backed the second winner Dearg which had won at 14/1. He was telling his two disciples that his father had told him Dearg had no chance and after it had won how he'd told his parent to go and sniff the daisies. As they were walking

away he was talking about putting all his winnings which I presume was €70 on the next race, while his two younger followers were pleading with him to stick to a €5 stake.
Rating: Average ★★★

How to get there:

To get there by road; from the south, on the approach to Sligo exit onto the R287 and follow signs for Sligo town, after first set of traffic lights turn right.
From Donegal, cross Hughes bridge and continue on the old road through Sligo via the cathedral.
From Enniskillen, take the first right at the traffic lights after Sligo Institute of Technology and join the main Sligo/ Donegal road, turn left and cross Hughes bridge and continue on the old road through Sligo via the cathedral.
Parking is free.
To get there by rail; Trains run from Dublin (Connolly) to Sligo station which is just over a mile from the course. Taxis are available from the station.
Nearest airport is Knock (34 miles).
There is plenty accommodation to be found in Sligo.

Tipperary Racecourse
Limerick Junction
Tipperary
County Tipperary
Tel: 353 62 51357
www.tipperaryraces.ie

Thursday morning and I opened the curtains only to see the rain was back. Before going down for breakfast we had a coffee in our room and switched on the news channel to get the weather predictions for the rest of the day. It didn't look good as the forecasters were predicting heavy rain throughout the day turning to showers in the evening.

After breakfast we packed the car and drove out of Sligo, our destination Limerick. I chose Limerick for our overnight stay for two reasons; first because we'd really enjoyed our previous two night stay in Limerick, and secondly it is only a short train ride from Limerick station to Limerick Junction which is right next to Tipperary racecourse.

The first time we noticed Tipperary racecourse was when we were on the train going to Mallow (Cork). Our train had stopped at Limerick Junction and we noticed some running rails and we quickly realised it was a racecourse. I asked the conductor which course it was and he told us it was the junction course. We had never heard of the junction course so we looked it up when we got home and found out that up until 1986 Tipperary racecourse was called Limerick Junction racecourse.

It rained for the majority of our 142 mile drive from Sligo to Limerick, but by the time we reached our hotel the rain had stopped. There hadn't been anything wrong with our accommodation on our last stay in Limerick, but this time we stayed the night in the Jurys Inn which is close to the river, and even though we could see the mighty Shannon from our room, some of the other rooms in the hotel would have had much better views.

After checking in and unpacking the cases there were still a few hours before we needed to head to the railway station for our train to the races. I would have been quite happy just lazing around in the hotel room but Angie thought it would be a good idea to have another look around the shops. It had only been a month since we last had a look around the shops in Limerick so I didn't know what she was expecting to be so different in such a short space of time. As it happens Angie didn't actually buy anything but I did; there are quite a few charity shops in Limerick and I think charity shops are great places to buy second hand books. I enjoy reading Dick Francis and John Francome novels and have nearly all their publications. I have bought one or two from book shops and some I have been given as gifts, but most of them I have picked up in charity shops.

Happy with my purchases we went for something to eat before returning to our hotel room to get ready for our evening at the races.

As we were walking from our hotel to the railway station we had to take shelter from a heavy rain shower. While we were there we even considered going back to the hotel for the car and driving to the races, but the shower passed over and we managed to get to the station without getting wet. Half an hour on the train and just a few minutes walk from the railway station and we were at the main entrance to the racecourse.

After the profitable night we'd had at Sligo and a quick read through the race card I was quite confident we would be building on our Euro kitty that evening. We were well in profit after our first two nights racing, but even though confidence was high we still had three meetings before the end of our trip so we stuck to our €20 stakes.

We did watch a couple of races from outside as the rain had stopped, but the temperature was well below what you would expect in August so we spent most of the evening indoors. Our confidence in backing winners gradually faded as race by race we managed to go through the card without a return. Although you do feel despondent in these situations you know you are going to have your share of bad days at the races. It's the bad days that make the good days feel even better, and you must remember the bookies are also out to win a few quid and you never see them turning up for the races on a pushbike. After racing we knew exactly where we were going for consolation; back to Limerick for a few drinks and a meal in the Chinese restaurant.

Angie's verdict:

It really did seem a long way to Tipperary; it's no fun travelling in bad weather and by the time we reached Limerick I was pretty much exhausted. It's not that I'm a bad traveller, I would call it more a nervous traveller which I think is the result of a motorbike accident I had when I was younger which put me in traction for eight weeks. A combination of the roads which we weren't accustomed to being wet, and statistically more road accidents occurring in wet conditions made the journey for me not a pleasant one.

Like Dave I thought our good luck from the previous night would continue, unfortunately it didn't but that's life and I can cope with that. What I couldn't cope with was being dressed in summer clothes in almost winter conditions; I was freezing cold which totally spoiled my night at Tipperary races.

There is a self service restaurant with quite a nice selection of food and a couple of bars where you can buy snacks as well as drink. I think a lot of people opted for the warmth of being inside that night but we weren't cramped for room and there was a nice friendly atmosphere.

The track itself is very flat over which you get very good views from both the stand and the running rails.

Disabled racegoers will find easy access around the enclosure where there are disabled toilet facilities and a viewing area.

Tipperary is a good course for a family outing as there is entertainment for the kids on Sunday and evening meetings.

Another track I would like to go back but in better weather conditions.

Rating: Average ★★★

How to get there:

To get there by road; the racecourse is about 2 miles outside Tipperary, from Limerick follow the N24 (approx. 22 miles).

From Dublin take the M7 then N8, at junction 9 take the N74 into Tipperary and continue forward onto the N24.

Parking is free.

To get there by rail; regular trains running from Dublin (Heuston) to Cork stop at Limerick Junction. The course is a short walk from the station.

Nearest airport is Shannon (38 miles).

There are a few hotels closer including the Ballykisteen Hotel which is right next to the course, but Limerick is also an option.

Friday 10 August 2007

Sports Wexford Ltd.
5 Selskar Street
Wexford
County Wexford
Tel: 353 53 4342
www.wexfordraces.ie

Friday morning and thankfully the rain had gone, there were still a few dark looking clouds in the sky but over all it didn't look too bad. We'd had a miserable night at Tipperary on all counts, and not managing to get even one return on the night had left a pretty big dent in our profit margin. But that was all in the past and we still had two more meetings to go to so there was plenty of time to make amends.

We had a three hour drive in front of us but we were both up pretty early, so after breakfast we went for a walk along by the river and found a shop to buy a Racing Post before packing the car and driving off to our next destination.

Our next stop was Wexford where we had a room booked at Townparks House, a Guest House in Coolcotts which is a very nice estate just outside Wexford town and just walking distance from the racecourse.

After the almost treacherous conditions we'd driven through on the previous day the drive to Wexford was a pleasurable one, and without any hold ups or delays we had reached Coolcotts and had been shown to our room by early afternoon.

I didn't even have to ask Angie what she fancied doing to kill a bit time before it was time to go racing because as soon as she had finished unpacking she put her jacket on; we were heading for the town centre.

By this time the skies had cleared and the sun was out and even though there was a slight breeze coming off the sea it was warm

333

and had turned into a really nice day. After a late lunch the rest of the afternoon passed quickly as we spent our time walking around the shops and before we knew it we were making our way back to the Guest House to get ready for what was going to be a great night at the races. Though to be perfectly honest if we'd managed to get our money back from one race it would have been a great night compared to the night before.

It was only a ten minute walk to the course and we were soon ready for the evening's action. We were sticking to our agreed €20 each a race, but we also decided to have a placepot between us, something we hadn't done for a while. The plan was to pick a horse each in every race and cross them to a €2 stake, a total of 32 bets and a stake of €64, Angie to have first pick in races 1,3 and 5 and me in races 2,4 and 6.

A great start to the evening when I had €10 e/w on the first winner Lupita at 8/1, and Angie had €10 e/w on the third Lookingforanalibi at 5/1.

We didn't get a return in the second race but the fourth horse First Symphony kept us in the placepot.

Another winner in the third when I backed North Shore €20 at 13/8.

Angie had the fourth winner Fiery Lord, €10 e/w at 7/1.

Another winner for Angie in the fifth, €10 e/w on Mudslinger at 6/1.

Three in a row for Angie with €20 on Farmer Brown at 8/13 in the sixth.

Nothing back in the last race, but not only did we have 5 winners between us we had the placepot up for €4.

The dividend paid €108.10 giving us a total profit on the evening of around €500.

After racing we walked into town where we went through our routine celebrations.

Saturday morning the rain was back and the landlady told us the forecast was for rain all day. Our last destination was Kilbeggan where we were stopping at Seber House, the only Guest House in Kilbeggan.

The journey I can only describe as wet and miserable and if anything the rain was getting heavier as the day went on. Once in Kilbeggan we had lunch then drove to the racecourse (just to find out its location).

When it was time to go racing we considered going by taxi but ended up taking the car. The racecourse car park was already quite full when we drove through the entrance gates and still the rain was coming down. One of the car park attendants flagged us down and told us we'd be better off turning round and going home as they were holding an inspection and racing was sure to be cancelled. So we took his advice and drove back to the Guest House and sure enough racing was abandoned for what we were told was the first time in over forty years.

Angie's verdict:

The more I was seeing of Ireland the more I liked it, and I really think Wexford is a nice town even though it is a bit hilly. We often said if we ever won a lot of money we would buy a second home in Ireland, but to be honest I wouldn't know where to buy one as there are so many nice places to choose from.

Thankfully the temperature seemed a good 10 degrees higher than it had been at Tipperary and we were able to enjoy our night at Wexford races standing outside.

We watched all the races that night from the stand from where the viewing is very good. We are both very superstitious people and followed the same routine for every race; we watched each race from the exact same spot then moved to the same location near the parade ring where I poured us a drink before placing our bets and moving back to our viewing position. It might seem a bit foolish but we often follow this type of routine and we did after all back 5 winners.

Wexford racecourse is another course we found to have a nice friendly atmosphere, there are a few bars, a carvery restaurant and a cafeteria selling hot and cold drinks and snacks as well as a few mobile catering units.

There is a viewing stand and toilet facilities available for the disabled.

Rating: Good ★★★

How to get there:

To get there by road; from Dublin get onto the N11 and continue all the way to the New Ross Roundabout (90 miles) at roundabout take the first exit onto the R769.

From Cork take the N8 then the N25. Follow N25 through Waterford until you come to the New Ross Roundabout and exit onto the R769.

Parking is free.

To get there by rail; trains run from Dublin (Connolly) to Wexford station which is a mile and a half from the course. Taxis are available at the station.

Nearest airport is Waterford (41 miles).

There is a good range of accommodation to be found in Wexford.

Laytown Racecourse
Laytown Strand
County Meath
Tel: 353 41 984 2111
For more information visit www.goracing.ie

Laytown races take place once a year usually early September, but it's amazing how many people know of its existence. In fact I wish I had a tenner for every time someone has asked us "Have you been to the one on the beach." Although not many of them can remember Laytown by name, they had nearly all watched the beach racing on BBC's Coast. Coast is a very popular documentary series telling interesting facts and stories as it follows the coastlines of Great Britain and Ireland. The programme on Ireland's east coast which had a feature on Laytown obviously had an impact on a lot of people.

With racing being held only one day a year it was hitty missy whether it would fall in with my shift pattern, but September 6th fell right in the middle of my days off work so the trip was on. We were staying overnight in our old haunt Dublin, and once again booked a room at the Celtic Lodge on Talbot Street, which is not only close to the bus station (Busaras) but is also close to Connolly Railway Station from where we were taking the train to Laytown.

The platform for Laytown was almost full by the time the train pulled into the station, but we managed to find a seat and were soon on our way to "The one on the beach."

Because of its location Laytown is very exposed to the elements, but we hit lucky as we arrived at the seaside town on a hot sunny day with not a breath of wind. This made the fifteen minute walk from the station very pleasant, in fact we walked most of it along the beach.

Horse racing is a lot of fun and Laytown's beach racing may seem like a bit of a novelty, but both the racing committee at Laytown and indeed the Irish Horseracing Authority take it very serious and strict safety measures must be adhered to.

There are a few interesting facts about Laytown races;

Laytown is the last surviving beach racing held professionally under rules in the world.

Races are held over a straight 6 or 7 furlongs, but the course used to be run on a U-bend until 1994 when a horrific pile up meant strict safety changes had to be made. As well as changing to a straight course other changes included a limited number of runners (10) ridden only by experienced jockeys.

The course has flagged poles at the furlong markers with only the final furlong having a running rail.

The time of the first race is totally dependant on the tide being fully out.

It may be a flat meeting but some of Ireland's top national hunt jockeys will be seen riding at Laytown, even Ruby Walsh was riding the day we were there.

Living in the north east we might not get the best weather in the UK, but we are blessed with some of the sandiest beaches with really soft sand. So when we walked the few hundred yards along the beach at Laytown we were surprised how firm it was, so with this as our guide and the going officially standard we agreed on €40 each a race.

We both had €20 e/w on Paris Sue in the first race which finished third at 9/2.

In the second race I had €20 e/w on Daramas which finished second at 7/2.

We both had €40 on the third winner Moon At Midnight at 6/4. Nothing in the next two races but I finished off a thoroughly enjoyable afternoon with €40 on the last winner Collingwood at 3/1 which just about broke us even on the day.

After racing we joined the crowds and walked back along the road towards the railway station, but we were in no rush to get back to Dublin and the trains were pretty regular, so we thought it would be nice to stay in Laytown for another hour or two. We'd passed a couple of bars on our way from the station to the races and it seemed only right that we should try them out. The first one we came to which if I remember correctly is called the Seaview Bar (for obvious reasons). The bar itself was quite busy, so we bought our drinks and took them round the back of the building where we sat on the grass just a couple of yards from the beach. During the afternoon we had been among thousands watching the racing, and just an hour later there was only us with not another person in sight. We had a couple of drinks in our romantic setting before heading to the next pub, the Cottage Inn which is quite close to the station. It was still a lovely warm evening so we went into the beer garden which was crammed and where we had no chance of finding a seat. It was a great atmosphere though, so we stayed a while before catching our train back to Dublin.

When our train pulled into Connolly Station Angie said she needed the toilet and couldn't wait until we got back to our hotel. We crossed the road and went into the bar of the North Star Hotel, and while Angie was away relieving the pressure from her bladder I ordered our drinks. We actually stayed for a few followed by our evening meal, and afterwards both agreed we would book a room at the North Star on our next overnight stay in Dublin.

Angie's verdict:

Most people enjoy a trip to the seaside even the dogs get very restless in the back of the car when they smell the sea air and sense they are going to have a run on the beach. But to combine a day at the beach with a day at the races is something that has to be experienced to appreciate.

I must however touch again on something Dave has already mentioned, "The Weather." Trips to the seaside are usually planned last minute on hot sunny days, but the show must go on and Laytown's racing will go ahead even if the weather isn't so kind, and to be perfectly honest I don't think I would have enjoyed it in bad weather conditions.

Alex liked looking at picture postcards and we'd been sending him them from the different places we'd been to in Ireland, so we thought it would be nice to send him a card with a picture of the horses on the beach. Easier said than done, we did manage to send one but most of the shops were closed with signs on their doors saying "GONE TO RACES."

One of the nicest memories I have of Laytown is while we were walking along the beach we could see a number of horses that had been ridden into the sea for a paddle before racing started and they were clearly enjoying themselves.

Marquees are erected to house a bar and a self service cafeteria; there are also a couple of mobile units.

When I said most of the shops were shut for the races, there was one couple who brought their shop with them. They were selling framed prints of the racing at Laytown and I couldn't resist buying a couple.

We thought the viewing from the steps in the dunes very good and in between races we enjoyed the sunshine sitting on the grass next to the parade ring.

Although not ideal for those with mobility difficulties, the enclosure is quite flat and the races are shown on a big screen. Laytown's fixtures and fittings may be temporary but it has left a permanent memory.

Rating: "Unique" ★★★

How to get there:

To get there by road; Come off the main Dublin/Belfast motorway (M1) onto R132 signposted Julianstown, Drogheda South, Laytown, and at roundabout take the R132 into Julianstown. Turn right onto the R150 signposted Laytown and head for the beach.

There is limited parking near the course entrance, a nearby farmers field is also used.
To get there by rail; there are regular train services to Laytown from both Drogheda and Dublin (Connolly). It is a 10-15 minute walk from the station.
There is a special bus service from Drogheda.
Nearest airport is Dublin (22 miles).
There is accommodation in the area, but with Laytown races attracting up to 10,000 visitors you may have to look further afield. Dublin is an obvious alternative.

Friday 5 October 2007

Dundalk Stadium
Racecourse Road
Dundalk
County Louth
Tel: 353 42 9334438
www.dundalkstadium.com

Although I'd spoken to my sister Elaine quite regularly on the phone, it had actually been a while since I'd seen her. It was during a phone conversation that we got onto the topic of horseracing, and I had been giving her an update of the latest tracks we'd been to when she said she could quite fancy going on another racing trip with us. We had often asked them to have a trip to Ireland with us, but Tam is a bad flyer and even though he has flown on a number of occasions he isn't the easiest of people to get airborne. The best of it is they go on cruises two or three times every year which I think is an even riskier way to travel. Anyway between us Elaine and I came up with the perfect solution, a trip to Dundalk Races. We planned to go racing on the Friday evening, and booked rooms for one night at the Fairways Hotel which is just a taxi ride from Dundalk Stadium. With Dundalk being almost the same distance from both Dublin and Belfast it didn't really matter where Angie and I flew to. But because we thought it would be better if we all turned up at the hotel together we flew to Belfast, and arranged to meet Elaine and Tam at Belfast Central Railway Station from where we would get the train to Dundalk.

We landed at Belfast International Airport at ten past eight, and the Airbus Express 300 had us at the Europa Bus Station before nine. Even after breakfast which we had in the bus station cafe we still had over three hours to kill before our rendezvous with my sister and brother in law. We spent an hour or so looking round a few shops before taking a slow walk towards the Central Station. On the way we came to St. George's Market, which is a weird and wonderful place and well worth a visit if you are ever in Belfast. I would have liked to have stayed longer, but it was really busy and not easy to get around while carrying a suitcase. We arrived at the station nearly an hour before Elaine and Tam pulled up in a taxi which had brought them from the docks. They had come from Stranraer to Belfast by ferry. If they'd been 5 minutes later we would have missed the train, but they weren't and we didn't and just over an hour later we pulled into Dundalk Station from where we hired a taxi to take us to our hotel. It was just after two o'clock when we checked in and the first race wasn't until quarter to seven, so we agreed to meet at the hotel bar at five.

 I took the opportunity to have an hour lying on the bed while Angie washed her hair, I can remember hearing her order a round of sandwiches from room service before I fell asleep. When I woke up she told me a man had opened the door to our room just as she had got out of the shower. He had been very apologetic and said reception must have given him and his wife a key to our room by mistake.

As arranged we met in the bar at five and had a quick drink while waiting for a taxi, Angie's earlier ordeal being a good topic of conversation to start the night off with.

The lit up Dundalk Stadium which had only been open a couple of months looked very impressive in the darkness of the evening. It was actually slightly hazy, and our driver told us dense fog was common in the nearby Dundalk Bay, and it often crept inland making the stadium very vulnerable to poor visibility.

It may have been hazy but it was very mild, though Elaine who was still doing a lot of talking but not as much as usual said she was freezing. Elaine can usually talk for five minutes non stop without taking a breath, and her being a bit quieter was a sure sign she wasn't feeling very well.

Angie and I had earlier decided to bet €40 each a race.

Elaine and I backed the first winner Russian Empress at 5/2. Elaine had put €20 on the winner and that was her only return on the night, partly because she only had two more bets as she was more preoccupied with finding ways to keep warm.

Angie and I both backed the second winner Lime Tree Valley at 2/1, and that was my last return of the night.

Angie and Tam backed the fourth winner Glowing at 7/2, Tam for €50 and Angie €20 e/w on what was to be her last return.

Tam had his second and final winner of the night in the fifth race with €50 on King Of Queens at 4/1.

No fortunes made and no fortunes lost, we stayed for one more drink after racing before going back to the hotel where we were hoping to have a meal. Unfortunately the restaurant was no longer serving, so we went into the bar where we had a few drinks while debating what to do about food.

Angie and I decided on Chinese, so Angie went to reception where they gave her a menu for a nearby Chinese takeaway, so we chose our food and Angie went up to our room to phone in the order.

Elaine wasn't that hungry as she'd been eating throughout the night at the races in her efforts to keep warm, but Tam, who doesn't like foreign food, was. Angie had told him that she'd enjoyed the sandwich she'd ordered from room service earlier in the day, so he asked the barman who'd been scoring for a tip every time we'd bought a round of drinks if it was possible to order a plate of sandwiches. I don't know if it was his ploy to keep us in the bar longer, but the barman whose wages had probably gone up by €20 an hour that night came back with a tray of sandwiches that wouldn't have looked out of place on the buffet table at a wedding reception.

It was ages before Angie came back into the bar, she told us that when she'd gone back to our room she couldn't get in, so went to reception where the receptionist told her there had been a mix up earlier in the day and two couples had been given keys for the same room. Angie told her she was aware of that as she had just come out of the shower when a man opened the door while she was standing there naked. So by the time she'd had a chat with the receptionist, sorted the key out and went back up to order our food, nearly half an hour had passed. It was nearly an hour before our delivery arrived during which time we had a few more drinks while helping Tam make a hole in his mountain of sandwiches.

The following morning Angie went to check out of the hotel and the same girl who had been on reception the night before was at the desk, she apologised again for the mix up with the keys and kindly knocked a few quid off our bill.

We hired a taxi to take the four of us to the railway station from where Elaine and Tam were heading north to Belfast and a couple of hours shopping before catching the ferry to Sranraer where their car was waiting.

We were heading south to Dublin from where we had an afternoon flight booked to take us to Newcastle.

Angie's verdict:

The atmosphere at a racecourse plays a major part in how much you will enjoy your day. Without being too harsh, our previous visit to a floodlit course had virtually no atmosphere and with it taking so long to tempt Elaine and Tam to come to Ireland with us I was hoping Dundalk wouldn't let us down. I should have known better, we were in Ireland where horse racing is in the blood and as usual the atmosphere was electrifying.

The whole set up is very impressive, and a lot of thought had been put into the redevelopment of Dundalk Stadium. As you would expect from a refurbished building everywhere is spotlessly clean.

There are a number of well stocked bars tended by very friendly staff; there is also a good selection of food ranging from a meal in the restaurant with its panoramic views to fast food.

Dave has always told me I'm a slow eater, and I'm sure Elaine won't mind me telling you this, but when we first arrived at the stadium I joined her for a bowl of Irish stew while the boys were at the bar. I don't know how she did it, but while we were eating Elaine never stopped talking and still finished her food long before I did, and that was Elaine on a bad night.

Viewing at Dundalk is also very good, but with their fixtures mainly being evening fixtures I would advise you to wrap up. Especially if you are planning to watch the racing from the terraces, as it got really cool as the night went on.

Disabled facilities include viewing platforms in the grandstand and on the rails close to the winning post. The entrances are wheelchair friendly and there are lifts to all floors.

Rating: Very Good ★★★★

How to get there:

Dundalk is situated just off the M1/N1, Dublin to Belfast motorway.

To get there by road; from the north follow the M1 and take the first left turn signposted Dundalk N52. At roundabout take the second exit, at the next roundabout take second exit for the N52, the stadium is located on this road.

From the south follow the M1 ignoring signs for Dundalk South and Dundalk Town Centre, take the last turn off for Dundalk signposted N52. At roundabout take the fourth exit over the bridge, at the next roundabout take the third exit for the N52 the stadium is located on this road.

Parking is free.

To get there by rail; Enterprise is a high speed rail network that runs an intercity service between Dublin Connolly and Belfast Central Railway stations. The service stops at Dundalk which is approximately halfway between the two. Taxis are available at Dundalk station which is two and a half miles from the stadium.

Nearest airport is Dublin (51 miles). Belfast City (55 miles). Belfast International (58 miles).
There is a good selection of accommodation in Dundalk.

Navan Racecourse
Proudstown
Navan
County Meath
Tel: 353 46 902 1350
www.navanracecourse.ie

Up to now we'd been very lucky in the way the Irish fixtures had been falling in with my days off from work. As I have already mentioned racing in Ireland doesn't take place every day like it does in the UK, and with some of the Irish courses only having a handful of meetings each year it was inevitable our luck would run out and fixtures would clash with my days of toil. Because of this there was only one rule we could follow, if a meeting was scheduled at a course we hadn't been to, if we had the money and I was off work we would go, the only thing that could break the rule of this simple policy was the weather. We knew only too well that Ireland suffers more than its fair share of rain, and hardly a year goes by without a number of meetings being called off due to oversaturated ground. So with this in mind we had to use the guidance of a new tool; the very unreliable long range weather forecast. There had been a mild spell of weather which was forecasted to continue and I was coming up to a few days off from work. Right in the middle of these days there was a meeting scheduled for Navan so I booked our flights to Dublin.
The reason I only booked flights and not accommodation was down to a meeting at Kilbeggan earlier in the year that had been abandoned due to a water-logged course. We'd actually driven into the car park at Kilbeggan racecourse that night, and on the advice of one of the car park attendants we turned around and drove back to our accommodation, parked up and walked back into town for a few drinks.

We went into a bar which was surprisingly quiet; I was expecting the place to be full of disgruntled punters who had been turned away from the races. We were ordering our drinks when a man standing alone at the end of the bar counter asked us if we'd been to the races. These few words had broken the ice, and although we were obviously disappointed that the racing had been called off, we spent a great night drinking in his company. It was amazing how much we had in common with our new found friend (Christy) and by the end of the night we were almost sorry to have to say goodbye. Before he left he wrote down his phone number and told us the next time we were staying in the Dublin area to give him a ring as he had an empty flat above the pub he ran which we were welcome to use free of charge, and he insisted we didn't look for any alternative accommodation. So for this reason I only booked flights for our trip to Navan.

So I rang Christy at his pub, and he was delighted to hear my voice. He told me there would be no problem with us using the flat and he would pick us up at the airport on our arrival. He took our phone number and said he would ring back to confirm arrangements, but he never did ring us back. Not knowing whether he'd lost our number or if I'd landed him in a totally embarrassing situation I didn't pursue the matter, and at the last minute I managed to book us a room for one night at the North Star Hotel in Dublin.

We landed in Dublin at our usual 09:00 and familiar with the routine by now had to leave our case in the hotels luggage lock up as we were far too early to check in. The forecasters had been right on this occasion and by the time we'd eaten breakfast the sun was out and it was surprisingly warm considering it was nearing the end of October.

Navan is another course that Bus Eireann runs a race day special to, and less than an hour after boarding the coach we were at the course. Ladbrokes were one of the sponsors that day and had banners and posters hanging up at the entrance gates. I don't know if it was down to Ladbrokes but admission was free, which was a good start to what was going to be a great day.

Once again we were betting €40 a race, and once again we got off to a flying start when we both backed the first winner Lady Meagan at 2/1.

Nothing in the second.

We'd had a brief chat with a man while waiting to be served at the bar, he asked us how our luck had been and told us to put all our money on The Fist Of God in the third race. We didn't follow his advice to the full, but we did put our money together and had €40 e/w at 9/2 on his tip. The Fist Of God won by 7 lengths.

Nothing in the fourth.

We both backed Bucephalus which finished second in the next race, I had €20 e/w at 13/2 and Angie €10 e/w, she also had €10 e/w on the fourth horse Passcini at 7/1.

With it being such a nice afternoon one or two people had brought seats out and were sitting in front of the grandstand enjoying the autumn sunshine. So we followed their lead and joined them, and sat enjoying a drink while watching Angie's horse Dolphin Bay win the sixth at 100/30.

It was while we were sitting deciding what to back in the last race that the man who gave us the tip came walking by. I thanked him for the information and offered to buy him a drink, but he declined my offer and said he was going to the betting ring to back Aiden O'Brien's horse Mississippian in the last. With nothing to lose we decided to follow suit, so Angie gave me her €40 and said she would keep our seats while I put the bet on. Mississippian was second favourite and trading around 2/1, I didn't put all my money on but I did put another €120 and managed to get 9/4 for my €200.

Mississippian won the race, and thanks to our fairy godfather we were showing a profit of around €600 on the day. I didn't actually tell Angie until after the race that I'd put €200 on the winner, she simply said, "I thought you would."

By the time we got back to Dublin it was dark, and the lack of cloud cover had allowed the temperature to drop to almost freezing point. So we cancelled our planned celebratory pub crawl and settled for an evening in our hotel's bar.

Angie's verdict:

It's a shame that communications broke down with Christy as we were both looking forward to meeting him again. I hope that he and his family are in good health, and you never know the world is a small place and our paths may well cross again.

It had been a rather wet disappointing summer compared to the long spell of good weather we'd experienced in 2006, but here we were at Navan Racecourse at the end of October the sun was out and it must have been at least 20° C.

Navan is another racecourse well designed with its public in mind, though I don't think the free admission could have been advertised very well as there wasn't a huge crowd there on the day.

With bars, a self-service restaurant and hot and cold snacks available there are plenty places to eat and drink at Navan. The enclosure is very clean and like most Irish courses the people are very friendly, as we found out to our good fortune.

Wherever you choose to watch the racing from the viewing is good, I quite enjoyed watching from the seats we'd pulled in front of the grandstand.

There are designated parking and toilet facilities for the disabled; there is also lift access to the upper level of the grandstand.

Rating: Good ★★★

My only disappointment on the day was the withdrawal of Patrick Oliver Brady's horse Takestan. I have seen P.O. Brady on television a few times, but haven't yet seen him at a racecourse. I have never seen any trainer celebrate a win like he does, he is a real character and he is what horse racing is all about; having fun.

I had every intention of backing his horse but when it was declared a non runner I had to switch, luckily I backed the winner, Dolphin Bay.

How to get there:

To get there by road; Navan is easy to reach from all directions as it is just off the N3 motorway which has links with all major routes. Once in Navan follow the R162 Kingscourt road for about 2 mile where you will find the course.
Parking is free.
There is a service bus that runs from Dublin Central bus station (Busaras) to Navan and stops about 2 mile from the course. Buses run every hour.
Bus Eireann also run a race day special coach which also leaves from Busaras.
To get there by rail; Drogheda which is on the main line running from Dublin to Belfast is the nearest station and is 15 mile away. From here there are bus transfers to Navan.
Nearest airport is Dublin (33 miles).
There are a number of hotels and Guest Houses in the area.

In April 2007 mission was accomplished, all 59 UK racecourses visited. We'd been proved to be good judges not waiting for Great Leighs to open as they were still having a lot of problems, and there was still no sign of their grand opening. There were also rumours of another course being under construction in Wales (Ffos Las).

We'd been concentrating on the Irish courses and had some great fun as we managed to visit 15 of the 27; we also had a couple of bonuses with a day racing in both France and the Czech Republic.
Again we hadn't done too bad with the betting, and apart from the odd rush of blood had pretty much stuck to our system.

We were looking forward to 2008 though we were envisaging a few costly events; Hollie and Michael had decided to make things official and tie the knot, Grant's 21st and a fortieth birthday celebration.

Angie's friend Mandy rang us and asked if we would like to go to her husband Graham's 40th. It was to be a week long celebration in Benalmadena on the Costa del Sol; and with Hollie's permission as she would again have the dogs to look after, we accepted the invitation.

Gowran Park
Gowran
County Kilkenny
Tel: 353 56 7726225
www.gowranpark.ie

March 2008 and like they say in the circus it was time to get the show back on the road. Hollie's wedding was scheduled for September and the winter months had been spent planning and organising, and so far things were all falling into place nicely. We still had six months before the big day so we still had time to put a few quid together. Michael and Hollie were paying some of the costs but naturally we were making a contribution as were Michael's parents.

The week in Spain to celebrate Graham's (Winchy's) 40th however was only weeks away. The flights and accommodation had already been paid for but we were going to need a few quid spending money, which we worked out to be about the same amount as we had in our Euro kitty. We knew it had to be used, but not before we had one more go at adding to it.

There was no way we were going to be able to afford to see all the remaining Irish courses during 2008, but we were hoping to fit a couple in around our busy schedule; Gowran Park was the first of them.

We'd quite enjoyed our stay at the North Star Hotel in Dublin on our previous trip to Ireland, so once again we booked a room there for one night along with our usual flights. All that was left to do was to organise the transport to take us the 80 miles from Dublin to Gowran Park.

I had read that Bus Eirran ran a race day coach from Dublin to Gowran Park for some fixtures, and was hopeful there would be one for the meeting we were going to. So to make sure I rang them, and after about a 10 minute wait while enquiries were being made at the other end I was eventually told there was no special coach planned in for Gowran Park that day.

There may not have been a race day coach to Gowran, but after a bit of net surfing I found out that service bus 004 Dublin to Waterford stopped at Gowran with a journey time of 2 hours. We also had a choice of the either the 10:30 or 11:30, both of which would have got us there in time for the first race, and being the cheapest option we decided that service bus 004 was to be our means of transport.

We arrived before 10:00 at the hotel where we left our case in the luggage store at reception before starting the short walk to the bus station. We considered going for breakfast and catching the 11:30 bus, but with the first race being at 14:10 we knew it would be a bit of a rush. So we skipped breakfast and bought sandwiches to eat while we were travelling on the 10:30 bound for Waterford. While we were waiting for the bus we started chatting with this young scruffy looking lad. He was actually quite a cheerful young man, but he had a really broad accent and spoke faster than anyone I have ever heard. It was actually hard work trying to make out what he was saying, but picking up the odd word gave us the general idea of what he was talking about. One word he did keep mentioning was "Circus" and every time he said it he seemed to get more and more excited and spoke even faster. He didn't sit near us on the bus and got off a few stops before us at Carlow where we presumed the circus was in town. As he got off the bus he bid us farewell, and waved showing a big grin as he walked by our window. To this day we don't know if he'd told us he was going to watch the circus or join the circus.

We were sitting near the front of the bus, and as we approached Gowran I asked the driver if he could let us know where to get off for the races. He told us his route took him alongside the racecourse and he kindly dropped us at the gates, but made sure we knew it wasn't a bus stop and the bus back to Dublin would only stop in the village.

The gates hadn't been open long when we arrived, and after a quick look around we sat and had a coffee while studying the form. €40 a race alternative picks was the method for the day and me to go first.

A winning start with Got Attitude at evens. Nothing in the second or third races.

Angie backed the fourth winner Clew Bay Cove at 9/4. Nothing in the fifth or sixth races.

I went to the betting ring to back Gaining Momentum in the last which was trading at around 9/2 but noticed there was a bit of a gamble going on. Mask Of Darkness which had been 5/1 was now down to 3/1, so I took my chance and put my €40 on the gamble.

Gaining Momentum the horse I had intended backing finished well down the field. Mask Of Darkness won the race by 8 lengths putting us up on the day by €90. We'd been hoping for more but at least we didn't lose.

It was only a ten minute walk to the bus stop in the village, and a short wait for our bus back to Dublin where we had a couple of drinks before going to bed.

Angie's verdict:

With such a big year in front of us we should have put our racing on the back burner, but we were so close to completing all the tracks we couldn't see any harm in having a couple of trips away. We'd had a lovely Christmas in 2007 but it had eaten away our sterling racing kitty, and we were expecting our Irish kitty to vanish in Spain. Dave said the flights and accommodation in Spain were paid for and indeed they were; but by credit card. Our flights and accommodation for our trip to Gowran Park were also paid for by our flexible friend, who would be coming to the rescue a few more times as the year progressed.

We'd become accustomed to a comfortable lifestyle more or less doing whatever took our fancy, and the sudden shortfall of money we thought was just a temporary hic-cup that would soon sort itself out.

It had been nearly 4 months since we'd been racing, in fact we'd hardly been anywhere over the winter months, so we were both ready to have a trip away whatever the cost.

The bus journey from Dublin to Gowran was better than I'd expected it to be; firstly because the bus was actually a comfortable coach, and secondly because there was some nice sights to take in on the way. I was only too glad circus boy didn't decide to sit beside us, as it would have given me a bad head listening to him talking in fast forward throughout our journey.

I was really impressed with the set up at Gowran Park, though I wished we had gone in the summer months. Not because it was cold but because there are a lot of trees around the course which would have looked even better with them in full bloom.

The facilities at Gowran are also very good and set in a nice clean environment. The main stand in the enclosure has a restaurant on the top floor and a self service restaurant on the ground floor where you will also find the well stocked bar. Fast food outlets can also be found around the enclosure.

Viewing is very good from both stands with the main stand overlooking the winning line; viewing from the rails is also quite good.

There are toilets for the disabled and a designated viewing area in the stand which is accessible via a lift.

The kids can also enjoy their day in the children's play area.

Rating: Good ★★★

How to get there:

To get there by road; from Dublin take the N7, turn left off the motorway for Waterford/Carlow. Drive through Carlow to

Paulstown where you turn left onto the N9 for Waterford. Drive through Gowran village and the course is on the left.

From Waterford take the N9 towards Kilkenny and turn right onto the N10 towards Dublin. Drive through Thomastown and Dungarven and you will see the course before you reach Gowran village.

Parking is free.

Gowran is on the service bus route from Dublin to Waterford.

To get there by rail; the nearest station is Kilkenny from where taxis will take you the 9 mile to the course.

There are regular trains to Kilkenny from both Dublin and Waterford.

Nearest airport is Waterford (34 miles).

Hotels and Guest Houses can be found in the area not too far from the course.

Sunday 1 June 2008
The Racecourse
Kilbeggan
County Westmeath
Tel: 353 506 32176
www.kilbegganraces.com

The wedding plans hadn't been going too bad, but a few days after we got back from Gowran Park Hollie rang us with some news. She has always been a one for entering competitions from newspapers and magazines and although she had won one or two nice prizes she had never won anything big; not until now. The Newcastle Evening Chronicle was holding a competition to win a dream wedding, and yes you've guessed it Hollie won the prize. This was the best news we'd had in a long time and obviously it would take the pressure off everyone financially, or so we thought at the time.

Since he was born Alex had been brought up with Cassie and Zak. He was two years old now, and even though the dogs were very protective of him for obvious reasons there was no way we would leave them together out of our sight. So we left the three of them in Hollie's capable hands while we jetted off to Spain for the week long birthday celebrations, where as predicted we spent our Euro kitty plus more.

A couple of months before we went to Spain I'd been surfing the net to see if there was any racecourses near to where we were staying. I hit the jackpot when I discovered a hippodrome at Mijas Costa which is only a few miles from Benalmadena, and according to their website hold race meetings all year round. We had planned to go racing on the Sunday morning, but we found out their racing season didn't start until a fortnight later (one for the future).

When we got home from Spain Hollie was worn out and told us never again. Alex was in his terrible twos and was into

359

everything, taking extra pleasure in constantly pestering the dogs while they were sleeping. She told us she was more than happy to look after the dogs for a day or two in the future, but a week was just too much for her to cope with.

A proposed trip to Kilbeggan races didn't go down too well with Angie at first. But when I told her we could do it comfortably on a day trip she showed a little bit more enthusiasm.

Flights to Dublin would have been preferred as Dublin is only just over sixty miles from Kilbeggan, but there was no early flight from Newcastle to Dublin that day. There was however cheap return flights to Belfast and even with the cost of a hire car it didn't work out that expensive. So with Angie's eventual approval and Hollie and Michael agreeing to walk and feed the dogs the trip was on.

We landed in a sunny Belfast at 08:55 and made our way to pick up the hire car stopping at an ATM where we drew €600 to replenish our now non existent Euro kitty, and to cover our expenses for the day. There was a small queue at the car hire desk, but it wasn't long before we had signed the paperwork and were handed the keys for our transport for the day; a Ford Focus. One thing I did think was a rip off was being charged an extra £25 because we intended taking the car over the border.

We had just over a three hour drive in front of us and our plan was to have lunch in the Pantry which is part of Locke's distillery in Kilbeggan. The problem was we'd been up and about since six o'clock and were both in need of something in our stomachs. Not wanting to deny ourselves the good food at the Pantry, we decided to stop for a bacon sandwich an hour or so into our journey. One thing you won't find in Ireland is a clutter of motorway service stations, so if you do feel the need for nourishment while on the road, look out for the signs for local services.

Our mid journey snack didn't spoil our appetite and we enjoyed a good lunch before the short drive to the course. Our previous attempt to go racing at Kilbeggan had been a total wash out; as we drove through the racecourse gates we were met by large puddles and sodden ground while the windscreen wipers were working overtime. This time in total contrast we followed a line of traffic that was kicking up dust from the sun baked ground. I'd had a look at the card on our flight across and Angie had been reading it while navigating the roads. We both came to the conclusion that it looked like being a good day for the favourites, so decided to go with them for a €40 stake. We also thought it best if we left after the sixth of the seven races to ensure we got back to Belfast in good time for our flight home.

€40 at evens and a winning start when Hamelsmead Lady won the first. Nothing in the second.

The next three favourites all won; King Rama at 4/6, Mr. Anderson at 7/4 and Nassaro at evens.

The sixth race was at 17:25 and with a 3 hour plus drive back to Belfast we didn't want to hang around. So we placed our bet with the Tote with the intention of collecting the winnings at our next Irish meeting if our horse won.

We watched the race from the centre of the course where we stood next to the ladies who already had their stalls set out with fruit and Toblerones. We left Kilbeggan with the fruit seller's blessings as soon as the horses crossed the line, but we didn't know the result. Our horse Coolnaharan was involved in a photo finish.

We got back to Belfast in good time for our flight, and arrived home to find out we had in fact backed the winner of the sixth race. Our Euro kitty was nowhere near the €2500 it once was, but at least we had enough to cover another day at the races.

Angie's verdict:

It seemed too good to be true that Hollie had won the "Win Your Dream Wedding" competition. What it did mean though was

starting the plans all over again, but at least part of the prize was
the use of a wedding coordinator to help sort things out. We still
weren't sure what the cost to us was going to be, so for that
reason I had reservations about having another trip away so soon
after our week in Spain.

Dave always makes things sound better than they really are, so
when he told me how much the trip to Kilbeggan would cost I
thought it was a bargain not to be missed. It ended up that the
final price of the trip was half as much again as what Dave had
originally told me, but he said it was due to the airport taxes
which he hadn't taken into account when working the fares out.
What he really meant was he hadn't included the airport taxes
when he told me the cost of the trip in case I said "No." What
made it worse was the €600 (roughly £500) we'd drawn from the
hole in the wall could have gone towards Hollie's wedding dress
which we'd already paid the deposit for.

Never-the-less what was done was done, and if nothing else I was
going to make the most of it and enjoy the day.

Kilbeggan itself isn't very big, what the cowboys would probably
class as a one horse town. But on our previous visit we'd had a
really good time even though the races had been abandoned due
to the foul weather. This time round the weather was nearly on
par with that we'd just experienced in Spain

Today it was an eighty five horse town and I had everything
crossed hoping that we'd picked six of the fastest.

Even though it was a red hot day I wasn't expecting there to be as
many people as what there was at the races, and most folk were
outside enjoying the sunshine. There is a large grassy bank which
overlooks the course and where we found ourselves a spot to sit
down among the many people who had already made it their base
camp for the afternoon.

I'd become to realise that apart from their general appearance
which gives the Irish tracks their own identity they nearly all
have something in common; bars, a restaurant, a self service

restaurant and a snack bar or two in their enclosures. Kilbeggan is no exception and all the facilities are spotlessly clean.

The view from where we were on the grassy bank is very good though it doesn't look directly over the winning line. The main stand however does look down at the post, but to be perfectly honest I liked watching from the bank where there was more room than in the packed stand.

Disabled racegoers will find easy access around the enclosure, there is designated parking and disabled toilet facilities.

Rating: Good ★★★

How to get there:

To get there by road; the racecourse is just over a mile outside Kilbeggan which itself is a midland town and easily reached from all directions;

From Dublin follow the N4 to Kinnegad and then the N6.

From Mullingar take the N52.

From Galway and Athlone take the N6.

From Potlaoise follow the N80 to Tullamore then the N52.

From Limerick follow the N7 to Nenagh then the N52.

There is plenty free parking.

To get there by rail; Tullamore is the nearest station from where you can hire a taxi to take you the nine mile to the course.

Trains running on the intercity line from Dublin (Heuston) to Westport stop at Tullamore.

Nearest airport is Dublin (62 miles).

Seber House (Guest House) was and I believe still is the only accommodation in Kilbeggan.

There is a few more to choose from in the nearby towns.

Ballinrobe Racecourse
Keel Bridge
Ballinrobe
County Mayo
Tel: 353 92 41811
www.ballinroberacecourse.ie

It turned out that Hollie winning her "Dream Wedding" wasn't exactly true, yes she'd won the competition that she'd seen in the Newcastle Evening Chronicle but the Chronicle wasn't supplying the prize. I won't go into all the details, but the prize was generously donated by several firms who had all agreed to offer their services to the competition winner. Their services however weren't entirely free from charge that is all except those of the florist who the Chronicle paid for after the original florist went out of business, and the photographer who was really good and made up the wedding album totally free of cost. The rest however did come with a cost; each company donated only part of their service free so what Hollie really won was a discounted "Dream Wedding." Don't get me wrong it was still a great prize to win as it would have cost about four times as much as what it did. But it was still going to cost nearly twice as much as what the original wedding was going to cost.

Angie reckons that money always turns up from somewhere unexpected when we really need it, and on this occasion it really was unexpected. I would have preferred the unexpected source to have been something else like winning the lottery, but it came by the rare need for my employers to put on overtime shifts to cover a busy workload. So I worked a number of extra shifts which helped towards the wedding costs and in my mind and with no argument from Angie I thought justified another day at the races, so I booked a trip to Ballinrobe.

We had read quite a bit on how nice a place Galway was and had more or less decided to leave Galway races and possibly the festival meeting as our final course. So with Galway being only 30 mile south of Ballinrobe we thought we would take the opportunity to have a look around and booked a one night stay in Galway's Jurys Inn. This Angie said she would pay for by her credit card and I would have to accept as an early Christmas present.

A flight from Newcastle to Galway would have been perfect, but with none scheduled we took our usual flight to Dublin and hire a car which was also being paid for as part of my early Christmas box. On arrival we went to Budget cars where we were told there were no medium size cars available, but were offered a Range Rover Sport at a discount price so we took up on the offer.

The 140 mile drive to Galway was made in extreme comfort and after making only one stop for breakfast en-route we arrived at our hotel early afternoon. We were racing at Ballinrobe that same evening but had a few hours to spare, so we went for a walk around town which really is a nice place to visit. So nice we lost track of time and when we eventually got back to our room to get ready for the races we were in a bit of a rush.

The first race was due off at 17:40 and at 17:30 we parked up and made our way from the car to the entrance gates. We had already decided on €40 a race alternative picks, and Angie had picked her horse for the first race while in the car on the way to the races. Slightly out of breath she managed to get her €20 e/w on Laura Celeb which won the first race at 11/2, and apart from the €100 we collected from the Tote when we handed in our winning ticket from Kilbeggan we didn't have another return.

A rather disappointing night which would have been even worse if we'd arrived a few minutes later. Once back in Galway we finished the evening trying a couple of the bars in town.

The following day when we took the car back we were told that whoever had offered us a discount on the car had no right to do so, and Angie was charged the full price. I think it was a few quid more than she had intended to spend on an early Christmas present and it showed in her face.

Angie's verdict:

Dave has already explained that there was a cost to Hollie's competition win, but can I just add the fact that if a person in a less fortunate position than Hollie had won they may well not have been able to afford the prize.

Dave always has a moan when his rest days (days off) are over and it is time for him to go back to work, but he does really enjoy his job. He actually gets over 200 rest days a year so working a few overtime shifts wasn't going to kill him, and the extra money did come in handy. But not for the trip to Ballinrobe as I was paying for that and we had our betting money which we brought back from Kilbeggan anyway. What I did do though was put a few hundred pounds to one side as we were hoping to go to Great Leighs with Dorothy and Billy later in the year.

I totally agree that Galway is a lovely place to visit, but I was having second thoughts about making the Galway festival our final trip, as the girl on reception at our hotel told me that during the festival everything in town including hotel room rates doubled in price.

It was mainly my fault we were running late so I can only blame myself for having to almost run from the car to get our first bet on.

Ballinrobe is another course well worth a visit. The enclosure is well set out and has all the now familiar catering outlets; a restaurant, a self service restaurant and fast food stands. There is a bar in the grandstand where there is a good friendly atmosphere. Ballinrobe has a nice parade ring and the viewing from the stand is very good. There are toilet facilities and a viewing area for disabled racegoers.

Rating: Good ★★★

How to get there:

To get there by road; Ballinrobe racecourse is north of the town on the N84 Galway to Castlebar road. From the south follow the N18 into Galway then the N84, from the west the N6 to Galway then the N84.

From the north follow the N17 to Claremorris then the R331 into Ballinrobe where you will pick up the N84 to Castlebar. The course is on the left about a mile out of town.

Parking is free.

To get there by rail; the closest station is Claremorris which is on the Dublin (Heuston) to Westport intercity line. There is a bus service from here; alternatively you can hire a taxi to take you the 13 mile to the course.

Nearest airport is Knock (30 miles) Galway (35 miles).

Nearby Galway, Westport and Castlebar between them will give you a large selection of accommodation.

By the end of September both big days had been and gone. Hollie and Michael's Black and White (Newcastle United) themed wedding had been a big success.

Apart from trying to keep Alex under control as he was fleeing around the church looking like an Al Capone mini-me dressed in his white suit and black tie, the wedding service went well, as did the following reception. Naturally a reporter and a photographer from the Newcastle Evening Chronicle turned up so the paper could have an article boasting the success of their "Win a Dream Wedding" competition.

The night time do was tremendous, there was that many folk there we had to bring in extra tables and chairs as three coach loads of guests arrived to join an already pretty full function room.

When the party was over the coaches were waiting to take those who needed transport back to Dudley. When we got back to the village us older ones were heading home to bed while a lot of the younger generation, including Grant still dressed in his morning suit decided to go back to someone's house to carry on partying. The following morning there was a knock at our door, and when I answered it I was confronted by two journalists from the Evening Chronicle. They asked if a Grant lived with us and if he was in a fit state to give then a statement so soon after being stabbed. Grant wasn't in and of course we knew nothing about it.

We found him at his girlfriend Kelly's house where he greeted us with a bandaged arm supported by a sling. While he had been at the party his friend got himself into a spot of trouble, so Grant went to calm the situation. He noticed someone out the corner of his eye thrusting something at him, so his reaction was to put his arm down to block whatever it was coming towards him.

His reaction probably saved his life as his assailant who was never caught had thrust a knife at him. The knife went straight through his arm which had deflected the blade from its intended target and ended up with the tip sticking in his hip. So the next edition of the Evening Chronicle had a write up on both Hollie and Grant.

It was actually quite amusing watching the tailor's reaction when we took the hired morning suits back, and had to tell him police forensics had held onto one of them as one of the ushers had been stabbed.

Grant's 21st wasn't quite as eventful. He didn't want a party as he had decided to spend his birthday with his mates on a trip to Amsterdam, his arm still in a sling.

Friday 16 October 2008
Great Leighs Racing
Moulsham Hall Lane
Great Leighs
Chelmsford
Essex
CM3 1QP
Tel: 01245 362412
www.greatleighs.com

I think everybody has ambitions in life, but some people's ambitions are nothing more than fantasies or wild dreams that they could never fulfil, but I strongly believe if your dreams are not too far fetched then there is no reason why you can't live them out. Visiting all the racecourses in the UK might not seem like much of an ambition to some people, but to me it was something special, and even in my wildest dreams I never thought I would be including all the courses in Ireland. My only other real ambition apart from one day being a wealthy man, which is a wild dream, is to one day cross the equator.

One person who did set his sights a bit higher was entrepreneur John Holmes, his ambition was to build and own a racecourse. With a personal investment of around £30 million his dream was to turn the old showground near Chelmsford in Essex into a world class racing venue; his dream turned out to be more of a nightmare.

Planning permission had originally been granted for the racetrack in 2002 and slowly but surely the development progressed. It was in 2005 when the British Horseracing Authority was willing to allocate a number of fixtures for the following year providing the course passed their final inspection. Set back after set back meant the licence for racing at Great Leighs was delayed many times and a licence wasn't actually granted until 2008.

In April 2008 John Holmes had his ambition fulfilled when Great Leighs Racecourse held its first meeting which was attended by a number of invited guests.

The first meeting open to the general public was on May 28th 2008 which I was hoping we could go to but it clashed with my shift pattern at work, so it would be a while longer before we could once again say we had been to all the courses in the UK. The big wedding and Grant's birthday had slowed down our racing plans, so it wasn't until October 16th and with Billy and Dorothy's agreement that we planned our long awaited trip to Great Leighs.

Our financial situation hadn't changed much, but Angie had put a few quid away for this trip so we decided to make the most of it by going to Great Leighs on the Thursday night followed by a day at Newmarket on the Friday. Since 2006 Great Leighs had been announcing opening dates and twice before we had booked a hotel in Chelmsford which is close to the Essex track only to find out the course still wasn't ready for racing. This time we booked rooms for the Thursday night at The White Hart in Braintree which I had worked out to be only 4 miles from the course, and rooms for the Friday night at the Travel Inn in Grantham where we were stopping on our way home from Newmarket.

So for our final trip of 2008 we set off for Braintree with Billy and Dorothy, leaving the now married Hollie to take care of the dogs. This time however Cassie was in need of extra care as she was on four different prescribed medications. Ten years is the average life span of a Boxer dog, and even though eight year old Zak was still behaving like a pup, Cassie who was nine and a half was showing symptoms of what the vet said was common in geriatric dogs and what could easily be treat with medication. Good company and good conversation made the drive down to Essex seem a lot shorter than it actually was, and after making only one stop for lunch we checked in at our hotel late afternoon. While we were checking in I asked the guy on reception how far it was to the racecourse and if he could book us a taxi to take us there, he told us it was 15 miles and booking a taxi would be no problem. 15 miles was a lot further than I'd worked it out to be and I was thinking I should have booked accommodation in Chelmsford. As it happens it was only 4 miles to the course, the hotel receptionist thought Great Leighs was a lot further away than it actually was. I don't know if all the locals thought Great Leighs was too far away or if they had been once and not liked it, but the racing fans of Essex stayed at home that night and didn't turn out to support their local track. I couldn't believe how quiet it was with only a few hundred people in the stand, even the bookies had stayed at home with only 4 standing in what you could hardly call a betting ring.

It was also quite apparent that the facilities at Great Leighs were nowhere near completion, and the magnificent state of the art grandstand displayed on their website hadn't even been started. Instead the De Boer stand had been erected on the inside of the course which would allow room for the new stand to be constructed on the outer. The De Boer stand is a two storey 150 metre long prefabricated structure which had been used once before when it stood alongside the seventeenth fairway of the K Club golf course in Ireland where it was used for hospitality during the 2006 Ryder Cup.

Whether it was these temporary facilities that kept the crowds away I'll never know, but like we've said before you never know what a place will be like until you get there and if you are like us and willing to adapt you can enjoy yourself in whatever surroundings.

Because we were going to Newmarket the following day and with there being 8 races at Great Leighs we decided on betting £20 each a race over the two meetings.

Billy who had now taken up betting e/w had a good night which he started by backing the first two winners; Accolation at 7/1 and Margot Mine at 3/1.He followed up with Marie Tempest which finished 3rd in the third race at 4/1, Atabaas Allure which won the sixth at 4/1 and Vineyard which finished 2nd in the last also at 4/1.

It looked like Dorothy was going to draw a blank on the night, but she found a winner in Suzi Spends which won the last race at 11/4.

We didn't do quite as well as Billy but we did show a profit on the night;

Nothing in the first.

Angie backed the second winner Margot Mine £20 at 3/1.

Nothing in the third or fourth.

None of us had a bet in the fifth race which was won by Audemar at 1/5.

We both backed Atabaas Allure which won the sixth and both had £20 at 11/4.

I backed the winner of the seventh Sabre Light £20 at 15/8.

Angie backed Suzi Spends which won the lucky last £20 at 11/4.

After racing we took a taxi back to Braintree and asked the driver if he could take us to a Chinese restaurant. He dropped us off at the old library building which had been converted into the China Dynasty restaurant and whose fixtures and fittings were definitely the finished article unlike the temporary surroundings in which we'd spent the earlier part of the evening. One thing we all agreed on though was we'd all enjoyed our night at Great Leighs. The following day Angie and I had a cracking day at Newmarket winning over £500, Billy and Dorothy didn't do so well. After a good night in Grantham we stopped off for an afternoon at Catterick races on the way home where Billy's luck returned and we put a big hole in our winnings from Newmarket.

Problems at Great Leighs carried on and the nightmare of John Holmes ended in January 2009 when its licence for racing was not renewed and the course went into administration.

Angie's verdict:

There's nothing much I can really say that the newspapers
haven't already said except that I think the closure of Great
Leighs was a real shame. There was obviously a lot of things
going on behind closed doors that we don't know about, but in
my opinion as an outsider looking in I don't think the course
should have been opened until the new grandstand had been built.
This would have quelled the negative comments from the press,
which must have been one of the reasons people were staying
away. Another unfortunate factor was they were trying to get the
new course up and running just as the country was going into an
economic recession, and I'm sure what little money people were
putting aside for entertainment they wouldn't want to spend at a
racecourse whose facilities weren't even complete.
When we got out of the taxi and made our way from the entrance
gate to the stand the layout of the area inside the course was very
impressive, I was particularly impressed with the number of
tables and chairs situated in a nice area near the entrance to the
stand Once inside there were a few bars, a cafe and a counter
where you could get hot and cold snacks. There were plenty seats
available inside, but this might have been because of the lack of
people to fill them. One thing I can say is everywhere was
spotlessly clean.
Facilities for the disabled include parking, access ramps and toilet
facilities.
The real negative thing I can say about Great Leighs is the
viewing is terrible. The stand at Great Leighs is in the centre of
the course from where you can see virtually nothing until the
horses are inside the final furlong, so the only way to watch the
racing was on the big screens.
When you go racing and a race is about to start the first place to
fill up is the grandstand, so Great Leighs opening without such a
facility has to be their biggest mistake.   Rating: Under
Construction. ★★

How to get there:

To get there by road; Great Leighs is about 5 miles north of Chelmsford on the A131.

Via M25/M11, exit the M11 at junction 8/8a and follow the A120 towards Colchester/Braintree. Exit the A120 at Panners roundabout and take the A131 towards Great Leighs/Chelmsford. At Great Notley roundabout turn right onto the A131 towards Great Leighs (the course is well signed).
Via M25/A12, Exit the M25 at junction 28 onto the A12 towards Chelmsford/Colchester. Exit the A12 at junction 19 Boreham interchange and follow the signs for A130/A131 towards Sudbury (the course is well signed).
To get there by rail; Chelmsford is the nearest mainline station and is on the line from Liverpool Street Station.
Bus shuttles operate to the course on race days.
Nearest airport is Stanstead (12 miles).
There is a good choice of accommodation within a 10 mile radius of the course.

.

What a year that turned out to be, we knew we wouldn't be able to fit many courses in around our busy year in 2008, so with us managing to visit four was a bit of a bonus.

Angie's craving for sunshine had been satisfied with a week in the Spanish Costa. It had been a great week but it cost us our Euro kitty plus more.

Apart from somebody trying to murder Grant on the night of Hollie's wedding, the wedding itself had been a big success, though financially we would have been a lot better off if Hollie hadn't won the "Dream Wedding" competition.

Grant's 21st didn't work out to be much of a financial burden as he didn't want a party, so it only cost us the price of his trip to Amsterdam plus a few quid spending money.

The year ended on a real sad note when Cassie's condition worsened. We don't know if it was her illness or a lethal cocktail of prescribed drugs, but on the 17th December 2008 she was put to sleep. One thing we did know was we had just lost the most loving, caring dog you could ever imagine. We had been her proud owners since she was five and a half weeks old and losing her was going to leave a big hole in all our lives. None more so than Zak's who couldn't understand why Cassie was no longer with us, and was constantly looking for his soul mate. His character changed; his puppy like behaviour stopped, and within a few weeks his young looking face was white with grey hair.

The recession had caught a lot of people by surprise, and overspending with the help of our credit cards to help finance our comfortable lifestyle found us caught up in the credit crunch. I know we only had ourselves to blame, but nearly everyone we knew was in a similar position, some a lot worse.

So 2009 was going to be our "Annus Horribilis," we needed to tighten the purse strings and we weren't expecting to go on many, if any, racing trips.

Thursday 7 May 2009

Clonmel Racecourse
Powerstown Park
Davis Road
Clonmel
County Tipperary
Tel: 353 52 72481
www.clonmelraces.ie

January 2009 and the closure of Great Leighs wasn't the best of news to start the New Year with, but at least there was a little bit of hope that the track would one day re-open as the administrators were looking for a suitable buyer.

More bad news came from Ireland as the racing fans of Tralee Racecourse had failed in their petition to keep their local course open, and the racecourse shareholders had agreed to sell the land to a consortium of developers who had plans to build a GAA stadium, retail units, a supermarket and residential property on the site. Tralee was actually one of the courses we were considering going to last as we quite fancied going when the Rose of Tralee festival was on, but unfortunately it wasn't to be.

Better news was coming from Wales as construction of Ffos Las Racecourse was on target and they were confident of being ready for racing by their scheduled first meeting on June 18th.

Losing Cassie had hit Zak so badly he was like a lost soul, and Angie was reluctant to leave him in the house for too long on his own. We phoned the vet to seek advice on how to deal with his condition, and were told he would eventually get over his loss, but it could take time. Take time it did, three months to be exact when he eventually returned to almost his old self, but with a grey face.

We'd been careful on how we'd been spending our money, and in the first three months of the year we had only been out once when we had a night out to celebrate our birthdays in February.

With our house being close to the flight path into Newcastle Airport the planes fly over very low as they are approaching and Alex was always fascinated by them as he watched them from our garden. So because it was coming up to his third birthday and we still had some Euros left after our trip to Ballinrobe, we decided to buy him a passport for his birthday and take him on a plane to Ireland.

Timing couldn't have been better as not only did Alex's birthday fall during my days off from work, but so did a meeting at Clonmel. We thought it would be nice to take him away for a couple of days, starting with a trip to the races on the Thursday and possibly a day at the zoo on Friday, so I set to work planning our trip. It had been nearly seven months since we were at Great Leighs and ten since we were last in Ireland, so were both ready and quite excited about having a few days away.

We booked our return flights to Dublin, a hire car, one night accommodation in McCarthy's B&B in Clonmel and one night in the Travel Inn, Dublin Airport. We'd been to Ireland quite a few times by now and had always considered it to be a reasonably inexpensive place to visit, but things had changed.

When we first went on our trips to Ireland cheap flights on the budget airlines really were cheap, but the introduction of airport taxes, plus the extra charges the airlines had brought in for what were once free services had more than doubled the cost of a so called cheap flight.

The Government "Green Taxes" in my opinion are a big con. I'm not disputing we should be taking more care of our environment, but I have watched many documentaries where top scientists have proved the global warming we are experiencing is the result of an increase in solar activity, and nothing to do with our neglect of our planet. But our so called wise politicians had found an excuse to rob us of our hard earned cash, and unfortunately we were going to have to live with it.

Another more significant reason why the cost of our trip to Ireland was increasing so much was the strength of Sterling against the Euro. Where we were once getting €1.4 to £1 we were now only getting €1, which meant everything was costing nearly half as much more than it did before the recession had caused the collapse in our economy.

Alex really enjoyed the short flight to Dublin, where we arrived just after nine and had breakfast in the airport before making our way to the car hire to pick up our car, and to be ripped off by one of the biggest scams you can imagine. With Alex only being a three year old he obviously needed a car seat, and the car hire companies know you have no alternative but to pay whatever they want to charge for the hire of one. The cost of the car seat for one day was actually the same price as what the cost of the hire car was, but there was nothing else we could do but reluctantly agree the price and drive off on our journey to Clonmel.

The car seat was expensive but it must have been comfortable, as Alex slept for most of our two and a half hour journey waking up just ten minutes or so before we pulled into our hotel car park. We were met by a warm welcome at our hotel where we spent a couple of hours relaxing in our room before driving off to the races for what we were hoping to be a profitable evening.

We had driven past Clonmel Racecourse once before on the day we drove from Limerick to Wexford so we had a good idea how to get there, but our landlady gave us a map anyway just to make sure we didn't get lost.

The card didn't look too hard so we thought €40 a race alternative picks would be the best option.

Hollie who was pregnant again was staying at our house with Zak, and was watching the racing from Clonmel on ATR to see if she could spot us in the crowd. After the first race in which our horse finished well down the field Hollie rang Angie's mobile.

She told us to stand near the winning post for the second race as the camera covering the finish gave a good view of the people standing along the rail. So I put Alex on my shoulders and we stood at the rails to watch the second race in which our horse once again finished down the field, but at least Hollie saw us on TV. We'd bought Alex a pair of binoculars which he thought were great for watching the horses, but he thought they were even better for watching the rabbits that were playing behind the stands.

We would have been better off spending the evening watching the rabbits as we managed to back five consecutive losers. It was just after the fifth race when the heavens opened up, and because Alex was starting to look a bit tired we decided to call it a day and made our way back to the car in the pouring rain.

It would have been nice to have backed at least one winner, but at least we had only lost €200 so it could have been worse. We got back to our room where Alex had half an hour running around pretending to be a jockey before we all had an early night.

The following morning after a substantial breakfast, we said our goodbyes to the landlady before driving back to Dublin. We drove straight to the Travel Inn where we checked in and put our cases in our room before returning the car and the gold plated, diamond studded car seat to the car hire company. We spent the afternoon at the zoo, and then had another early night as we were catching the early flight to Newcastle the following day.

We'd all thoroughly enjoyed our trip, but it had cost a lot more than we had budgeted for, which meant all the cost cutting and money saving we'd managed in the first three months of the year had all been in vain, and financially we were now back to "Square One."

Angie's verdict:

I must agree with what Dave said about the trip to Ireland being a lot more expensive than what we had been used to paying, but it wasn't just the cost of travelling that had gone up in price. You tend to notice theses things more when you are trying to be careful with your money, and even the basic necessities had jumped up in price.

The money we spent on our trip to Clonmel however, we both thought was money well spent as we really enjoyed taking Alex along with us, and to be able to spend quality time with your grandchildren is priceless.

As you can see Clonmel is another racecourse in a picturesque location, and another with easy access around a well designed enclosure. There are a couple of bars, a self service restaurant and a snack bar where you can get hot and cold food and drinks. When we first arrived at the course it was dry but there was a bitter cold breeze blowing, so we went into the self service restaurant for something to eat and to get a warming drink of coffee. With Alex being so young we asked if they served children's portions but were told they didn't, so we then asked if they could just put less on the plate and we would pay the full price. The girl at the counter said she couldn't do that either, so three year old Alex ended up sitting in front of a full serving which he only managed to eat about a quarter of. The food was quite expensive anyway, but to put a plateful of food out knowing for a fact it wasn't going to be eaten, in my mind was a total waste.

We watched one race from the rails, but that was more so Hollie could look for us while she was watching the racing on the television. The view from the rails is okay, but the view from the grandstand from where we watched the rest of our races is excellent. There is a viewing stand for the disabled as well as parking and toilet facilities.

The parade ring is quite nice but Alex spotted the small play area on the grassy area behind it, so whoever's turn it was between Dave and I to have a bet got the opportunity to look at the parading horses, while the other was on playground duties. Clonmel Racecourse is another course I would like to put on my ever increasing "Like to go back on a Nice Day" list.
Rating: Good ★★★

How to get there:

To get there by road;
From Waterford; take the N9 out of Waterford and continue forward onto the N24 signposted Limerick. At Killheffernan roundabout take the first exit onto the N24 signposted Limerick/Clonmel; continue forward entering Clonmel. The racecourse is just off the N24.
From Cork; take the N8 followed by the M8 signposted Dublin. Leave the M8 at junction 10, at the first roundabout take the fifth exit, and at the second roundabout take the second exit onto the N24. Follow the N24 into Clonmel.
From Dublin; take the N7 Naas road and continue onto the M7, at junction 17 take the N8 signposted Cork and continue onto the M8. Leave the M8 at junction 10 and take the first exit onto the N24, continue on the N24 into Clonmel.
Parking is free.
To get there by rail; there is a direct line from Waterford to Clonmel, trains from Cork and Dublin Heuston change at Limerick Junction.
Taxis are available at the station to take you to the course which is just over a mile away.
Nearest airport is Waterford (32 miles).
There are a number of hotels and B&B's in and around Clonmel.

Ffos Las Racecourse Ltd
Trimsaran
Camarthanshire
SA17 4DE
Tel: 01544 811092
www.ffoslasracecourse.com

The year ticked by slowly, and it was so frustrating being in the situation we had landed ourselves in. We were so close to completing all the tracks, but in the same breath we were so far away. There were a few occasions when I was on my rest days from work that one of the four Irish tracks we still had to visit were holding a meeting, but there was no way without totally breaking the bank we could have possibly gone. It felt like nothing short of a lottery win was going to get us out of the situation we were in, but that was a four million to one shot. We might not have won the lottery but we did have one or two returns off the bets we were having on a Saturday. Never a fortune but enough to put a little bit away until we had enough saved to pay for another trip. By the middle of August we'd managed to save a few hundred quid, this wasn't quite enough to pay for a trip to Ireland, but Ffos Las was now up and running and a meeting they were holding on September 12th which fell right in with my days off from work looked very inviting.

After the visit to Great Leighs with Billy and Dorothy we'd all agreed we would go to Ffos Las together, so two minutes after we told them we were thinking about going to the September fixture, the trip was on. When we'd been away with Billy and Dorothy in the past we'd managed to fit more than one meeting into the trip, this time we were just going to the one. This was partly because there were no suitable fixtures on either the day before or the day after the Ffos Las meeting, but more because we didn't want to stretch the money we had too far. We were driving straight to the course on the morning of the races, then staying the night in the Travel Inn, Port Talbot before travelling home the next day. The weather on the days leading up to our trip had been unsettled and very cold for the time of year, and from what we'd read about Ffos Las being very open to the elements we decided to wrap up warm in woolly jumpers and top coats.

Ffos Las when translated into English I believe is blue ditch, which was the name of the farm that once existed on the land before mining operations took over in the early eighties. It is a very large area and was once the site of the biggest open cast mine in Europe until 1997 when mining ceased and the area was in-filled and landscaped, so what we had read was right it really is open to the elements.

It is 380 miles from Dudley to Trimsaran so we were going to have to make an early start, because of this Hollie collected Zak on the Friday night and took him round to her house where he was going to stay for a couple of nights with herself, Michael, Alex and not to forget Max, our new grandson who was born on July 30th.

At 04:45 on Saturday September 12th Billy and Dorothy who only live about 50 yards from us, walked to our house as we were once again setting off on a journey that would allow us to say we had been to all the racecourses in the UK. We were outside standing by the car when they approached and it was obvious by the way Billy was hobbling along he was in a lot of discomfort. Earlier in the year I had an operation on my dodgy knee after it totally give way on me while coming down a ladder at work, an incident that prompted me into finally getting it seen to. Knee problems seem to come with the job, as there are quite a few of my workmates who have had similar operations. Billy who works in the same industry but for a different company was having the same problem, but he unfortunately was suffering with both knees. A slight consolation was his knees were less painful when he was sitting down, which at least meant he wasn't going to be in total discomfort during our six hour drive. Because we'd set off so early the roads were very quiet and we were making really good time, which allowed us to make a couple of stops to break up the journey. We made our first stop at Trowell Service Station where we had breakfast, and where we were pleasantly surprised at how warm the weather was. By the time we made our second stop at Cardiff West Service Station it was a red hot day and our jumpers and coats were without a doubt surplus to requirement. We arrived at the course in good time and joined a really good crowd who had turned out to support the new track. With there being such a good attendance it made me wonder if the credit crunch really did have a part to play in the closure of Great Leighs, or if it was simply because people weren't impressed with the temporary facilities at the track

Because we were being careful with our money, Angie and I had considered betting £20 a race alternative picks, but in the end just went for £10 each a race on the eight race card. Before racing started I decided I was just going to back the favourites, so I placed eight £10 wins with the bookmaker in the betting hall.

None of us had what you would call a brilliant day betting wise, but we all found at least one winner, Billy the only one showing a profit.

Angie started the ball rolling by backing the first winner Morgans Choice at 3/1; she also had £5 e/w on the sixth winner Haajes at 4/1.

Billy backed the second winner Glen Shiel at 13/2, and also had e/w bets on the first and second in the last race; Arlene Philips which won at 8/1, and the second Arabian Silk at 22/1.

Dorothy had the seventh winner Chichen Daawe for which she managed to get 9/2.

My idea to back the eight favourites didn't turn out to be a good one, I did have two returns but neither one of them went off clear favourite. In the fourth race Ela Gorrie Mou won returning the 7/2 joint favourite, and in the seventh race the winner Chichen Daawe which was eventually sent off 3/1 co-favourite of three.

After racing we drove to the Travel Inn in Port Talbot, and with the nice weather continuing into the evening we spent the rest of the night in the hotel's beer garden. Once again we'd been to all the courses in the UK, but that didn't mean we couldn't do them again, and we decided it would be a good idea to have regular racing trips away together. I was trying to talk Billy into coming to Ireland with us though he didn't seem too keen, but there again he didn't say no, so I thought I would leave it a while before mentioning it to him again.

We stopped three times on the long journey home the next day, a journey that Billy didn't find so comfortable, but this had nothing to do with his knees. All the creepy crawlies residing in Port Talbot must have had a gathering the previous night in the Travel Inn's beer garden and chose Billy as their evening meal, he was absolutely covered in real nasty looking insect bites.

Angie's verdict:

It had been a bad summer weather-wise, so bad that we only managed to have a couple of barbecues during the whole summer when we would normally be expecting to have at least two or three a month. But at least we put Dave's days off work to good use as we decorated the whole house from top to bottom.

We were expecting another dull miserable day when we went to Ffos Las as the weather forecast didn't look too promising, so it was a real surprise when it turned out to be such a nice sunny day. It was a long journey but the stops we made broke it up nicely, and we were all in a fine fettle when we pulled into the car park of Britain's newest racecourse.

The first notable thing about Ffos Las apart from the nice entrance is how friendly everyone is, we had quite a few conversations with some of the locals as the afternoon went on, and they all made us feel very welcome. Can I just say at this point that one local couple we were talking to told us we were very lucky to be there on such a nice day, as on some days you would need to be wearing no less than oilskins(but I suppose you could say that about anywhere in the UK).

Another thing I like about Ffos Las is there is only one enclosure, so your admission price allows you access to all public areas. Once inside you will find a couple of bars serving a good selection of alcoholic drinks, and where you can also get hot and cold food as well as tea and coffee. Mobile catering units and trade stands can also be found parked up around the enclosure. There is good access for disabled racegoers, other disabled facilities include; parking, toilets, viewing areas (parade ring and course) and a lift to the restaurant situated on the upper level of the grandstand.

The grandstand from where the viewing is excellent isn't very big, and with there being so many people there it was filling up very quickly just before a race was due off, so we watched most races from the rails where the viewing is also very good.

I was surprised to read picnics aren't allowed in the enclosure, but entertainment is put on for children at certain fixtures, so Ffos Las races can still be a fun day out for the whole family.

Rating: Good ★★★

How to get there:

To get there by road; Ffos Las lies between Llanelli and Carmarthen, coming from the east plan your route to join the M4 into Wales, come off the M4 at junction 48 and take the A4138 to Llanelli, from here you will pick up the brown signs directing you to the course.

From the west take the A40 to Carmarthen followed by the A484 to Llanelli where you will pick up the brown signs (the brown signs start quite a few miles from the course).

Parking is free.

To get there by rail; Swansea is the nearest mainline station, from here you will get a connecting train to Llanelli Station which is probably your best option and from where you can get a taxi to take you the six miles to the course.

Service bus 197 which travels between Llanelli and Carmarthen Monday to Saturday drops off at the racecourse entrance.

Kidwelly station which is also on the line from Swansea and four mile from the course is a request stop only and doesn't have many transport links.

Nearest airport is Cardiff (63 miles).

There is a good selection of accommodation in the area.

2010, and a year had passed since the closure of Great Leighs who were still hopeful of finding a buyer, though as time was going on it was looking less likely. More significantly to just how quickly time was passing us by was it had been a decade since the Millennium, ten years that seemed to have gone by almost within the blink of an eye.

2009 as we predicted hadn't been a great year for us but it could have been worse, a lot of factories and businesses had been closing down or enforcing redundancies as they were falling victim to the credit crunch, at least I still had a job and a salary coming in, which was just about keeping our heads above water.

Looking back on it we'd been pretty fortunate to have been able to fit a couple of racing trips into what had been a difficult year financially, plus we'd still been having a bet on the weekends when I wasn't at work. Watching the racing on the telly doesn't hold the same excitement as actually being there, but it's better than nothing. We also managed a couple of days out at our local tracks, including spending the anniversary of our first date at Newcastle's Fighting Fifth meeting.

So everything wasn't total doom and gloom, and one bit of happiness that did come our way was the birth of Max Robert Stanley our new grandson, a chunky little chappy who was born on July 30th. His middle name Robert was given to him in memory of Sir Bobby Robson, a soccer legend and a folk-lore hero in Newcastle, who sadly died aged 76 on July 31st the day after Max was born.

Grant and his girlfriend Kelly live less than a mile from us, but we were lucky if he popped in to see us more than once or twice a week. He did take the time however to come and let us know that Kelly was pregnant, and we should be expecting a new addition to the family in August 2010.

It had also been a year of ups and downs for Zak. Once he was over his grieving for the loss of Cassie he returned to pretty much his old self, but he developed spondylosis which meant he would be permanently on tablets. Then in the last week of the year he went lame, and the vets were still investigating the reason for his lameness into the turn of the year.

So with a new year in front of us and still four tracks to visit, the fixture list didn't look very promising against my shift pattern but we were hoping to get at least one trip to Ireland during 2010.

The last two weeks of 2009 and the first few weeks into the New Year brought the worst weather conditions we had seen for thirty years, and the predictions were it was going to be the coldest winter for over a century (so much for global warming). Needless to say racing was hit hard, and apart from the odd turf meeting that managed to survive the wintry conditions, it was the all weather tracks that were keeping the sport alive. National hunt trainers were becoming almost desperate to find a race for their horses, so when Southwell came up with the idea to stage a couple of national hunt bumper (flat racing) meetings on there all weather surface it came as a bit of a godsend. So much so that 242 horses were entered for the six race cards on the first day of their all weather NH flat fixtures.

The dates in the Irish fixture list in 2010 for the four tracks we still had to visit didn't work out too well with my shift pattern at work. In fact the only fixture we could fit in was a meeting at Tramore on April 17th, so needless to say we planned the trip. Angie's mam and her partner Joe had decided to come with us so I started looking for the most economic way for the four of us to travel. The basic cost of flying across to Ireland was still very reasonable but the taxes were pushing the price right up, so I started looking elsewhere. It worked out that taking our car across on the ferry was going to be the cheapest option, and because we were going to hire a car anyway it made sense to sail across. I sat down at the computer to make the booking, but thought I would just check the flights once more and was amazed to see Ryanair had made the flights we were looking at free from taxes. So the plans all changed and I booked return flights for our trip. Two days before we were due to fly, two eruptions from the volcano beneath the Eyjafjallajokull glacier in Iceland sent a plume of ash towards Europe. This had a devastating effect on air travel, and yes you probably guessed it, ours was one of the flights to be grounded.

So we ended up not making any trips to Ireland in 2010, though if I'd stuck to the original plan and booked the ferry we could have at least travelled over once.

X-rays had revealed Zak's lameness to be more serious than we'd expected, a damaged cruciate ligament surrounded by an arthritic joint was the problem we were faced with. We were told that because of his age an operation, though not out of the question would be the last resort and only if all else failed. So the old boy was prescribed with painkillers and put on a diet with a target of losing 2 to 3 kilos, and more importantly his walks had to be cut right down and on his lead only so as to rest his leg as much as possible. We were hoping that by the time he had lost some weight his knee would have naturally repaired itself enough for surgery to be unnecessary.

Short walks on a lead aren't the best form of exercise for a dog and we were finding it hard to get his weight down, though he seemed to be coping with his lameness quite well. But over the months his health deteriorated and blood tests revealed he had liver problems. Sadly we lost Zak on May 24th.

I had offered to get another dog for Angie, mainly to keep her company while I was at work especially on night shift, but she had said no. I think that having to take both our dogs within less than a year and a half for their final visit to the vets and coming home with just their collars and leads had taken its toll. We are renowned for being a nation of animal lovers with almost half the homes in the United Kingdom owning a pet. Of course we also have the extremists (animal rights) who have got a few valid arguments, but I think their views on horse racing being a cruel sport is totally wrong. It seems to me that most horses enjoy their days at the races, and for a racehorse to be successful it has to be given the best of care 24 hours a day by dedicated staff. The sport does however have its low points and it is inevitable that throughout the season horses will die. Naturally we feel sorry for the horses as we do for the owners and trainers, but I can relate to how the stable lads and lasses who look after their horses day in and day out must feel when they return home from the races with nothing but a bridle.

Things did brighten up as the year progressed, first with Grant and Kelly announcing the birth of baby Liam on August 7th.

Secondly our financial situation had stabilised, and thirdly the Irish fixture list for 2011 looked a lot healthier against my shift pattern and all going well we could visit the last four courses in two trips.

Saturday 4 June 2011

Waterford and Tramore Racecourse
Tramore
County Waterford
Tel: 353 51381425
www.tramore-racecourse.com

The end of the road was in sight; by mid April I had already
booked the flights for two weekends away, the first in June to
visit Tramore and Listowel, and the second in August for
Killarney and Galway which would complete our venture. We
had finally talked Billy and Dorothy into coming along to get a
taste of Irish racing, so they were travelling with us in June. On
the August trip Angie's mam Daisy and her partner Joe were to
be our companions as it fell on the weekend of Daisy's 70th
birthday.

Both meetings on the June weekend were afternoon fixtures
which gave us a problem with flight schedules. We had decided
to stay two nights in Cork; firstly because it was a pretty central
base for the two tracks, and secondly we had never stayed there
before and were quite looking forward to looking around
southern Ireland's second biggest city. I ended up booking
outbound flights to Cork for the Friday afternoon, but the only
return flight from Cork was Sunday evening which we couldn't
have made in time so I booked one night accommodation in
Dublin for Sunday and return flights from Dublin for the Monday
morning. Barring a natural disaster we were all set for a good
weekend.

Déjà Vu – Just over a week before we were due to fly we heard
some devastating news, Iceland had closed its main airport as the
islands most active volcano Grimsvotn began erupting sending a
plume of smoke 12 miles into the sky. By the following morning
a few flights had been cancelled to and from Scotland as the ash

cloud drifted towards the U.K. We feared the worst, but thankfully the eruptions stopped and the ash cloud dispersed within a few days.

The nice thing about flying to Ireland is it takes less than an hour so you don't have time to get bored or restless like you do on longer flights. Within 2 hours of landing (3 hours from taking off) we had picked up our hire car, driven to the Belvedere Lodge a really nice B&B on the outskirts of the city, unpacked, freshened up and took the short taxi ride into town. We spent the evening finding seats in the sunshine as we made our way round some of the city centre pubs.

The weather across the British Isles had been unsettled for a couple of weeks leading up to our trip, but the Friday had been glorious and this carried on into the Saturday. Perfect weather for a day near the coast, so after our full Irish breakfasts, we set off on our 120km. drive to the seaside resort of Tramore.

Helped by a trouble free journey along quiet roads we drove by the racecourse with an hour to kill before the gates opened. So we took the opportunity to go down to the strand where we drank coffees while enjoying the sunshine on the sea front. It really was hot, so much so that Billy who isn't a great lover of the sun found it necessary to buy a hat to protect his head from the burning rays.

We made our way back to the course and parked up not long after the gates had opened. Arriving early for a race meeting has its advantages, one of them being you are more likely to find a seat. This we done and we couldn't have asked for a better one. There were tables and chairs out on the grassy area in front of the stands, and the one we chose was right on the rails in front of the winning post, which between us we managed to hang on to for the full day.

Without a shadow of doubt, the most successful system we had used that would most frequently give us returns was to back two horses a race and betting e/w on anything priced 7/2 or over. We were confident we were never going to lose a lot, but we also knew we were never going to make a fortune, though we sometimes made a tidy profit and most days done no worse than break even.

Billy and Dorothy used this system and with their win and place money finished the day slightly in front of the bookies.

We too used this system but in a way I later regretted. During the week leading up to our trip Angie and I had decided to bet €10 each a race over the two days, which was fair enough until I came up with one of my good ideas. I had been reading the statistics on the success rates of the favourites at the two courses we were visiting and both have a 40% strike rate, so I decided I was just going to back the favourites in all races over the two days. This too would have been fair enough if I hadn't also thought it would be a good idea to place my bet (14 tenners) with our local bookmakers before we left home. This wasn't one of my better ideas and a decision I would later regret.

There were three favourites won on the day;

Dimona which won the second race at 4/9, Beliar which won the fifth at 5/2 and Alayir which won the seventh at 4/6.

Angie managed to do a bit better with €5 e/w on the first winner Apt Manor at 9/2, she didn't have a bet in the second as she fancied the favourite but not at 4/9, and said she would keep the €10 for a later race.

After nothing in the third or fourth she then went on to back the last three winners, €10 on Beliar at 5/2, €5 e/w Grand Cru at 9/2 followed by €20 on Alayir at 4/6.

So we ended up showing a profit on the day though I might as well have been betting at the track as I was in the betting ring prior to every race anyway.

After racing we drove back to our hotel in Cork and once again took a taxi into town to carry on where we'd left off the previous night.

\

Angie's verdict:

It was nice to be in the position to plan another trip away, and I was especially looking forward to staying in Cork. It would have been a shame to have completed all the tracks in Ireland and not have stayed at least one night in what we had been told was a lovely city to visit. When we did get there I didn't get the opportunity to spend any time in Cork's retail outlets, but we did have a good walk around the city centre and it really is a nice place. One thing that stood out was just how clean it was compared to other towns and cities we have been to.

I have mentioned before what a big part the weather plays when you are going racing and the day we went to it was red hot which really made the day.

The enclosure at Tramore is nicely laid out with all the amenities close at hand. Apart from the hospitality suites there are three bars as well as a self service and a takeaway restaurant. All the facilities including the toilet facilities are clean and well kept.

The course itself is undulating so although we had seats right at the winning post we couldn't see much of the action. There are two stands, but the only place you can get a good view right round the course is from the main stand which in my mind would be better with safety barriers as the steps are quite steep.

The whole enclosure which includes toilets for the disabled is wheelchair accessible.

A couple of interesting facts I read about Tramore racecourse are; It was the first track to stage a meeting in the new millennium, and it was the first track to use the new currency when Ireland changed to Euros.

Rating: Good ★★★

How to get there:

To get there by road; the course is a short distance outside the seaside town of Tramore and is only 8 miles from Waterford which has good transport links from all directions.
From Cork; head south on the N7 then join the N8 signposted Dublin/N8/Rosslare/N25. Continue to follow the N8 for approx. 60 miles then join the N25 signposted Rosslare/Waterford. Follow the N25 through 8 roundabouts then turn right onto the R682 which will take you into Tramore.
From Dublin; take the N7 Naas road and continue onto the M7, exit at junction 11 onto the M9 then the N9 towards Waterford. Continue from the N9 onto the N24 signposted Waterford/N9. At roundabout take the second exit onto the N25 towards Cork. Follow the N25 then take a left turn onto the R675 Tramore road, continue on R675 into Tramore.
Parking is free.
To get there by rail; Waterford Plunkett is the nearest railway station from where there is a regular bus service to Tramore, taxis are also available at the station.
Waterford Plunkett is on the Intercity line between Limerick and Rosslare, there is also a direct service from Dublin Heuston
Nearest airport is Waterford (7 miles).
There is a good selection of accommodation in both Tramore and Waterford.

Sunday 5 June 2011

Listowel Racecourse
William Street
Listowel
County Kerry
Tel: 353 68 21144
www.listowelraces.ie

Most of the Irish courses we have been to have had a real good
racing atmosphere, and we have always been made to feel
welcome by the people we have spoken with. Tramore didn't
seem to have that atmosphere so didn't give us the same buzz as
usual. Billy and Dorothy had enjoyed their day however, though
deep down I knew they hadn't yet felt the real Irish racing
experience. This was partly due to the fact that a large group of
people had set their stalls out on the tables next to us and for
some reason were having an Australian theme day, and partly due
to the fact that the only people we had spoken to on the day were
not only English but live only a few miles from our village in
Northumberland. Even the lady fruit sellers were missing as we
exited the course. So I was hoping that Listowel was going to
have the racing atmosphere that with the exception of maybe
Cheltenham can only be experienced in Ireland.
Another thing that was missing on the Saturday was the Racing
Post. As usual I was out of bed early on the Saturday morning
and went out to buy our racing paper. There were no shops close
to our hotel, and the two service stations that were nearby only
sold the national morning papers. Thinking we could purchase a
Racing Post at the track we didn't try anywhere else before we
got there only to find there was none on sale.
One thing that hadn't been missing on the Saturday but was
certainly missing on the Sunday morning was the clear blue skies
and glorious sunshine. The clouds had crept in overnight and

399

although it wasn't raining it certainly looked like it was going to. "What a difference a day makes." The TV weather forecast was as we'd thought it would be; cloudy with scattered showers, heavy at times. The one good thing was the best of the weather would be in the south west and that was where we were bound. After breakfast we packed the car and set off on our journey west, making a few unsuccessful stops on the way to try to find what was fast becoming the elusive Racing Post. We did drive through a few rain showers, but as the TV weather girl predicted the further west we drove the brighter the skies became. By the time we reached Listowel the sun was shining though there were one or two clouds still hanging around. We drove past the racecourse and into town for one last ditch attempt to get our racing paper, "Success" we found a shop that had one copy, so with a feeling of achievement we drove back to the racecourse car park. It may well have been sunny but there was a strong cool breeze bringing the temperatures down considerably, but at least it wasn't raining. Once inside the enclosure Billy went off to explore while the girls and I went for a coffee and a look through the runners for the day. After our refreshments Angie and Dorothy went to the powder room while I went off looking for Billy. After a while I spotted him coming down the stairs at the back of the grandstand with a big smile on his face. The reason for his grinning face was because he'd found the ideal spot from where to watch the afternoon sport. Inside the grandstand on the top floor are bench seats right next to the windows overlooking the course, so it was here we set up camp for the rest of the day. Not only did we have unobstructed viewing but we were well and truly sheltered from the wind. There was also Tote betting just a couple of yards behind where we were sitting, so to save them going up and down the stairs to the betting ring the three of them were happy to place their bets for the afternoon on the Tote. One thing we found out while we were there was the Tote in Ireland which used to pay the first four places in all races with sixteen or more runners now only pays the first four in handicaps with sixteen or more runners. Apparently this changed in May 2010.

Billy got off to a good start when he backed the first and second home e/w in the first race: Liberty Gift €7.10 a win €3.20 a place and Mcmonagle €5.80 a place. This set them up for the day and after having a couple more returns they were once again up on the day.

The idea I'd had to back all the favourites over the two days at our local bookies before we left home turned out to be a bad idea. I'd had three winners on the Saturday at Tramore but because two of them were odds on I finished up slightly down on the day, thankfully Angie had put us in a winning position. Sunday at Listowel was a disaster when the only favourite to win was in the last race when House Rules won at 8/15.

Angie just managed to keep our heads above water and ensured we broke just better than even over the two days; she had €5 e/w on the third winner Royal Blue Star which paid €7.10 a win and €2.10 a place, €5 e/w on Pires which finished second in the fourth paying €1.40 a place, €5 e/w on Worldly Wise which was third in the sixth race paying €1.70 a place and €20 on the last winner House Rules which paid €1.50.

So the end of another days racing and we now had the long drive to the Premier Travel Inn at Dublin airport where we were staying the night before our flight home on Monday. Once again the system hadn't let us down though my contribution hadn't helped much; the best of it is when I looked through the racecards I didn't fancy many of the favourites.

 One thing I was pleased about however was there was a really good atmosphere at Listowel which made the day even more enjoyable and gave Billy and Dorothy a true taste of Irish racing.

Angie's verdict:

I suppose it would have been asking too much to have three consecutive hot sunny days, and when Dot dropped our newspaper off and told us how cold it was outside my immediate thoughts were on what to wear for the day. With Dave and I both preferring the national hunt season a days racing in the cold isn't new to us, but you don't expect cold weather in June. Because the weather forecast was predicting fairer weather in the west and with Listowel being situated in Kerry, Ireland's most westerly county I took a chance on the summer clothes I had planned to wear with a cardigan for extra protection against the elements. With Listowel being a market town, and Listowel racecourse not holding many fixtures each year I thought the enclosure would be quite small but this is not the case, the enclosure at Listowel is big, spacious and modern. There are plenty bars and food outlets including the self service restaurant where most people were opting for the Sunday roast lunches. The meals looked very nice, but although there are plenty of tables in the restaurant there aren't any seats so you have to stand at the table while eating your food.
As well as the New stand where we spent our afternoon there is the Lobb stand and the Hannon stand, which all give good viewing. Two wheelchair viewing platforms are located in the stands.
 I had just been to the parade ring when I noticed something which I thought was quite nice. We had came in through the entrance off the main car park, but walking in through the entrance from the town you come through the gate then cross a footbridge over the river to the enclosure.
Talking of rivers, our drive after racing took us north towards Limerick before heading east to Dublin, it was on the road to Limerick that we followed the bank of the Shannon for a few miles where we enjoyed some breathtaking views.
Rating: Good ★★★

How to get there:

To get there by road; the course is just outside Listowel town off the N69 between Limerick and Tralee.

From Dublin; take the M50 southbound coming off at junction 9 signposted Limerick N7. Follow the N7 following the signs for Limerick, after Birdhill (approx.125 miles) take the second exit onto the Limerick by pass (N7). At the next roundabout take the first exit onto the N20 signposted Cork/Tralee/N21. Branch left, then merge onto the R526 signposted Galway N18. Follow the signs for Galway N18 for 4 roundabouts passing through Limerick, and then at the next roundabout take the second exit onto theR510. At the next roundabout take the first exit onto the N69 signposted Foynes. Follow the N69 for approx. 40 miles to Listowel.

From Cork; Head west on the N22 to Tralee (approx. 60 miles) from where you will pick up the N69 north to Limerick which passes through Listowel.

Parking is free.

To get there by rail; Tralee is the nearest railway station and can be reached from Dublin Heuston, Cork, Limerick/Limerick Junction changing trains at Mallow.

There are special bus services from both Tralee and Limerick to the races during the festival meeting.

Nearest airport is Kerry (35 miles).

There is a good selection of accommodation to choose from in and around Listowel.

Friday 26 August 2011

Killarney Racecourse
Killarney
County Kerry
Tel: 353 6431125
www.killarneyraces.ie

With a little bit of planning which by now had become almost second nature and with the help of the internet everything was set in place for our final trip. The two remaining courses we had left to visit fell on corresponding days and both within my seventeen day break from work. The two meetings we were going to were an evening meeting on the Friday night at Killarney followed by an afternoon fixture at Galway on the Saturday. Unfortunately they were on the last weekend of my seventeen day break which meant we had to cut the trip a day shorter than we would have ideally liked. We would also have preferred to fly to Cork as it is a lot closer to Killarney than Dublin but the flight schedules to Dublin worked out better for our racing plans.

Our itinerary was to fly out on the Thursday morning and stay the first night in Dublin before picking our hire car up on the Friday morning for our journey west to Killarney. Our travelling companions Daisy (Angie's mam) and her partner Joe had never been to Ireland before, so we thought an afternoon and evening in Dublin would be a good introduction for them to the Emerald Isle.

The weather forecasters had once again predicted a long hot summer and once again got it seriously wrong. The few weeks leading up to our trip saw some very heavy spells of rain across the British Isles and I couldn't help thinking that the chances of both meetings surviving this deluge were slim. Thankfully though there were enough dry breezy days in between the downpours to cancel out any possibilities of abandonment due to waterlogged courses.

When the big day came, everything went smoothly and our morning flight into Dublin arrived ahead of schedule at around 11:30am. We had thought about booking a hotel in the city centre but we had to pick up our hire car at the airport the following morning so we booked rooms in the Premiere Travel Inn which is close by. The hotel shuttle bus had soon dropped us at our accommodation where luckily our rooms were ready, and by mid afternoon we had taken Daisy and Joe by taxi to show them round the big city.

After an hour or so taking in the sights and a light lunch we thought it was time to take the weight off our feet and continue with the second part of our tour around Dublin's pubs. On the occasions Angie and I have been drinking in Dublin we have met many a character which has always made the experience more enjoyable. I was hoping Daisy and Joe would have a similarly good time, and I was not let down as the characters were out in force. One guy who sat in our company for about an hour claimed to be an ex Chicago cop who had been retired on medical grounds and still lived in America but had come home on holiday to visit his parents who live in Drogheda. He seemed genuine enough until he told us his grandmother had left his father a lot of land which he had sold for €14,000,000. Even this could be believable, but I smelled a rat when he told us his father had spent some of his fortune on a racehorse called Oscar Schindler which had proved to be a profitable investment. He told us that the horse had won a race last year but was now in semi retirement in Newbury but they were considering bringing him back to retire to pasture in Ireland. I later discovered that Oscar Schindler died at 15 years old in 2007 ten years after his victory in the Irish St. Ledger. Sitting in good company whether they were telling tall stories are not made it a great night which we finished off with a couple of night caps in our hotel bar.

After a good sleep and a good hearty breakfast we boarded the shuttle bus and set off back to the airport to pick up the hire car. We were soon on our way and made good time as the majority of the roads from Dublin to Killarney are either motorways or "A" roads. Even after stopping for lunch we arrived at our hotel (Muckross Lodge) in Killarney by mid afternoon with plenty of time to freshen up before hiring a taxi to take us to the racecourse where the first race was due off at 4:30pm.

It was pretty quiet when we arrived at the track even though the gates had been open almost an hour, which was surprising as it was ladies day but at least it gave us a chance to have a look round. What wasn't surprising was the official going was declared as soft. There hadn't been a great deal of rain but this was the fourth consecutive days racing and what rain there had been had got into the ground.

We had fully intended staying for all eight races on the card but the cool wind which was coming from the north bringing with it the odd shower helped us make up our minds to call it a day after six.

It looked like Angie and I were in for a good night when we both had €20 on the first winner Hurricane Ridge at 5/2, but it didn't turn out to be a bumper evening as we only managed to find one more winner when we both backed Galileo's Choice which won the fourth at 4/5. Angie also saved her money in the third race with €10 e/w on the third horse Beauty Express at 6/1.

Without any real damage done to our pockets Angie and I were quite happy with our evenings racing. Daisy also seemed quite pleased as she'd picked up on a few occasions from her e/w bets on the tote (small stakes). Joe however I think took a bit of a clattering.

Nobody had to pick up off the sixth race which allowed a quick exit and a short taxi ride into town, or should I say on the town. It was the day before Daisy's 70th birthday and we knew we would be having a reasonably early night the following night as we were flying home on Sunday morning so we toasted her birthday a day early.

Angie's verdict:

After the ash cloud had ruined our planned trip to Tramore races in 2010 which my mam had booked to come along on, we had talked about a possible trip later in the year but she seemed to have gone off the idea, as it happens we never made it anyway. So it really surprised me when she said she and Joe would come with us on this trip, especially as it was the weekend of her 70th birthday which meant she wouldn't see the rest of the family all weekend. On top of it being my mam's birthday weekend Grant's partner Kelly was expecting to have our first granddaughter Jessie who was already a week late. It would have been nice if she had been born on my mam's birthday but it wasn't to be and we were back home when she was born on 31/8/ 2011.

All and all it was going to be a big weekend and for Dave and I the end of an epic journey. I was sad in a way it was coming to an end, but all good things must come to an end according to the proverb.

Naturally I was looking forward to Galway which was to be our final track, but Killarney was a course I couldn't wait to see. I had read in a couple of racecourse guides that Killarney racecourse is the most scenic racecourse in Ireland and probably the world, and I raise my hat to those who have visited all the world's racecourses and who are in a position to make such a comparison. After all it has taken us six years to visit all the tracks in the UK and Ireland.

On arrival I could see the reasons for this bold statement as the views over the course are really spectacular with the mountains being so close to the track. So who am I to argue, and in some people's eyes Killarney may well be the most scenic though most of the courses in Ireland and quite a number in the UK can also boast about their surrounding views, and I am sure there are one or two out of the hundreds of racecourses around the world that will think they have a valid claim to top spot.

What I did like about Killarney is the layout of the enclosure; it is pretty basic but more than adequate for the needs of its racing public. There are a couple of well stocked bars tended by very friendly staff and on the night we were there a marquee with a champagne bar inside (don't know if this is a regular feature).There is a large self service restaurant with plenty seating and also a few snack outlets.

The viewing over the course from the grandstand is very good, and viewing from the rails is also quite good, this being enhanced by a big screen in the centre of the course. I also thought the parade ring at Killarney was quite nice.

Disabled facilities include toilets, parking (phone in advance) easy access to facilities in the main stand and a viewing area.

Rating: Average ★★★

How to get there:

To get there by road; the course is a short walk from Killarney town, just off the road to Kenmare.

From Dublin; head south on the N7 Naas Road signposted Limerick/The South. Continue on N7 for approx. 120 miles, and then at roundabout after Birdhill take the second exit onto Limerick by-pass-N7 signposted Cork/Killarney. At roundabout exit onto the N20 signposted Cork/Talee/N21 and continue forward onto the N21 entering Castleisland from where you join the N23 signposted Killarney. At Farranfore turn left onto the N22 which will take you into Killarney.

From Cork; from the South Ring Road take the N22 which will take you directly into Killarney.

From Limerick; take the N21 from where you will pick up the N23 then N22 into Killarney. Parking is free.

To get there by rail; Intercity trains from both Dublin Heuston and Cork will take you to Mallow from where you will get a connecting train to Killarney. Taxis are available to take you to the course.

Nearest airport is Kerry (10 miles)

Killarney is a very popular holiday town with an abundance of hotels and B&B's many of which are within walking distance of the racecourse.

Galway Racecourse
Ballybrit
County Galway
Tel: 353 91 753870
www.galwayraces.com

Saturday 27th August 2011, the big day, Daisy's 70th birthday and the day Angie and I would be finally crossing the finishing line. Before we went down to join the birthday girl for breakfast we sat in our room having a coffee while looking out of our window, which more or less overlooked the entrance to Killarney National Park. As we watched a couple of deer grazing in the field opposite I was thinking about all the different places we had stayed in both Ireland and the UK while on our travels, and I was feeling quite chuffed with myself at being almost at the end of what I reckoned had been quite an achievement.

When we very first started out on our venture a few people asked how long it was going to take, obviously I couldn't give them an exact answer but told them we hoped to complete our tour in five or six years. Later when we added the Irish courses to our target we were probably looking at ten to twelve years, which would mean visiting a new course on average every 6-7 weeks. So to be only a few hours away from being at our final course only six and a half years down the line surpassed all expectations especially when you take into consideration we didn't visit any new courses in 2010.

Another question I was asked during the weeks leading up to our final trip was how many miles did I think we had covered while travelling to and from the courses we had been to. The answer to this one was anyone's guess but I thought it would be interesting to know, so I sat down one afternoon in front of the computer and calculated the miles we had clocked up. It worked out that without including the trips to France and the Czech Republic and by the time we reached Killarney we would have travelled just under 28,500 miles, and the final 130 mile drive from Killarney to Galway would take it just over.

Studying Genealogy seems to be a popular pastime these days and there are a couple of people I know who have been quite successful in building their family trees. So much so that talking to them made me curious enough to have a go. To do this properly takes a lot of time and the few weeks I spent sifting through the archives I found very frustrating as I was looking for instant results. I did however manage to trace part of my mother's family back to the mid 1800's but with my fathers family who originated in Ireland I had little success, so I gave it up as a bad job.

So taking what we had been told by a girl we met in a bar in Sligo that the Conroys were from the west of Ireland and the information I had found on the internet stating that the Conroys originated in Galway was good enough for me. This in my eyes made Galway the perfect course to finish on, a sort of homecoming.

Daisy had already opened her cards and presents on the Thursday morning before we flew to Dublin as she didn't want to take them along with her on our trip so she had nothing exciting to wake up to on her birthday, but at least we'd celebrated it in style with a decent drink the night before.

There had been quite a lot of rain overnight which thankfully had cleared away and apart from the odd cloud it was a nice day for racing. The forecast for the day was nothing more than a few light showers so there was little chance of racing not going ahead. You might be wondering why I have this fixation on meetings being postponed, cancelled or abandoned but believe me you will be surprised at how many times it actually happens, and for this reason Angie and I decided that as long as we watched three races at Galway we could say we had attended a meeting at every racecourse.

Once again we made good time on our journey so had time to stop for refreshments and a quick look at the Racing Post before arriving at the track well before the first race.

While putting this book together we have contacted every racecourse in one way or another and have found almost everyone we have either written to or spoke to very helpful, and for their help we are truly thankful. Just as I had done with Sandown when we had completed all the UK courses I contacted Galway to see if they could give our names a mention in the programme on the day we were there and just like Sandown they kindly obliged.

We'd soon settled in to our new surrounds and found a good spot as a meeting place as a decent crowd had gathered for the day's sport.

Daisy continued just as she had the night before at Killarney by collecting on a few win and place bets that she'd placed with the tote. Joe also had a couple of winners so he was quite happy.

We were hoping to finish our final course on a winning note and I got us off to a reasonable start with €20 on the first winner Sam Bass at 9/4, we had nothing in the second.

Before the third race Angie who was holding the racing kitty said this race signifies the end of our journey so we should celebrate with a decent bet and gave me €100 with which I toddled off to the betting ring feeling like it was my birthday and not Daisy's. I thought the favourite Laganbank looked like a good thing so had my €100 on at 9/10. When I rejoined Angie in the grandstand she told me she too had €50 on Laganbank on the tote.

It couldn't have been a better ending to our racecourse tour as Laganbank won easily by seven lengths paying €2.70 a win on the tote.

Our luck continued into the fourth race in which we both once again backed the winner Adropaupep, €20 each with the tote, which paid €3.70.

We stayed for two more races without success but just as we had hoped we had finished well in front on the day. It would have been nice to have stayed the night in Galway but we had to get back to Dublin as we were flying home the next morning as I was back to work on the Monday.

As we sat in the hotel bar that night Daisy asked us what we were going to do with ourselves now we had been to all the courses. Angie and I had already discussed this and told her we would still be having trips to the races but in 2012 we were going on a proper holiday.

Six years isn't a really long time but a lot of water had passed under the bridge and with it some major changes in both what is going on in our lives and what is happening in the world around us. Now that we don't have the dogs we have a lot more free time, but the ever-increasing number of grandchildren are giving us a new focus on life.

One major change that has not just had an impact on our lifestyle but it has had an effect on just about everyone we know, and that is the current crisis in the global economy. When we first set out on our journey we were in the middle of an economic boom with everyone including us enjoying the rich pickings. Sadly this has come to an abrupt end with the world's economy in utter turmoil. One of the biggest sufferers is the Euro zone, which has hit Ireland with a severe blow and I think it is fair to say that at today's prices it would be a costly venture to travel to all the Irish tracks from the UK.

Because of the poor value in the Euro a lot of people we know are going to places like Turkey and Bulgaria and even though they all come back saying what wonderful holidays they have had neither of theses two countries have had any appeal to me.

One place I've never been to and have always fancied visiting is Jersey, and when I suggested it to Angie who doesn't like long haul flights she was all for it.

So in 2012 we are heading for Jersey, and it just so happens that the dates I am looking at corresponds with a meeting being held at Le Landes, the racecourse run by the Jersey Race Club. What a coincidence!

Angie's verdict:

For as far back as I can remember and certainly all my adult life I have loved spending a day at the races, but I'd never have dreamt that one day I'd be able to say I'd been to all the courses in both the UK and Ireland. It had been Dave's ambition to visit all the UK tracks that triggered it all off, but midway through 2006 with over 40 courses crossed off and with the Irish tracks added to our to do list it became a joint passion.

Out of all the trips we have been on I have always enjoyed the ones that have included two race meetings best of all, and I would suggest to anyone with their hearts set on visiting all the courses that two at a time is well worth considering, if nothing else it's more cost effective.

This trip so far was proving to be a great success and as far as Dave and I were concerned the highlight was still to come. Actually I think the highlight of my mam's weekend was also because Dave and I were visiting our final course and not the fact that it was her birthday. She was thrilled to bits when she read our names in the programme at Galway, and still to this day she carries it around with her in her handbag so she can show people. They say you should always keep the best until last and although I can't put my hand on my heart and say Galway is the best course in Ireland in my opinion it is certainly one of the best, and was a great course to finish our journey on.

Nine times out of ten when we have visited a new course I didn't know what to expect and to me that was part of the fun. But we have watched the Galway summer festival on television over the last few years and after seeing the huge crowds it draws I had an idea that the facilities would be of a high standard and I wasn't wrong.

The large enclosure houses two big stands, first there is the impressive Killanin Stand which has four floors. The top two floors are where the hospitality suites are, but anyone can use the lower floors where you will find food and drink facilities and access to a seated balcony.

Secondly there is the Millenium Stand and this is where we spent most of our day. This too has numerous bars and eating places and also a seated balcony from where we watched most of our races, and from where we enjoyed a great view over the whole course with Galway bay in the distant background. The seats we were in however were numbered so I suspect these will need to be reserved for the summer festival. I didn't think the view from the rails was brilliant but it was okay, but I did like the parade ring.

There is a viewing stand for the disabled as well as toilet facilities and lifts and escalators to the upper floors.

So that was Galway, absolutely marvellous and we didn't see it at its best, when the festival is on there is so much more going on for the public to enjoy; Champagne bars, Oyster bars etc. etc. and even a fun fair for the kids.

Something we see regularly at the races in England but I had never seen it in Ireland before were groups of young people in fancy dress whose presence just added to what was a great atmosphere, to top it all we had a profitable days racing. We couldn't have wished for a better ending.

Rating: Very Good ★★★★★

How to get there:

To get there by road; the course is approximately three and a half miles from Galway and very well signposted, from the city centre follow the routes to the N17, continue on the N17 passing the City West Business Park on the right. Take a right turn towards Parkmore and stay on this road continuing forward at the roundabout, the racecourse is on your right.

From Dublin; leave Dublin on the M4 then exit onto the N6 signposted Galway. Continue on the N6 through Craughwell until you reach the Oranmore roundabout where you take the third exit towards Galway City. At the next roundabout (Quality Inn) continue forward then at the next take the second exit following the N6 west towards Galway. At Lynch roundabout take the last exit signposted Carnmore/Galway Airport, shortly after the roundabout take the left hand turn for Parkmore, this will take you to the racecourse.

From Cork and Limerick; the N20 is a direct route north from Cork to Limerick. From Limerick follow the N18 towards Galway until you reach the Oranmore roundabout where you take the second exit towards Galway City. At the next roundabout (Quality Inn) continue forward then at the next take the second exit following the N6 west towards Galway. At Lynch roundabout take the last exit signposted Carnmore/Galway Airport, shortly after the roundabout take the left hand turn for Parkmore, this will take you to the racecourse.

Parking is free.

To get there by rail; Inter City trains run direct from Dublin (Heuston) to Galway, travelling from Cork and Limerick change trains at Portarlington. Taxis are available at Galway Station to take you to the course which is approx. four and a half miles. There are shuttle buses that run from Galway City to the racecourse on race days.

Nearest airport is Galway (2 miles).

There is a large selection of accommodation to choose from in and around Galway.